THE ARCHITECTURE OF MASTABA TOMBS IN THE UNAS CEMETERY

sidestonepress

THE ARCHITECTURE OF MASTABA TOMBS IN THE UNAS CEMETERY

THE MUNRO ARCHIVE PROJECT
STUDIES ON THE UNAS CEMETERY IN SAQQARA 01

Ashley Cooke

Series Editors André J. Veldmeijer & M. Sählhof

Published by Sidestone Press, Leiden
www.sidestone.com

Lay-out & cover design: Sidestone Press
Photograph cover: André J. Veldmeijer

ISBN 978-90-8890-894-1 (softcover)
ISBN 978-90-8890-895-8 (hardcover)
ISBN 978-90-8890-896-5 (PDF e-book)

Contents

Foreword 9

Introduction 10

1. The Unas Cemetery 13
1.1. Introduction 13
1.2. Gazetteer of Tombs in the Unas Cemetery 21

2. Sources of Stone at Saqqara 46
2.1. Pyramid Cemeteries 46
2.2. Geology 49
2.2.1. Limestone Quarries in Egypt 49
2.2.2. Likely Sources of Limestone at Saqqara 50
2.3. Delivery Routes of Building Materials 52
2.4. Archaeological Observations Relating to Masonry Materials 57
2.4.1. Imitation of White Stone 60
2.4.2. Imitation of Stone 60
2.4.3. Imitation of Organic Material Using Stone 61
2.5. Acquisition of Stone 62

3. Masonry in Tombs at Saqqara 64
3.1. Introduction 64
3.2. Masonry Classification 64
3.2.1. Masonry by Cross-Section: Freestanding Walls within Mastabas 65
3.2.2. Surface Appearance 77
3.3. Masonry Techniques at Saqqara 102

4. Roofing 105
4.1. Introduction 105
4.1.1. Roofing in the Tomb of Mehu 106
4.1.2. Roofing in the Tomb of Seshseshet Idut 107
4.1.3. Roofing in the Tomb of Niankhba 108
4.1.4. Roofing in the Tomb of Mitri 110
4.1.5. Summary 112

5. Doorways 113
5.1. Introduction 113
5.2. Doors from Old Kingdom Tombs 113
5.3. Representations of Doors in the Old Kingdom 115
5.4. Doors Within Tombs 117
5.5. Fastening Doors 119
5.6. A Survey of Doorways Within the Unas Cemetery 121
5.6.1. The Tomb of Kairer 122
5.6.2. The Tomb of Khenut 123
5.6.3. The Tomb of Nebet 127

5.6.4. The Tomb of Seshseshet Idut 131
5.6.5. The Tomb of Iynefert 132
5.6.6. The Tomb of Nebkauhor 133
5.6.7. The Tomb of Mehu 136
5.6.8. The Tomb of Ptahshepses Impy 137
5.7. Other Memphite Tombs 139
5.7.1. The Tomb of Mereruka 139
5.7.2. The Tomb of Kagemni 141
5.7.3. The Tomb of Khentika 143
5.7.4. The Tomb of Ankhmahor 144
5.7.5. The Tomb of Debehen 145
5.8. Doorkeepers 145

6. Courtyards, Columned Halls and Storerooms **151**
6.1. Courtyards and Columned Halls 151
6.2. Storerooms for the Mortuary Cult 154
6.3. Storerooms in Pyramid Temples 157
6.4. Tombs with Five Storerooms 160
6.4.1. The Tomb of Nebet 160
6.4.2. The Tomb of Nebkauhor 161
6.4.3. The Tomb of Kagemni 163
6.4.4. The Tomb of Mereruka 164
6.4.5.The Tomb of Ptahhotep (LS 31) 164
6.5. Tombs with Less than Five Storerooms 165
6.5.1. The Tomb of Khentika 166
6.5.2. The Tomb of Seshseshet Idut 167
6.5.3. The Tomb of Kairer 169
6.5.4. The Tomb of Akhethotep and Ptahhotep (D 64) 170
6.6. Storerooms Adjacent to Offering-Rooms 172

Synopsis **176**

Bibliography **178**

Foreword

André J. Veldmeijer & Martin Sählhof

Peter Munro (Kestner Museum in Hanover/Freie Universität Berlin) started working in the Unas necropolis at Saqqara in 1973 and continued to work there until his retirement in 1995. Although the concession included earlier and later levels, Munro's main interest was the 5th Dynasty necropolis. Despite the fact that he worked on the publication of the fieldwork up to the end of his life, due to his illness and premature death, only one monograph saw the light of day (in addition to several preliminary reports and articles). The archive, containing the published and unpublished documentation of these excavations, was transferred to the Netherlands with a view to its final publication (Munro Archive Project [MAP]; Sählhof & Veldmeijer, 2018). One of the first steps in dealing with the archive was its digitisation and the creation of an online presence, making the material easily accessible (see also Veldmeijer *et al.*, 2015).

The MAP does not limit itself to work on Munro's archive, and is open to collaboration with other scholars who deal with the area of the Unas necropolis, and offers the possibility of publication within their series, "Studies of the Unas Cemetery in Saqqara. One such example is the present volume by Dr. Ashley Cooke, to whom we are grateful for inaugurating the series with his work: "The Architecture of Mastaba Tombs in the Unas Cemetery". We thank Kunst- und Kulturstiftung Hannover for the financial support to make this publication possible.

Sählhof, M. & A.J. Veldmeijer 2018. The Architectural Record of the Munro Archive. - Saqqara Newsletter 16: 23-30.

Veldmeijer, A.J., M. Sählhof & C.E. Loeben. 2015. De Oenas-begraafplaats in Sakkara. - Ta-Mery 7: 2-15.

American University in Cairo/German University in Cairo
Dwingeloo/Cairo
September 2019

Kunst- und Kulturstiftung Hannover

PalArch Foundation
Munro Archive Project
hosted by the

Introduction

For well over a century Memphite tombs of the Old Kingdom have been among the most intensively-studied of ancient monuments, yet curiously a detailed understanding of their architecture remains lacking. There are a number of reasons why this is the case. The most obvious seems to be the outstanding quality, both aesthetically and in terms of the information they contain, of the texts and relief decoration on their walls. They are the most coherent collection of 'art' from the Old Kingdom and (along with Theban tomb paintings of the New Kingdom) they are one of the most important datasets, albeit biased in terms of topic and selected moments of these topics, of visual depictions of what might generally be referred as 'everyday life' from the ancient world. This concentration of archaeological attention on one admittedly important aspect of these tombs – what their texts and illustrations can tell us about life as it was lived in the Old Kingdom and what the afterlife might hold for a non-royal member of the Egyptian elite at that time – has diverted attention from the walls on which these images appear, and the rooms constructed from those walls. This is especially the case for the later part of the Old Kingdom; Dynasties Five and Six have the most architecturally complex and interesting of these so-called mastaba tombs, particularly at Saqqara, but that is precisely the period when the physical coverage and thematic range of wall-decoration is also at its most extensive. It is generally the rule that a publication of an Old Kingdom mastaba is essentially the publication of its texts and decoration, with relatively little attention given to the architecture.

There is a good deal of justification for this practice. It is undoubtedly true that the texts and relief carvings are more vulnerable to physical damage than the bulk masonry of the mastaba as a whole, and so treating the recording of these possibly ephemeral elements as a priority seems reasonable enough. Such selectivity in recording is not, of course, justified in the case of monuments which have been deliberately excavated from the preserving sands of the desert. Part of this is to do with the priorities of individual scholars. As a crude rule of thumb it is probably true to say that, as far as Old Kingdom mortuary monuments are concerned, in the period up to the 1970s, Egyptologists whose interest was in deriving information from texts and visual images worked in non-royal tombs, while those who wished to concentrate on architectural and constructional form studied the (mostly) mute royal pyramid tombs. It is now much more the accepted norm that a holistic approach to the study of any monument requires an understanding of all its elements, and especially the way they relate to each other. However, the vast bulk of the published record for Old Kingdom mastabas is one where a study (or even description) of architectural detail is an uncommon bonus.

Once more this is especially the case for the later, more complex mastabas. The detailed comparative work on the form of Old Kingdom tombs which was carried out in the heyday of large-scale mastaba clearance chiefly concerned tombs from the first half of the Old Kingdom at Giza (especially Junker and Reisner). A similar comparative task for the second half of the Old Kingdom remains to be carried out. In part this is because of the complexity of the archaeological situation and the greater architectural variety of tombs from during and after the reign of Nyuserra.1 Saqqara is the main locus for multi-roomed mastabas of the late 5th and 6th Dynasties but, although they can be grouped in convenient clusters in association with royal tombs (the Unas Cemetery is the main focus for the present work), they do not have the same chronological closeness as, say, the mastaba fields associated with Khufu's pyramid at Giza. In addition, as their name suggests, the multi-roomed mastabas at Saqqara are architecturally more complicated than their 4th Dynasty predecessors and they are also subject to much more individual variation (Snape, 2011: 51-85). A multi-roomed mastaba is not more complex simply because it has more rooms, but rather through the way in which the arrangement and variation of those rooms makes every mastaba of any size from the late Old Kingdom at Saqqara very much an individual monument. Design of multi-roomed mastabas stretched the imaginations of Old Kingdom architects who were no doubt intimately aware of royal mortuary temple layout (Jánosi, 1999: 27-39). Aside from satisfying all the needs for the afterlife the architect had to accommodate the desires of a new class of high official, keen to express their wealth and growing independence through their tomb and mortuary cult. Closer inspection of tomb plans and architectural elements not only sheds light on building technology but places tombs within the wider context of the cemetery and the interplay with society. Even though it is accurate to say that no multi-roomed mastaba is exactly the same as any other multi-roomed mastaba, all these monuments were created within an existing and evolving tradition. It is therefore not only valid, but crucial, that the relationship between individual mastabas within this tradition is studied. This approach has been taken with regard to the decoration of these tombs, and it can also be taken for the architecture of those same tombs (Harpur, 1987).[2] Until comparatively recently, there has been no real attempt to produce a detailed study of the architectural make-up of these multi-roomed mastabas and the implications of these observations for understanding the ways in which these tombs were actually used.[3]

The aim of the present study is to reveal the finer details of tomb building and to understand how the masonry was used to produce a particular structure. This will include a close analysis of extant remains in order to postulate now-missing elements which were important to the functioning of the mastaba. A concentration of attention on such minutiae, which is then widened to examine the detail tomb design, can begin to work towards a greater understanding of how these tombs were intended to appear and how they were used.[4] Features such as doorways and the security of the tomb, as well as other aspects such as the provision of storage

---

1 See Bárta (2005: 105-128) for discussion on the major changes in non-royal tomb architecture and in society from the mid 5th Dynasty down to the 6th Dynasty.

2 Also, for the frustrations of tomb publications, see Harpur (2005: 115-127).

3 See Munro (1993a) for an exceptional standard recording of tomb architecture; likewise for Ziegler (2007) and Brovarski (2001).

4 See Harpur & Scremin (2006) for the Oxford Expedition to Egypt strategy of selecting detail over entire wall scenes for appreciating individual craftsmanship.

space for the maintenance of the mortuary cult, are all considered. For it must not be forgotten that multi-roomed mastabas, like most tombs in ancient Egypt, were not built so they could be buried and lost, but rather for a continuation of use for a variety of practical purposes which were carried out by the living in order to service the cult of the dead.

My special interest in the Unas Cemetery goes back to my work as surveyor in the University of Liverpool fieldwork project at the multi-roomed mastaba of Kairer. In trying to find comparative material for the architectural elements I was recording, I was struck by how little published material was available compared to the voluminous literature concerning the decoration of similar tombs. The present work has the tomb of Kairer and others in the Unas Cemetery very much as its core, using my detailed observations of the architecture in these tombs for the comparative examination of other multi-roomed mastabas at Saqqara. This comparative work was carried out in part through what published work was available, but also through further personal observation I was able to carry out during a project of archaeological survey within the Unas Cemetery between 2003 and 2005. For this publication new illustrations have been produced throughout (all figures are by the author unless mentioned otherwise) and additional references to newly published tombs added. There are now new technologies available to the archaeologist include virtual reconstruction and visualisation. In 2019 the Leiden-Turin Expedition to Saqqara began recording in 3D their entire excavation process. Creating 3D models of monuments is a great advance for archaeological survey and one that I hope will be used more with Old Kingdom tombs.

1. The Unas Cemetery

1.1. Introduction

The Unas Cemetery is located at Saqqara - part of the vast Memphite necropolis that stretches for more than 30 km from Abu Rawash, to the south of Dahshur, incorporating other cemetery sites at Giza, Zawyet el-'Aryan, Abu Ghurab, Abusir, and Kom el-Fakhery.[5] The pyramid complex of Unas defines the western edge of the Unas Cemetery, a burial ground for elite individuals of the late Old Kingdom which grew beside the south enclosure wall of the Step Pyramid complex of Djoser (figure 1.1) (Università di Pisa, 2003: 116, 382-385; Edwards, 1996: 173-176; Labrousse *et al.*, 1977). A distinctive covered causeway about 666 m. long connects Unas's pyramid temple with the valley temple at the mouth of a natural depression, or wadi (Hassan, 1955: 136-139, pls. XII-XIII; Moussa, 1985: 33-34; Raslan, 1973: 151-169; Labrousse & Moussa, 1996). The east escarpment of this wadi had been previously utilised as a quarry and this continued during the construction of Unas's pyramid complex. Unas built upon two Early Dynastic gallery tombs whose extant substructures contained the names of 2nd Dynasty kings inscribed on clay sealings: Hetepskhemui and Raneb in Tomb A (Porter & Moss, 1981: 613), Nynetjer in Tomb B (Porter & Moss, 1981: 613). Tomb A, the 'western gallery', is located beneath the eastern side of the pyramid and the pyramid temple of Unas; Tomb B, the 'eastern gallery' is located beneath the south of the causeway of Unas, to the east of Unas's pyramid (Munro, 1993a: 1-2; Spencer, 1993: 105, fig. 80; Wilkinson, 1999: 240-244; Jeffreys & Tavares, 1994: 150-151). The series of underground corridors and storerooms have been likened to the layout of an underground palace by Günter Dreyer (2005: 26).[6] The superstructure of the tombs would have been a mastaba structure but the size and style of the tomb's external appearance is unknown and Peter Munro (1993b: 49-50) does not believe that they could have covered the entire vast subterranean network of chambers. The masonry may have been used in the construction of the Step Pyramid Complex and by time of the 5th Dynasty the monuments were most likely in ruins before Unas decided to level the area for his own mortuary complex (Wilkinson, 1999: 242). In doing so Unas transformed the landscape of this part of the necropolis and provided his funerary monument with a prominent position on the Saqqara plateau (Jeffreys & Tavares, 1994: 151). The location allowed Unas to associate his monument with earlier structures such as the Step Pyramid Complex and the Sekhemkhet complex (besides the previously-mentioned Early Dynastic remains he had built upon). Symmetry is also created by building the pyramid at

5 For a detailed discussion see Lauer (1976), Ray (1979: 149-157) and Smith (1997: 379-93).

6 Meanwhile, after many years of work, later directed by Claudia Lacher-Raschdorff, the tomb of Nynetjer has been published (Lacher-Raschdorff, 2014).

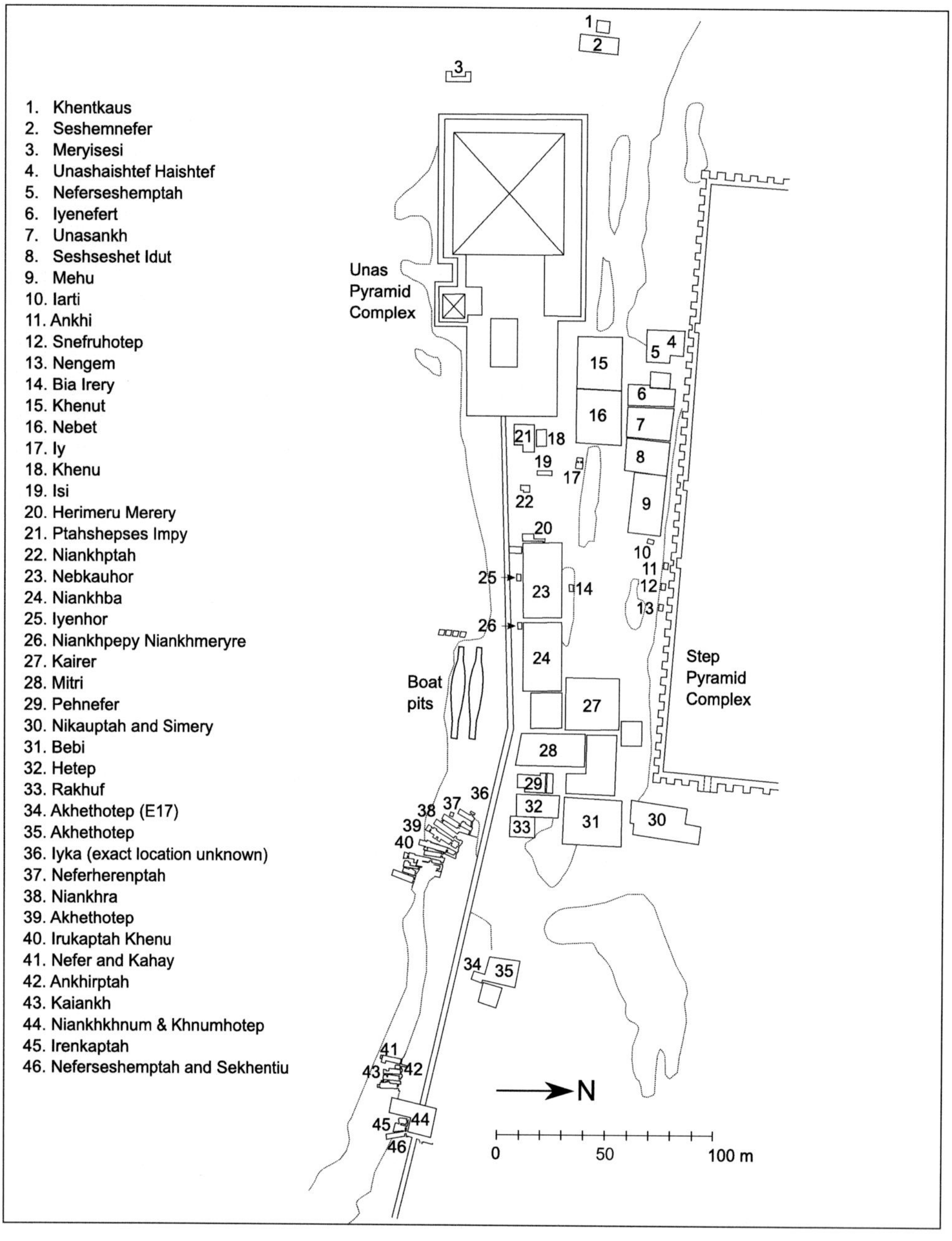

Figure 1.1. Location of tombs in the Unas Cemetery included in the gazetteer.

the south-west corner of the Step Pyramid Complex, opposite Userkaf's pyramid at the north-east corner. Unas's decision to locate his pyramid near the founder of the 5th Dynasty is deliberate and the return of the royal cemetery to Saqqara recommenced the practice of officials building their tombs close to the king's pyramid, unlike during the reign of Unas's predecessor, Djedkara Isesi (Daoud, 1998: 5; Roth, 1988: 201-214). Prior to Unas's building programme the site was a popular burial ground for officials working in the royal household, such as royal butchers and overseers of palace manicurists (Porter & Moss, 1981: 637-648; de Rachewiltz, 1960; McFarlane, 2000; Moussa & Altenmüller, 1971; 1977; Moussa & Junge, 1975). These tombs are partly constructed in masonry and hewn into an escarpment on the south side of the causeway. Swelim (1988: 12-24) thought this was the southern edge of an incredibly deep 'dry moat' surrounding the Step Pyramid Complex enclosure. McFarlane (2000: 7, 16) better describes the rock outcrop as the southern slope of a natural ravine; a natural feature worked as a quarry, probably from the reign of Djoser, as suggested by Moussa and Junge (1975: 9) who excavated in this area (figures 1.2-1.3). In this respect they are similar to rock-cut tombs at Giza, hewn within the faces of former quarry sites, such as those at the site of the Khufu/Khafre quarry and to the south of the Menkaure mortuary temple. The twenty or so known tombs in this area are broadly divided into terrace levels. The tombs of the lowest terrace level must have been closed when Unas developed the cemetery and built his raised causeway through this

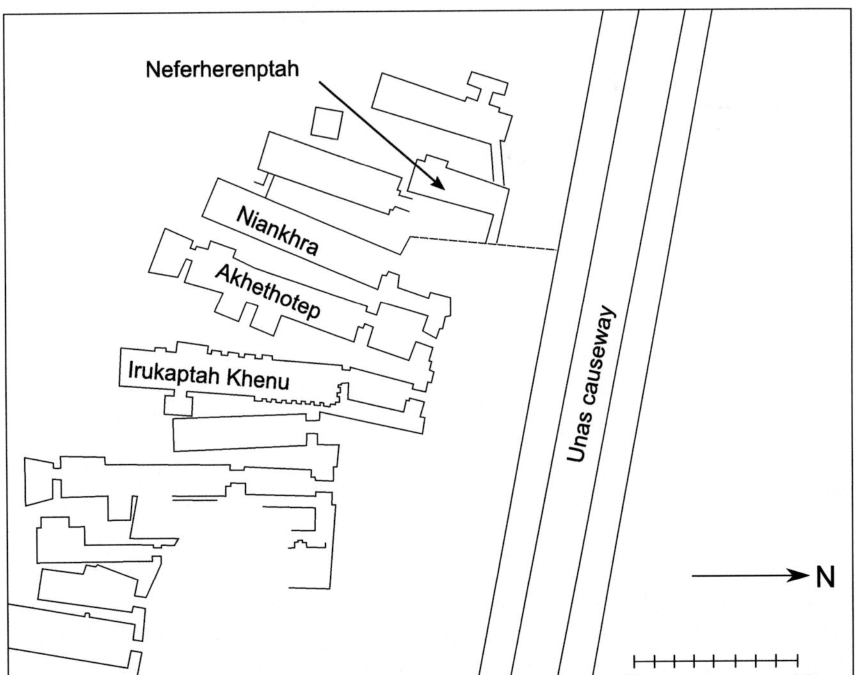

Figure 1.2. East group of rock-cut tombs.

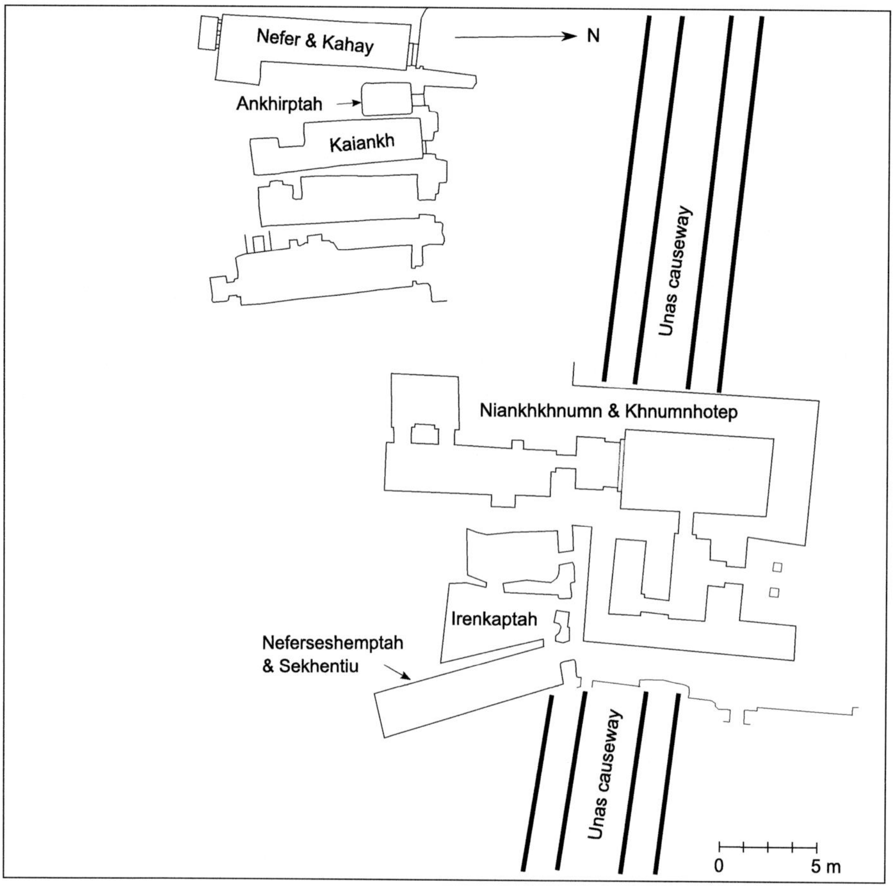

Figure 1.3. West group of rock-cut tombs and the mastaba of Niankhkhnum and Khnumhotep.

area, destroying parts of tombs and obscuring others. Indeed, Unas used masonry from earlier structures, including the enclosure wall of the Step Pyramid Complex, to build the causeway that required a great deal of filling material to raise its level above the height of the wadi floor (Hassan, 1955: 137; Moussa, 1981: 289-295, pl. IX; 1983: 273-276, pls. VIII-IX; Moussa & Nasser, 1979: 155-161, pl. XII).

Mastabas were built in prominent positions along the north side of the causeway during the reign of Unas and in the 6th Dynasty (Munro, 1993a: 1-8; Roth, 1987: fig. 10). The cemetery can be divided into five distinctive zones to aid discussion of the cemetery topography and development (figure 1.4). Unas's building programme included provision of a twin-mastaba for his two wives, queens Khenut and Nebet (Munro, 1993a; Saad, 1940: 683-685). Built from fine white limestone they are impressive mastabas occupying a prime position in the cemetery beside the pyramid temple. Each shares a complicated internal plan featuring a courtyard, storerooms and statue niches (Munro, 1993a: 31, plan 2; Saad, 1940: 683, pl. LXXX).[7] They mark the beginning of a sequence of tomb building in the

7 *Cf.* the statue-niches built in the 5th Dynasty mastaba of Ptashepses at Abusir (Verner, 1994: 175).

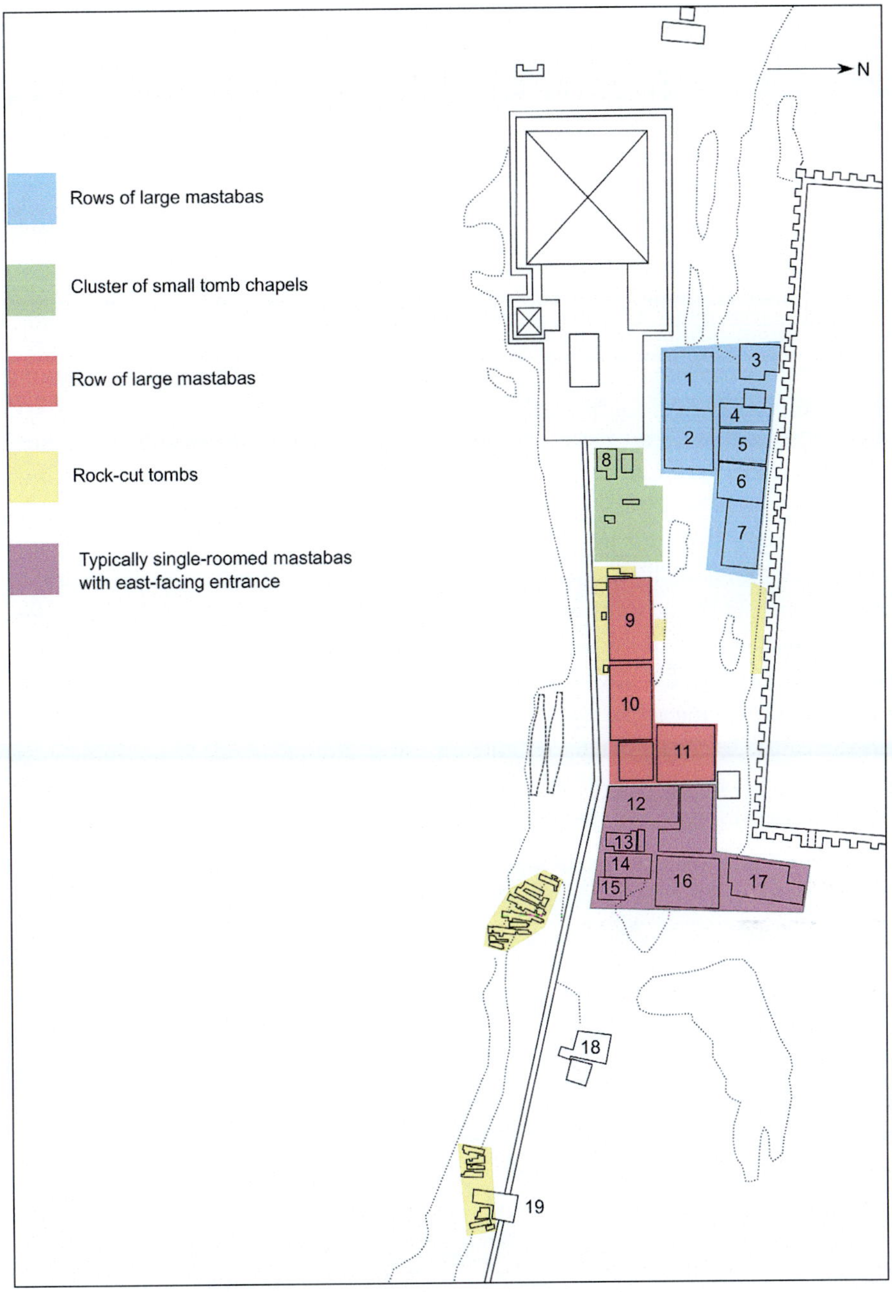

Figure 1.4. Tomb type distribution in the Unas Cemetery.

cemetery. Perhaps next to be built was a row of three mastabas, forming a narrow street directly behind the tombs of Khenut and Nebet. All were built for high officials of Unas, and in a similar size with entrances on the south side. At the east end of the row is a tomb built for a vizier called Ihy, later usurped by the king's daughter, Seshseshet Idut, during the reign of Teti (Kanawati & Raziq, 2003). In the middle is the tomb of Unasankh, an overseer of Upper Egypt, and completing the row at the west end is the tomb of a vizier called Iynefert. The south façade of the three tombs gives the appearance of a unified terrace. Modern restoration hinders close examination of the masonry between these tombs but it has not stopped discussion on the building sequence (Baer, 1960: 66-67, 289; Strudwick, 1985: 56-57; Harpur, 1987: 38-39; Munro, 1993a: 4). Following a programme of archaeological work by Kanawati and Abder-Raziq in this part of the cemetery, they consider there is no evidence of dividing walls within the core between each mastaba and therefore all three tombs were intentionally planned as a terrace unit - construction commenced with the tomb of Iynefert and work moved eastwards, with the tomb Ihy built last (Kanawati & Raziq, 2003: 13-14, 37). In contrast Onderka (2009: 21-27) presents greater supporting evidence for a sequence of work moving in the other direction, starting with the tomb of Ihy. A final addition in the building phase for this row of tombs was added in the 6th Dynasty. A tomb for Mehu, a vizier of Teti, was built against the east wall of Sesheshet Idut's tomb. However, unlike the others Mehu's tomb is orientated east-west, with an entrance on the east side. The mastaba is built on lower ground beside the sloping edge of the escarpment on which the Step Pyramid Complex enclosure wall is built (Altenmüller, 1998: 17-34, plans B, C, D and E). To compensate for this a 2.75 m.

Figure 1.5. Mastaba of Mehu and rock-cut tombs beneath the enclosure wall of the Step Pyramid Complex. Note the narrow street between the two rows of mastabas in the distance.

tall parapet was built to bring the height of the tomb up to the level of the neighbouring tombs to the west. In front of Mehu's mastaba are a series of rock-cut tombs carved within the face of the rock escarpment underneath the enclosure wall of the Step Pyramid Complex (figure 1.5). These rock-cut tombs and the mastaba of Mehu make up a distinct area between the Step Pyramid Complex and the trench (or 'dry moat') that runs between here and the causeway (discussed in Chapter 2).

Family and work affiliations would influence where an official was buried and there have been several discussions concerning genealogy of the tomb owners in the cemetery, which includes three generations of a non-royal family buried within the cemetery: Niankhpepy, Iy and Iarty are father, son and grandson respectively (Altenmüller, 1998: 34-86; Daoud, 1998: 281-283; Fischer, 1965: 49-53; Munro, 1993a: 20-25; Saad, 1940: 690-692). In part of a study of the spatial organisation of cemeteries Roth (1987: 208) considered the high number of viziers buried within the Unas cemetery: "This cemetery is especially interesting in that there appears to be some spatial organization within it. The tombs of king's wives are arranged next to the causeway, the viziers are located in a parallel row behind them, and the tombs of the Overseers of the Judiciary and other judicial offices are located along the causeway to the east." Roth (1987: 202-214) concluded that on some level the cemetery was organised by a bureaucratic function and that the more prestigious tomb plots were those closest to the king's pyramid, with land north of the causeway being premium.

Located further away from Unas' pyramid, directly beside the causeway are two impressive mastabas belonging to Niankhba and Nebkauhor. Both men were viziers during the reign of Unas and their high status is immortalised by the location and architecture of their tombs. The tombs share an architectural style suggesting that both were built at a similar time by the same construction team (Strudwick, 1985: 56-57). At the front of each mastaba are the more humble rock-cut tombs of priests: Niankhpepy before Niankhba, and Iyenhor before Nebkauhor (figure 1.6). Each tomb is accessed via a staircase descending to an open forecourt constructed partly from hewn rock and masonry. Beside the west wall of Nebkauhor's tomb is the rock-cut tomb of Herimeru, which is built in the same 'subterranean' typology as Iyenhor and Niankhpepy. These three later tombs of the 6th Dynasty utilise underground space in the cemetery, with small forecourts and chapels squeezed in beside wealthy tombs popular with visitors to the cemetery, who may be enticed to step down below (into the shade) and make an offering.

To the east of the tomb of Kairer is a cluster of mastabas of a similar style, all with an entrance located facing east. The tombs are built close together and form tight 'streets' in places. With their use of large limestone blocks and small recessed chapels the style is reminiscent of earlier 4th Dynasty mastabas at Giza. Their orientation to the east suggests they are facing the way visitors approach the cemetery, and may indicate a greater chronological difference between this cluster and the west side of the cemetery.

Figure 1.6. The rock-cut tomb of Iyenhor in front of the mastaba of Nebkauhor.

The area between the tomb of Nebkauhor and the pyramid temple is unlike other part of the cemetery; it contains a large quantity of small simple mastabas and rock-cut tombs dating between the late Old Kingdom and the First Intermediate Period (c. 2345-2055 BC), with many later intrusive burials. The area was partially excavated by Zaki Saad in the early 1940s and re-examined in the 1980s and 1990s by Peter Munro (1983a: 81-109; 1984a: 59-94; 1984b: 73-91; 1993a: 5-6, plan 1). Termed 'Zone C' by Munro he has shown how the area was organised into two rows with a narrow central street 2.00 m. wide orientated east-west (figure 1.7). It is curious that this area was not particularly utilised for a large building plot during the late 5th Dynasty and early 6th Dynasty. There is a definite gap between the pyramid temple of Unas and the mastaba of Nebkauhor. The location of the trench (discussed in Chapter 2) or some other architectural relic from the earlier history of the cemetery could have initially hampered the construction of a substantial structure. Tombs in this area reuse masonry from earlier funerary structures which could suggest that earlier monuments in this area were dismantled during the later part of the Old Kingdom. Like so much of the Memphite necropolis, the Unas Cemetery was in use beyond the Old Kingdom through to the Roman Period, giving rise to a sequence of tomb building and complicated vertical stratigraphy. The gazetteer below attempts to give an overview of tombs built around the pyramid complex of Unas during the Old Kingdom and First Intermediate Period.

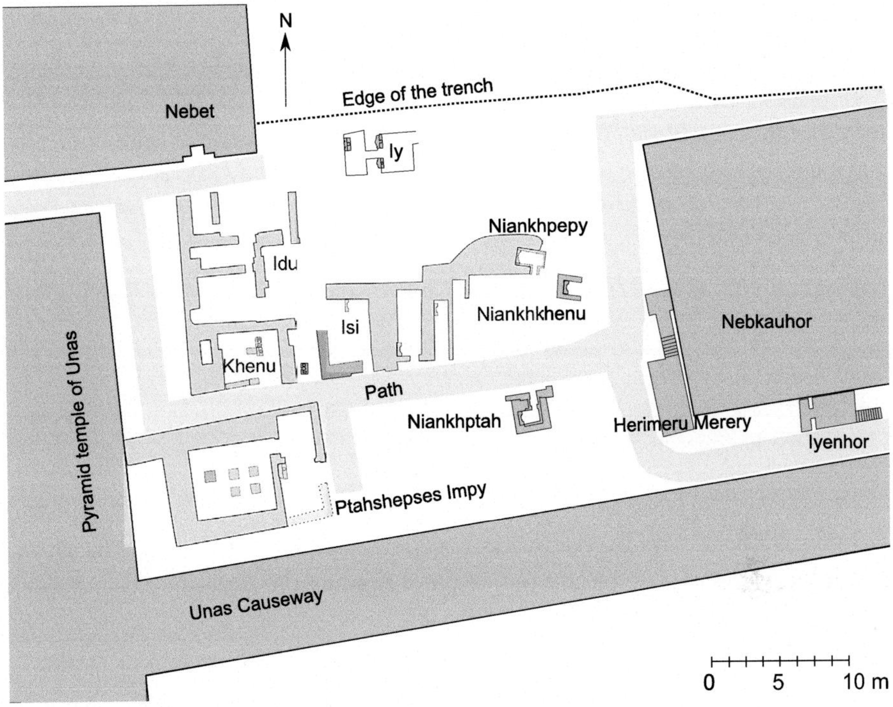

Figure 1.7. The area between the pyramid temple of Unas and the mastaba of Nebkauhor (Munro's Zone C).

1.2. Gazetteer of Tombs in the Unas Cemetery

This gazetteer of the tombs within the Unas Cemetery in the order presented in Porter and Moss (1981). For each tomb selected titles of the owner is included as well as a note on the location. Tomb entries contains the date provided within Porter and Moss (1981) and, where useful, other authors have been included, most notably: Harpur (1987), The Oxford Expedition to Egypt Scene-details Database/OEE Database (Linacre College, 2006; henceforth referred to as OEE Database), Strudwick (1985), Baer (1960) and Kanawati (1977). Where applicable there is a short description of the excavation history, any subsequent archaeological work, and a brief description of the architecture. Bibliographic references are not intended to be exhaustive and those provided are ones that relate specifically to the excavation and architecture of the tomb. Full references for each tomb can be found in Porter and Moss (1981) and in this way the lack of published material on tomb architecture and archaeology is more apparent.

Khentkaus

Selected Titles: King's eldest daughter of his body.

Date: Porter and Moss (1981): probably 6th Dynasty.

Location: At the west of the tomb of Seshemnufer, near the rear of the north-west corner of the pyramid of Unas (figure 1.1)

Architecture: Partly rock-cut and partly built with mudbrick. The chamber was roofed with three blocks of limestone and contained a limestone false-door that had been painted to imitate the appearance of granite. The same effect had been applied to the underside of the roofing slabs and the walls of the tomb plastered with mud and whitewashed. It would appear no plan has been published.

Bibliography: Saad (1947: 62-6, pls. xxvi and xxix-xxxi [a]).

Seshemnefer

Selected titles: Overseer of the department of tenants of the great house; Master butcher of the great house.

Date: Porter and Moss (1981): 6th Dynasty; OEE Database: 6th Dynasty, reigns of Pepy I to Pepy II, years 1-34?

Location: At the west of the pyramid of Unas (figure 1.1).

Architecture: Rock-cut tomb with a descending staircase leading to a rectangular shaped courtyard. The south wall of the courtyard is built from limestone masonry with a large inscribed lintel above a doorway to an offering-room that has a north-south orientation and a limestone false-door at the southern end of the west wall.

Bibliography: Barsanti (1900: 150-152, 160, figs.1-3, 5, 16; 1901: 246); Saad (1947: 56-62, pls. xviii-xxiii).

Meryisesi

Selected titles: Supervisor and inspector of priests of the pyramid of Unas.

Date: Porter and Moss (1981): early 6th Dynasty.

Location: About 50.00 m. to the west of the pyramid of Unas and to the south of the tomb of Seshemnefer (figure 1.1).

Architecture: Mastaba with a decorated rectangular shaped entrance chamber orientated on a north-south axis. At the north end is an undecorated room, and opposite at the south end is the offering-room with an east-west orientation and a false-door. The tomb was usurped by Meryisesi.

Bibliography: Lauer (1937: 110-111).

Unashaishtef Haishtef (originally for Kai Seni)

Selected titles: Unashaishtef Haishtef: Overseer of commissions of the pyramid of Unas; Kai Seni: Inspector of priests of the pyramid of Unas.

Date: Porter and Moss (1981): Probably Middle Kingdom. Munro considers that the tomb can hardly be older than the second half of the Herakleopolitan Period (1993b: 55-58).

Location: Built beside the enclosure wall of the Step Pyramid Complex, west of the tomb of Iynefert (figure 1.1).

Architecture: Uncovered during excavations of the Antiquities Service directed by Zaki Saad (season 1939-1940). Thought to be built over the earlier tomb of Neferseshemptah and originally intended for the owner's father, Kai. Hölscher and Munro planned the full extent of the tomb which extends southwards with two chambers.

Bibliography: Saad (1940: 685-686); Munro (1993a: insert 1; 1993b: 55-58); Hölscher and Munro (1975: 122-123).

Neferseshemptah

Date: Porter and Moss (1981): 5th or 6th Dynasty; OEE Database: 5th Dynasty, reign of Unas, to 6th Dynasty, reign of Teti; Munro gives a date of the time of Unas (1993b: 55-58).

Location: Underneath Unashaishtef Haishtef (figure 1.1).

Architecture: The tomb was destroyed for the construction of the tomb of Unashaishtef Haishtef and his family. Hölscher and Munro recorded a plan of the tomb in the early 1970s. It consisted of at least five chambers, with the entrance located on the southern face. With a large open courtyard the tomb plan is reminiscent of others in the cemetery, such as the neighbouring mastaba of Iynefert. The courtyard contains a staircase to the roof, rather similar in style to the nearby tombs of Niankhba and Nebkauhor.

Bibliography: Munro (1993b: 55-58); Hölscher and Munro (1975: 115-117, 121, 126).

Iynefert

Selected titles: Chief justice and vizier.

Date: Porter and Moss (1981): 6th Dynasty; OEE Database: 5th Dynasty, reign of Unas; Harpur (1987): 5th Dynasty, reign of Unas; Strudwick (1985): 5th Dynasty, middle to late reign of Unas; Kanawati and Raziq (2003): 5th Dynasty, early to middle reign of Unas for the construction of the tomb.

Location: Within a row of tombs between the enclosure wall of the Step Pyramid Complex and the tombs of Nebet and Khenut (figures 1.1, 1.8).

Architecture: Large mastaba uncovered and recorded during excavations by Zaki Saad (season 1939-1940). The interior consists of five rooms, one of which is an open courtyard. An east-west offering room with false-door occupying the west wall, carved from limestone painted reddish-brown to imitate the appearance of granite. The offering-room has no attached side-room and for this reason Harpur (1987) dates the tomb to the reign of Unas. The mastaba was part of a fieldwork project led by Kanawati (Macquarie University) and Abder-Raziq (University of Suez Canal), with a full report published in 2003.

Bibliography: Saad (1940: 686-687); Hölscher and Munro (1975: 126); Kanawati and Raziq (2003).

Unasankh

Selected titles: Overseer of Upper Egypt; King's son.

Date: Porter and Moss (1981): 5th Dynasty, reign of Unas; OEE Database: 5th Dynasty, reign of Unas; Baer (1960): 5th Dynasty, year 16 Isesi – year 10 Unas.

Location: Within a row of tombs between the enclosure wall of the Step Pyramid Complex and the tombs of Nebet and Khenut (figures 1.1, 1.8).

Architecture: Large mastaba first uncovered by James Quibell in 1907, with Rooms 4 and 5 (offering-room) dismantled and sold to The Field Museum of Natural History, Chicago (A 24448), by the Egyptian Government in 1908. The mastaba was cleared again during work in the area by Cecil Firth, 1925-1927; and by Zaki Saad, 1939 -1940 who made a record of the remaining rooms. The tomb consisted of six rooms, one of which is an open courtyard; very similar in design to the neighbouring tomb of Iynefert. The north-south orientation of the offering-room is also similar to that within the neighbouring tomb of Sesheshet Idut. Peter Munro's team made investigations in this area between 1973 and 1982. A full record of the tomb has been published using Munro's documentation and new data collected by Pavel Onderka between 2004 and 2006.

Bibliography: Onderka (2009); Saad (1940: 687).

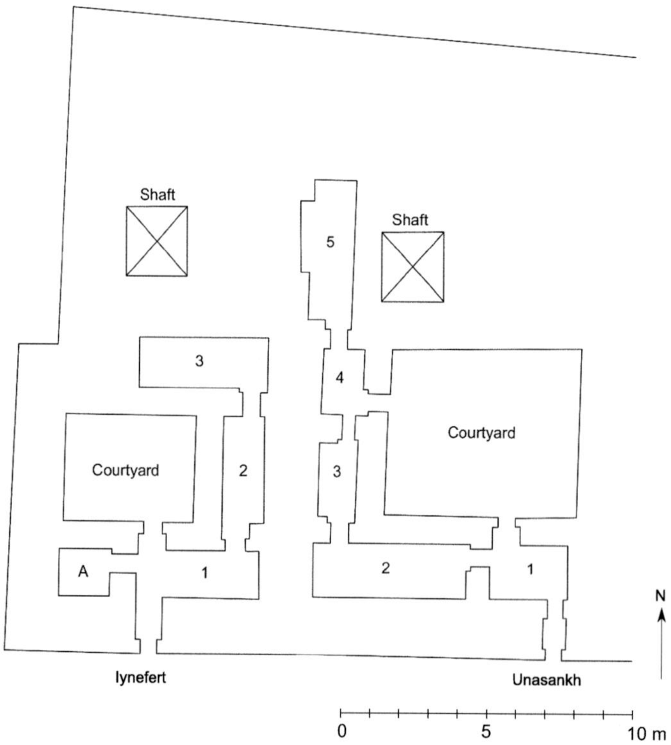

Figure 1.8. The mastabas of Iynefert and Unasankh.

Seshseshet Idut (originally for Ihy)

Selected titles: Ihy: Chief justice and vizier; Seshseshet Idut: King's daughter of his body.

Date: Ihy: Porter and Moss (1981): 6th Dynasty; OEE Database: 5th Dynasty, reign of Unas; Kanawati and Raziq (2003): 5th Dynasty, late reign of Unas; Harpur (1987): 5th Dynasty, reign of Unas; Strudwick (1985): late reign of Unas; Baer (1960): 6th Dynasty, Merenre to Pepy II year 15.

Seshseshet Idut: Porter and Moss (1981): 6th Dynasty; OEE Database: 6th Dynasty, reigns of Teti to early Pepy I; Kanawati and Raziq (2003): 6th Dynasty; Harpur (1987): 6th Dynasty, no later than the reign of Pepy I; Strudwick (1985): 6th Dynasty; Baer (1960): 6th Dynasty, probably middle or late reign of Pepy II.

Location: Within a row of tombs between the enclosure wall of the Step Pyramid Complex and the tombs of Nebet and Khenut (figures 1.1, 1.9).

Architecture: Large mastaba uncovered by Cecil Firth whilst clearing areas near the enclosure wall of the Step Pyramid Complex, 1926 -1927. The mastaba has a complex internal layout that includes a north-south offering room with false-door occupying the west wall; three storerooms; and a staircase leading to the

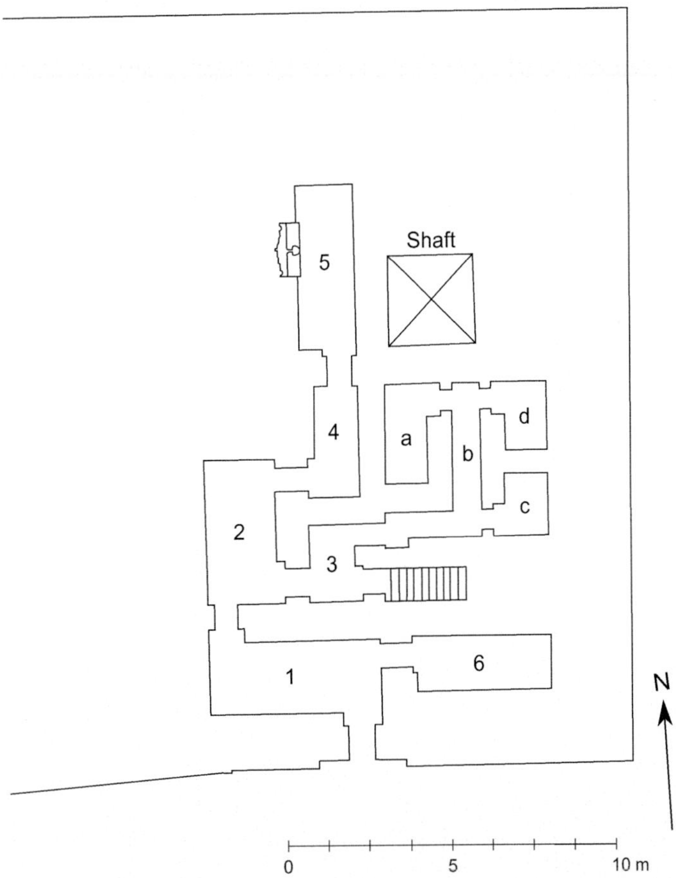

Figure 1.9.
The mastaba of Seshseshet Idut.

roof. Originally built for a vizier called Ihy, late in the reign of Unas; then usurped for the king's daughter Seshseshet Idut in the reign of Teti. The tomb was part of a fieldwork project led by Kanawati (Macquarie University) and Abder-Raziq (University of Suez Canal), with a full report published in 2003.

Bibliography: Firth (1927: 107); Macramallah (1935); Kanawati and Raziq (2003).

Mehu

Selected titles: Chief justice and vizier.

Date: Porter and Moss (1981): 6th Dynasty, reign of Pepy I; OEE Database: 6th Dynasty, middle reign of Pepy I to reign of Merenre?; Strudwick (1987): 6th Dynasty, reign of Pepy II.

Location: Adjoining the east wall of the tomb of Seshseshet Idut and forms the east end of the row of tombs between the enclosure wall of the Step Pyramid Complex and the tomb of Nebet (figures 1.1, 1.10).

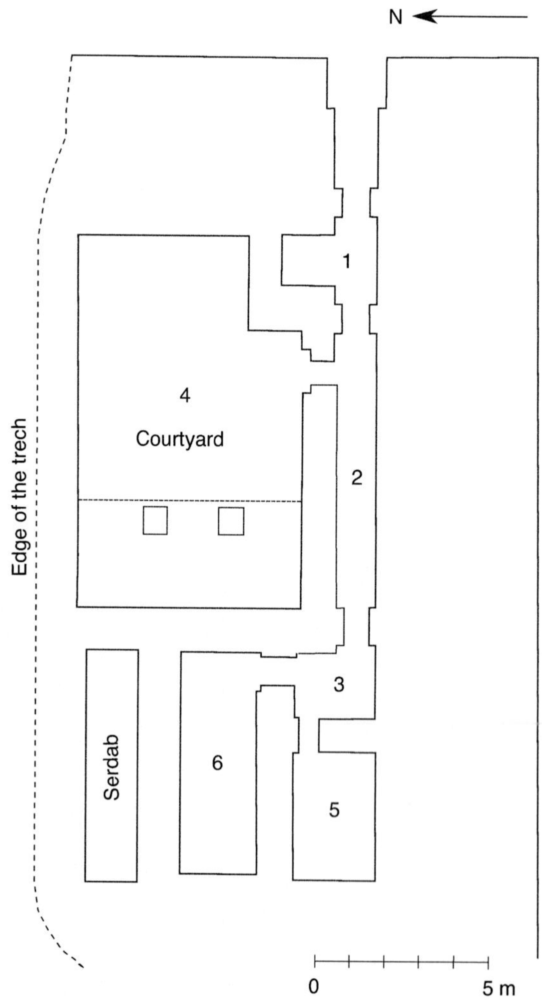

Figure 1.10. Mastaba of Mehu.

Architecture: Large mastaba uncovered during excavations of the Antiquities Service directed by Zaki Saad, (season 1939-1940), with restoration work directed by Abdel Hussein. Between 1977 and 1980 the tomb was studied by Munro and Altenmüller. The tomb measures 29.40 m. east to west, and 16.50 m. north to south. It is built against the east wall of the tomb of Sesheshet Idut and the rear of the tomb meets the vertical face of the rock that supports the enclosure wall of the Step Pyramid Complex. The tomb was certainly constructed after the tomb of Sesheshet Idut, as no western wall was constructed. The southern half of the floor is carved from the bedrock. A mudbrick wall and a wall of consolidated rubble and mud encircle the limestone walls on the eastern and southern sides. The entrance lies on the east side, and leads towards an open court at the front of the tomb, and the two east-west offering-rooms at the rear. The largest offering room is for Mehu and a magazine was converted into an offering-room for his son during later modifications to the original tomb plan, which included the addition of a portico in the courtyard. Rather unusually the roofing in each chamber is intact and includes windows set between the top of the wall and the ceiling (discussed in Chapter 4).

Bibliography: Altenmüller (1998); Hussein (1942: 417-425, fig. 114, pls. xxiv-xxxiv); Saad (1940: 687-690).

Iarti

Selected titles: Inspector of the priests of the pyramid of Unas; Overseer of tenants of the great house.

Date: Porter and Moss (1981): middle of the 6th Dynasty or later; Daoud (1995): no earlier than the 8th Dynasty or early Herakleopolitan Period (he is the son of Iy and grandson of Niankhpepy, who are both buried in this cemetery).

Location: One of a group of four rock-cut tombs belonging to officials, many serving as priests under Unas, Teti and Pepy I. The tombs are hewn into the rock face below the enclosure wall of the Step Pyramid Complex (figure 1.1). The tomb of Iarti is nearest to the mastaba of Mehu and the others are positioned in a row to the east of this, with the tomb of Nengem being at the end. This escarpment is now concealed by sand and many of the tombs are not visible. Very little attention has been given to the architecture of the tombs. Iarti's tomb is a single square chamber with a narrow entrance (Hussein, 1942: pl. XXXIII). In his account of the 1939-1940 excavations Selim Hassan (1940: 683) comments: "Twenty-seven limestone false-doors of different types and measurements were found; some were thrown out of their original places, while some were found *in situ*. They are all nicely inscribed and some traces of colour still appear on some of them. They are all for officials who lived under kings Unas, Teti and Pepi. The majority of these officials were priests and priestesses who served the cult after the death of the king." The number of false-doors that Hassan reported does not match with the actual total (Personal

Communication Khaled Daoud, 2000). The false-doors of Ankhi, Sneferuhotep and Nengem were found in an area to the east of the tomb of Mehu, with only that of Iarti being found in its original position.

Architecture: Rock-cut tomb hewn into the rock face below the enclosure wall of the Step Pyramid Complex.

Bibliography: Altenmüller (2012: 1-20); Daoud (1998: 281-283); Saad (1940: 683, fig. 73).

Ankhi

Selected titles: Priest of the pyramid of Unas; Overseer of tenants; Noble of the king.

Date: Porter and Moss (1981): 6th Dynasty.

Location: See above for the tomb of Iarti (figure 1.1).

Architecture: Rock-cut tomb hewn into the rock face below the enclosure wall of the Step Pyramid Complex.

Snefruhotep

Date: Porter and Moss (1981): 6th Dynasty.

Location: See above for the tomb of Iarti (figure 1.1).

Architecture: Rock-cut tomb hewn into the rock face below the enclosure wall of the Step Pyramid Complex.

Nengem

Selected titles: Royal chamberlain; Inspector of scribes of sacrificial cattle.

Date: Porter and Moss (1981): 6th Dynasty.

Location: See above for the tomb of Iarti (figure 1.1).

Architecture: Rock-cut tomb hewn into the rock face below the enclosure wall of the Step Pyramid Complex.

Bia Irery

Selected titles: Noble of the King; Companion of the house.

Date: Porter and Moss (1981): end of the 6th Dynasty; OEE Database: 6th Dynasty, reign of Merenre to reign of Pepy II, years 1-34?

Location: Behind the tomb of Nebkauhor (figure 1.1).

Architecture: Rock-cut tomb with a limestone architrave Wilson (1954) believed was positioned above the false-door. The location of the tomb is related to the owner's relationship with the vizier Mehu as Fischer (1965) believes Bia and his son were both funerary priests of the vizier. In Mehu's tomb Bia appears three times as one of Mehu's funerary servants and because of the distinctive nature of the name Fischer believes they are the same individual and that Mehu was Bia's master and someone whom he wished to be buried next to.

Bibliography: Fischer (1965: 49-53, pl. xxix); Wilson (1954: 243-264).

Nebet and Khenut

Selected titles: Nebet: King's wife; Companion of Horus; Khenut: King's wife.

Date: Nebet: Porter and Moss (1981): 5th Dynasty, reign of Unas; Khenut: Porter and Moss (1981): 5th Dynasty, reign of Unas.

Location: Directly beside the northern wall of the funerary temple of Unas (figure 1.1, 1.11).

Architecture: Large adjoining mastabas excavated by Zaki Saad, whilst he was directing work for the Antiquities Service in a season between 1939 and 1940. Excavations between 1973 and 1982 by Peter Munro revealed that the plan of each mastaba paralleled each other very closely. Both were built from fine white limestone masonry but now little survives of the western side of Khenut's tomb as the masonry was removed during the Saite Period. Together the two tombs have an east to west length of nearly 50.00 m., with each being about 22.00 m .in width. Both tombs contained statue niches and an east-west offering room with side-room to the south. The configuration of a series of storerooms within the two tombs appears identical.

Bibliography: Munro (1993a); Saad (1940: 683-685).

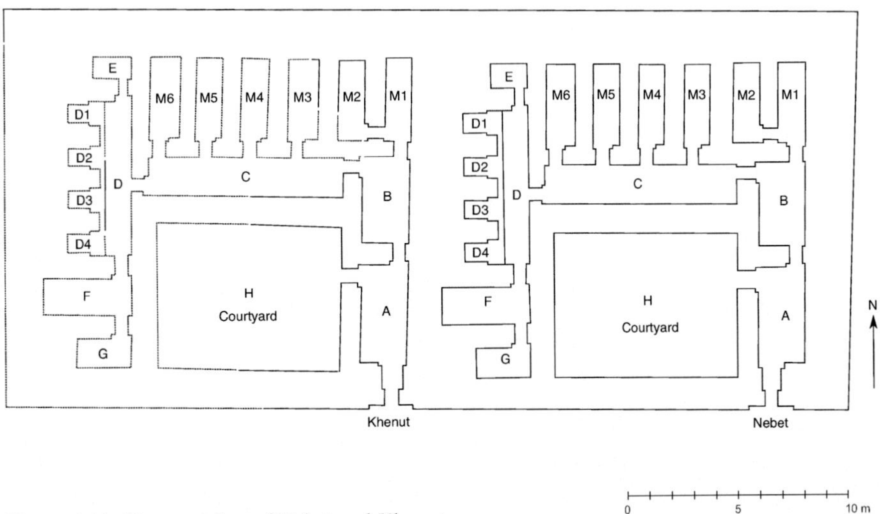

Figure 1.11. The mastabas of Nebet and Khenut.

Iy

Selected titles: Tenant of the pyramid of Pepy I; Companion of the house; Noble of the king.

Date: Porter and Moss (1981): 6th Dynasty, reign of Pepy I or later.

Location: One of a group of small tombs clustered between the pyramid temple of Unas and the west wall of the tomb of Nebkauhor (figures 1.1, 1.7).

Architecture: Rock-cut tomb with inscribed door jambs, but little else has been published about the architecture of the tomb. Iy is the son of Niankhpepy who is buried in a rock-cut tomb in front of the mastaba of Niankhba.

Bibliography: Munro (1984a: 61-64; 1993a: 5-6); Altenmüller (1974: 5-6).

Khenu

Selected titles: Tenant of the pyramid of Unas; Noble of the king of the great house.

Date: Porter and Moss (1981): Late 6th Dynasty or Middle Kingdom; Munro (1993a): end of the 12th Dynasty; Daoud (1998): end of the Old Kingdom.

Location: One of a group of small tombs clustered between the pyramid temple of Unas and the west wall of the tomb of Nebkauhor (figures 1.1. 1.7).

Architecture: Three inscribed columns support a portico containing one false-door for Khenu and a later false-door positioned in front of this. The structure has been heavily restored.

Bibliography: Daoud (1998: 275-278); Munro (1983b: 283-295; 1984a: 73-77; 1993a: 5-6); Altenmüller (1974: 6-8)

Isi

Date: Porter and Moss (1981): 6th Dynasty.

Location: Beside the mastaba of Khenu (figures 1.1, 1.7).

Bibliography: Munro (1993a: 5-6).

Herimeru Merery

Selected titles: Priest and tenant of the pyramid of Unas.

Date: Porter and Moss (1981): end of the 6th Dynasty; OEE Database: 6th Dynasty, reign of Pepy II year 1 to late 6th Dynasty.

Location: Close to the south-west corner of the tomb of Nebkauhor (figures 1.1, 1.7).

Architecture: This is a rock-cut tomb entered by a descending staircase and consists of two rooms. The front of the tomb is built from limestone masonry and mudbrick and contains two false-doors within the west wall.

Bibliography: Munro (1993a: 5-6); Hassan (1975c: 69-81, figs. 36, 43, pl. lii).

Ptahshepses Impy

Selected titles: Lector priest.

Date: Porter and Moss (1981): 6th Dynasty.

Location: Immediately beside the east wall of the Unas's pyramid temple and the end of the causeway (figures 1.1, 1.7).

Architecture: Small mastaba uncovered by the Antiquities Service during 1929-1930 clearance of the Unas pyramid temple. The interior of tomb is constructed from masonry with a thick mudbrick wall on the exterior. An entrance room on the east side leads to a small columned hall. The false-door has recently been identified in the collections of the Museum of Archaeology and Ethnology, University of Sao Paulo (de Araújo Duarte, 2018: 231-242).

Bibliography: Munro (1984a: 77-88; 1993a: 5-6); Firth (1930: 187).

Niankhptah

Selected titles: Secretary of all works; Priest of the pyramid of Unas.

Date: Porter and Moss (1981): 6th Dynasty; OEE Database: 6th Dynasty.

Location: To the west of the mastaba of Nebkauhor, on the south side of the narrow 'street' of tombs that runs between the funerary temple of Unas and the mastaba of Nebkauhor (figures 1.1, 1.7).

Architecture: Little has been published on the architecture of this mastaba. It is a single chambered tomb with long entrance passage on the north side. Stone masonry survives at the front of the tomb and for part of the interior walls.

Bibliography: Munro (1984a: 88-90; 1993a: 5-6).

Nebkauhor (originally for Akhethotep Hemi)

Selected titles: Akhethotep Hemi: Chief justice and vizier; Nebakauhor: Chief justice and vizier; King's eldest son of his body; Inspector of the priests of the pyramid of Unas.

Date: Akhethotep Hemi: Porter and Moss (1981): late 5th Dynasty/early 6th Dynasty; OEE Database: 5th Dynasty, reign of Unas; Strudwick (1985): middle reign of Unas; Baer (1960): 5th Dynasty, reigns of Djedkara to Unas (assuming the range of titles belong to the original owner).

Nebkauhor Idu: Porter and Moss (1981): 6th Dynasty; OEE Database: 6th Dynasty, reign of Pepy II years 1-85; Strudwick (1985): 6th Dynasty, no earlier than the reign of Pepy II; Baer (1960): 6th Dynasty.

Location: On the north side of the causeway, beside the tomb of Niankhba (figures 1.1, 1.12).

Architecture: Large mastaba uncovered during excavations directed by the Antiquities Service directed by Selim Hassan, 1937-1938. The complex plan is a classic example of multi-roomed mastaba tombs of the late Old Kingdom. The tomb originally belonged to a 6th Dynasty vizier called Akhethotep and was usurped by another vizier called Nebkauhor during the reign of Pepy II or later (Strudwick, 1982: 89-94). Nebkauhor concealed the original owner's names and titles around the entrance with a new course of masonry; all trace of Akhethotep's name was removed from the interior except in one place. The architecture of the tomb is very similar in plan to that of its neighbour belonging to Niankhba. The whole of the mastaba varies in height, with some rooms only surviving to a height of two or three courses. In most rooms the walls are built using a lower course of rougher local limestone, surmounted with finer white limestone. The walls of the large pillared hall (9.45 m. x 9.80 m.) have mostly been restored following Hassan's clearance of the tomb in 1937-1938. Other internal chambers include an east-west offering room with an attached side-room, and a complex of five storerooms.

Bibliography: Hassan (1938: 512-514, 519; 1975a).

Niankhba

Selected titles: Chief justice and vizier.

Date: Porter and Moss (1981): 6th Dynasty; Strudwick (1985): 5th Dynasty, middle reign of Unas.

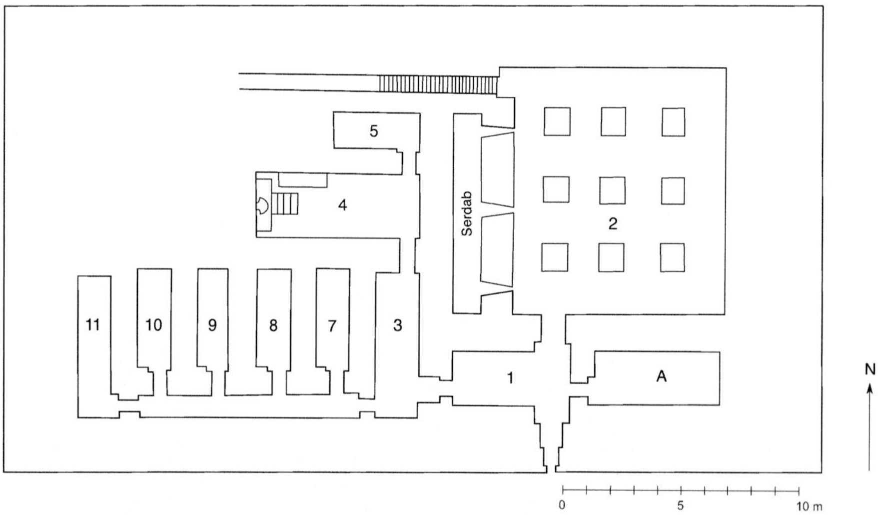

Figure 1.12. The mastaba of Nebkauhor (Akhtihotep).

Location: To the north of the causeway, beside the tomb of Nebkauhor (figures 1.1, 1.13).

Architecture: Large mastaba uncovered during excavations by the Antiquities Service directed by Selim Hassan, 1937-1938. It has a complex plan which includes a large roofed hall supported by sixteen square pillars. The tomb contains an east-west offering room with an attached side-room to the north. The internal and external masonry consists of a mixture of imported and local limestone. Wall heights vary though few are over two or three courses high. The walls of the pillared hall survive to the greatest height, in some places six courses.

Bibliography: Hassan (1938: 506-508; 1975c: 41-48, fig. 25, pls. xxvi and xxxi).

Iyenhor

Selected titles: Lector-priest of the mit-bark of Horus and the *ḏ3t*-bark of Horus

Date: Porter and Moss (1981): end of the 6th Dynasty.

Location: Between the tomb of Nebkauhor and the causeway (figure 1.1, 1.7).

Architecture: Rock-cut tomb uncovered during excavations by the Antiquities Service directed by Selim Hassan during the 1937-1938 season. This small tomb is hewn from the rock floor against the south wall of Nebkauhor's tomb, revealing the rock surface foundation of this tomb. A staircase leads to the open courtyard with an offering-room cut into the rock on the west side. Above the doorway to the offering-room are two inscribed limestone lintels. The floor of the offering-hall is 0.28 m. lower than the courtyard and the walls were covered with plaster. Two false-doors are located on the west wall, one of which is inscribed for Iyenhor while the other remains uninscribed.

Bibliography: Hassan (1975c: 59-67, figs. 32, 35, pl. XLV-LI).

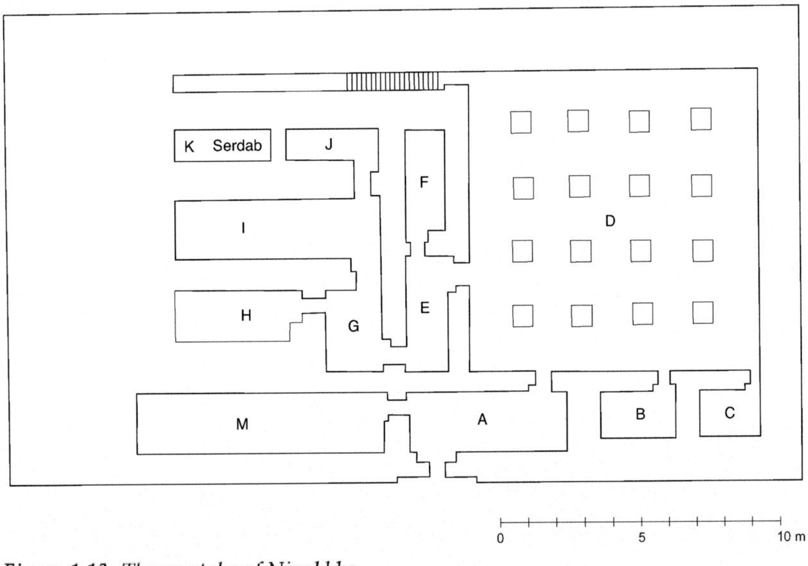

Figure 1.13. The mastaba of Niankhba.

Niankhpepy Niankhmeryre

Selected titles: Overseer of commissions of tenants of the Pyramid of Pepy I.

Date: Porter and Moss (1981): end of the 6th Dynasty (usurped tomb).

Location: Between the tomb of Niankhba and Unas's causeway (figure 1.1).

Architecture: Rock-cut tomb uncovered during excavations by the Antiquities Service directed by Selim Hassan during the 1937-1938 season. Stairs lead down to a small open courtyard with an offering-room cut into the rock on the west side. The entrance to the offering-room is constructed from two inscribed limestone doorjambs and a lintel. The tomb is partly hewn from the rock and partly built from limestone blocks, all originally plastered over and white-washed. Within the offering-room the northern end of the western wall contains a recess that accommodates the false-door. The door was not completed but the surface is inscribed with black ink. The shaft of the tomb is located directly behind the false-door, descending to a burial chamber cut on the eastern side. Interestingly the shaft narrows in the middle to form a narrow circular 'waist' that supported a large plug of granite.

Bibliography: Hassan (1938: 508-512; 1975b: 1-23, fig. 1, pls. I-V).

Kairer

Selected Titles: Vizier; Hereditary prince.

Date: Porter and Moss (1981): 6th Dynasty; OEE Database: 6th Dynasty, reign of Pepy I.

Location: Beside the north-east corner of the tomb of Niankhba, set back from the causeway behind the tomb of an anonymous person (figures 1.1, 1.14).

Architecture: Large mastaba cleared by Cecil Firth whilst working in the area around the tomb between 1925 and 1926. Parts of the tomb were restored and the burial chamber cleared between 1936 and 1937 by Jean-Philip Lauer on behalf of the Antiquities Service. Between 1993 and 2000 Khaled Daoud and Christopher Eyre of the University of Liverpool carried out epigraphic work, including an architectural survey. The entrance is on the south side of the tomb with two small obelisks on either side of the doorway. The tomb originally covered an area in the extent of 570 m^2 and is built upon a raised platform of rubble that provided a level area on the sloped ground to the south of the southern enclosure wall of the Step Pyramid Complex. The superstructure is built from limestone masonry, surrounded by a mudbrick enclosure wall. Only four of the eight restored rooms are decorated, with an undefined room layout in the north-west part of the tomb which was not included in Lauer's restoration work. To the north-east is an east-west offering room, with an attached side-room to the north. The false-door is now missing, with only a few fragments remaining.

Bibliography: Daoud (1995: 35-48; 1997: 6-7); Lauer (1937: 107-109, fig. 2).

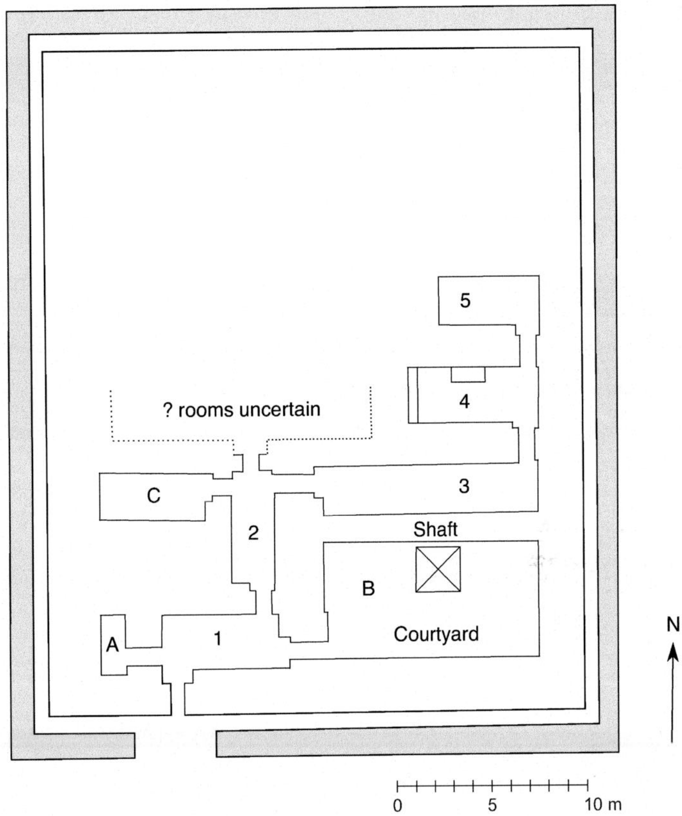

Figure 1.14. The mastaba of Kairer.

Mitri

Selected titles: Boundary official; Priest of Maat.

Date: Porter and Moss (1981): end of the 5th Dynasty or early 6th Dynasty.

Location: An area between the south-east corner of the enclosure wall of the Step Pyramid Complex and the causeway (figure 1.1). At the beginning of December 1929, Cecil Firth of the Antiquities Service made an examination of this area and reported that the tombs were "comparatively unimportant, and in some cases, unfinished" (Firth, 1930: 185). He noted that some of the burial chambers had not been finished and that red marks were still visible on a number of false-doors that had not received a final dressing. It was during 1937-1938 that the Antiquities Service made a complete clearance of this area, and Selim Hassan states that twelve mastabas of the 5th and 6th Dynasty were discovered on the eastern side of the Pyramid of Unas (Hassan, 1938: 503-521).

Architecture: This solid structure mastaba is more typical of the 4th Dynasty mastabas found at Giza. The tomb is oriented north-south, with a recessed chapel entered at the southern end of its eastern façade. There are two small niches along the east wall to the north of the entrance. The exterior masonry has been removed from the tomb exposing a core of large sized roughly dressed limestone blocks.

Three limestone roofing slabs survive on the western half of the serdab. Several statues were removed from the serdab but very little has been published on the structure of this tomb.

Pehnefer

Selected titles: Director of the broad hall.

Location: To the west of the mastaba of Hetep.

Date: Porter and Moss (1981): 6th Dynasty.

Location: The area between the south-east corner of the Step Pyramid Complex enclosure wall and the causeway (figure 1.1).

Architecture: Mastaba built from mudbrick, measuring 10.55 m. x 8.50 m, with a present height of 2.06 m. A small offering-room, measuring 2.75 m. x 8.50 m. is located at the north-east corner of the tomb, and it is accessed at the east side of the tomb. An inscribed false-door is located on the east face of the offering-room wall. The shaft is positioned south-west of the offering-room, and no sarcophagus was found in the burial chamber.

Bibliography: Hassan (1975c: 49-51, fig. 26, pl. xxxii).

Nikauptah and Simery

Date: Porter and Moss (1981): 6th Dynasty.

Location: The area between the south-east corner of the Step Pyramid Complex enclosure wall and the causeway (figure 1.1).

Architecture: This tomb was excavated in December 1929 by the Antiquities Service. In Jean-Philippe Lauer's report of work, conducted at Saqqara between 1936 and 1937, he commented on the good quality of painted reliefs but other than this, these tombs have received little attention.

Bebi

Date: Porter and Moss (1981): 5th Dynasty.

Location: The area between the south-east corner of the Step Pyramid Complex enclosure wall and the causeway (figure 1.1).

Architecture: Like other tombs in this cluster the recessed offering-room is entered on the eastern façade. The offering room has a north-south orientation and a false-door set back within a recess. To the north of the entrance is a small niche.

Bibliography: Hassan (1938: 505-506).

Hetep

Selected titles: Director of the broad hall; Inspector of priests of Hathor of the Meret-temple.

Date: Porter and Moss (1981): end of the 5th Dynasty or later.

Location: The area between the south-east corner of the Step Pyramid Complex enclosure and the causeway (figure 1.1).

Architecture: A more substantial mastaba than to its immediate neighbours, with a greater number of internal rooms. The eastern façade is well preserved and surviving to a height of nine courses of limestone blocks. An entrance chamber gives access to one room to the south; and on the north a doorway leading to the offering-room which has a north-south orientation. Behind the west wall of the offering-room is serdab, with two sealed rooms beyond this, which the excavator presumed were further serdabs or sealed magazines.

Bibliography: Hassan (1938: 503-505; 1975c: 53-58, fig. 28, pls. XXXV-XLIV).

Rakhuf

Selected titles: Royal chamberlain; Overseer of the great court.

Date: Porter and Moss (1981): 6th Dynasty.

Location: The area between the south-east corner of the Step Pyramid Complex enclosure and the causeway (figure 1.1).

Architecture: A mudbrick superstructure with an entrance on the east side that leads to one room.

Bibliography: Hassan (1938: 506).

Akhethotep (E 17)

Selected titles: Royal chamberlain; Priest of the pyramid of Isesi; Priest of the pyramid of Unas.

Date: Porter and Moss (1981): 5th-6th Dynasty; OEE Database: 5th Dynasty, reign of Unas to 6th Dynasty, reign of Pepy I.

Location: The north side of the causeway near the tomb of Niankkhnum and Khumnhotep (figure 1.1).

Architecture: Small mastaba with a offering-room built against a rock face of exposed limestone. The masonry uses two lower courses of greyish limestone topped with blocks of finer white limestone. The excavation took place in 1905, though the report was not published until 46 years later, in two volumes that included nine other tombs cleared by a team directed by Margaret Murray.

Bibliography: Petrie and Murray (1952: 7-8, pl. xxi).

Akhethotep

Selected titles: Secretary of the toilet-house; Priest of Khnum in all his places.

Date: Porter and Moss (1981): 5th Dynasty or early 6th Dynasty; OEE Database: 5th Dynasty, reigns of Nyuserra to early Djedkara.

Location: The north side of the causeway near the tomb of Niankkhnum and Khumnhotep (figure 1.1).

Architecture: Large rectangular mastaba orientated north-south with an offering-room entered on the east side. The offering-room was acquired by the Musée du Louvre, Paris (E 10958), from the Egyptian government in 1903. Since 1991 Christiane Ziegler of the Louvre Museum has been directing fieldwork at the area of the tomb and revealed further structures of the Old Kingdom and later.

Bibliography: Ziegler (1993; 2006: 20-24; 2007); Janot *et al.* (2001: 249-291); Ziegler *et al.* (1997).

Iyka

Selected titles: King's wab-priest; Chief of the great estate.

Location: Beneath the causeway, probably in an area east of the boat pits opposite the tombs of Mitri, Pehnefer and Hetep (figure 1.1).

Date: Porter and Moss (1981): 5th Dynasty.

Architecture: Mastaba with mudbrick wall with an offering-room containing a wooden false-door (Egyptian Museum, Cairo, JE 72201). No further detail was recorded about the architecture or the exact location of the tomb revealed during clearance of the causeway during excavations of the Antiquities Service directed by Zaki Saad (season 1939 -1940).

Bibliography: Saad (1940: 675-680, pls. lxxiii, lxxiv).

Neferherenptah

Selected titles: Overseer of hairdressers of the great house.

Date: Porter and Moss (1981): 5th Dynasty; OEE Database: 5th Dynasty, reigns of Djedkara to Unas.

Location: Beside a group of rock-cut tombs hewn within the escarpment on the south side of the causeway of Unas (figures 1.1-1.2).

Architecture: One of a group of tombs excavated by Abd el-Salam Mohammed Hussein in 1940. A rectangular shaped tomb built in masonry orientated north-south with an uninscribed false-door cut into the southern end of the west wall.

Niankhra

Selected titles: Royal acquaintance of the great house; Secretary of Neferirkare.

Date: Porter and Moss (1981): 5th Dynasty.

Location: Rock-cut tomb hewn within the escarpment on the south side of the causeway of Unas (figures 1.1-1.2).

Architecture: Outer forecourt partly built of masonry, built before a rectangular shaped rock-cut chamber orientated north-south cut into the rock face.

Bibliography: McFarlane (2000: 20).

Akhethotep

Selected titles: Director of wab-priests of Sekhmet of the great house; Priest of Buto.

Date: Porter and Moss (1981): 5th-6th Dynasty.

Location: Rock-cut tomb hewn within the escarpment on the south side of the causeway of Unas (figures 1.1-1.2).

Architecture: An outer forecourt which is partly built of masonry, built before a rectangular shaped rock-cut chamber orientated north-south cut into the rock face.

Bibliography: Badawi (1940: 495-501, pls. XLVI-XLVII); McFarlane (2000: 20); Zayed (1958: 127-137).

Irukaptah Khenu

Selected titles: Master butcher of the great house; King's wab-priest.

Location: Immediately south of the Unas causeway (figures 1.1-1.2).

Date: Porter and Moss (1981): 6th Dynasty; OEE Database: 5th Dynasty, reign of Djedkara; McFarlane (2000): 5th Dynasty, reigns of Menkaure to Djedkara; Harpur (1987): 6th Dynasty; Strudwick (1985): 5th Dynasty, reign of Djedkara.

Architecture: The outer forecourt is partly built of limestone masonry, and built before a rectangular shaped rock-cut chamber orientated north-south cut into the rock face. The inner-most room contains false-doors and engaged rock-cut statuary.

Bibliography: McFarlane (2000); de Rachewiltz (1960).

Nefer and Kahay

Selected titles: Nefer: Director of singers; Inspector of the wab-priests; Kahay: Director of singers; Priest of Meret in Upper Egypt.

Date: Porter and Moss (1981): middle to late 5th Dynasty; OEE Database: 5th Dynasty, reign of Nyuserra; Moussa and Altenmüller (1971): 5th Dynasty, reign of Nyuserra or shortly afterwards in the reign of Menkauhor.

Location: The east part of the cemetery, cut in the escarpment on the south side of the causeway (figures 1.1, 1.3). Part of an upper terrace of tombs which was uncovered during work for the Antiquities Service in 1966 directed by Ahmed Moussa.

Architecture: A rock-cut tomb with L-shape layout, typical of the 4th and 5th Dynasties corresponding to Reisner's type RC IV (1942: 241). The western end of the south wall is built from fine white limestone behind which is a serdab. The tomb contains six false-doors. Moussa and Altenmüller (1971: 10-11) believe that the outer wall of the tomb was originally cased with limestone blocks, and that a lintel stood above the door. In front of the entrance were lower courses of a mudbrick rectangular outer court, which were destroyed during the construction of the causeway.

Bibliography: Moussa and Altenmüller (1971).

Ankhirptah

Selected titles: Overseer of beef fat.

Date: Porter and Moss (1981): 5th Dynasty.

Location: East part of the cemetery, cut in the escarpment on the south side of the causeway (figures 1.1, 1.3). Part of an upper terrace of tombs uncovered during work for the Antiquities Service in 1966 directed by Ahmed Moussa.

Architecture: A rectangular rock-cut tomb of small size (1.40 m. x 2.20 m.) A lintel depicts the owner and his wife receiving the offerings.

Bibliography: Moussa and Altenmüller (1971).

Kaiankh

Selected titles: Butcher of the great house.

Date: Porter and Moss (1981): 5th Dynasty.

Location: The east part of the cemetery, cut in the escarpment on the south side of the causeway (figures 1.1, 1.3). Part of an upper terrace of tombs uncovered during work for the Antiquities Service in 1966 directed by Ahmed Moussa.

Architecture: Situated beside the tomb of Aankhirptah, this tomb measures 1.80 m. at its largest width, and 7.60 m. in length. At the rear there is a smaller chamber carved into the rock. A drum above the door in incised with the name and titles of the owner.

Bibliography: Moussa and Altenmüller (1971).

Niankhkhnum and Khnumhotep

Selected titles: Niankhkhnum: Priest of Ra in the sun temple of Nyuserra; Overseer of manicurists of the great house; Khnumhotep: Priest of Ra in the sun temple of Nyuserra; Overseer of manicurists of the great house.

Date: Porter and Moss (1981): 5th Dynasty, probably reigns of Nyuserra or Menkauhor; OEE Database: 5th Dynasty, late reign of Nyuserra to reign of Menkauhor.

Location: In the east part of the cemetery in a depression, c. 290 m. from the beginning of the causeway (figures 1.1, 1.3). Moussa found the tomb of Niankhkhnum and Khnumhotep in October 1964 in an area where the depression of the wadi widens to the south to form two reclining terraces.

Architecture: This tomb is an interesting combination of a rock-cut-tomb and mastaba. The rear of the tomb is hewn into the limestone escarpment. The front was then extended outwards with masonry, creating a north facing pillared portico entrance. The extension included an entrance room, with an undecorated storeroom to the north, and an open courtyard to the west which leads on to the original rock-cut offering chapel. The superstructure of the mastaba was covered over during the construction of the Unas causeway.

Bibliography: Moussa and Altenmüller (1977).

Irenkaptah

Selected titles: Master butcher of the great house; Overseer of beef fat.

Date: Porter and Moss (1981): 5th Dynasty; OEE Database: 5th Dynasty, reigns of Nyuserra to Unas.

Location: The east part of the cemetery, 290 m. from the beginning of the causeway, cut into the southern face of escarpment, where the wadi widens to the south to form two reclining terraces (figures 1.1-1.2). Uncovered during work for the Antiquities Service in 1965 directed by Ahmed Moussa.

Architecture: A rock-cut tomb of a trapezoidal shape, with the longest wall being the east wall and measuring 5.10 m. This wall runs parallel with the west wall of the adjacent tomb of Neferseshemptah; both are separated by a wall with a thickness of c. 0.22 m., and adjoin at the north-east corner where the wall has been broken through. The west wall has also been destroyed in place to link through into the undecorated tomb. The entrance to the tomb is positioned at the western end of the north wall, and the drum above the doorway was undecorated. The northern end of the west wall is cased with limestone blocks, and features a false-door for Irenkaptah and his wife cut into the limestone. The other half of the wall is uncased cut rock and contains a false-door carved within the wall. Both the east and west walls were decorated, though the work was not completed in their northern parts.

Bibliography: Moussa and Junge (1975: 31-46, fig 1).

Neferseshemptah and Sekhentiu

Selected titles: Overseer of metal-workers; Overseer of gold-workers.

Date: Porter and Moss (1981): late 5th Dynasty; OEE Database: 5th Dynasty, reign of Unas.

Location: In the east part of the cemetery, 290 m. from the beginning of the causeway, cut into the southern face of escarpment, where the wadi widens to the south to form two reclining terraces (figures 1.1, 1.3). Uncovered during work for the Antiquities Service in 1965 directed by Ahmed Moussa.

Architecture: A rectangular rock-cut tomb with maximum length 8.70 m. and width 1.82 m. The entrance is positioned at the extreme west side of the north wall, and contains no distinctive architectural or decorative elements. The west wall contains three false-doors, and the beginnings of a carved niche. It would appear that the southern end of the tomb was a later addition that did not see completion. The walls and ceiling are roughly cut, and remain unfinished.

Bibliography: Moussa and Junge (1975: 13-27, fig. 1).

Corpus of Tombs

The present work attempts to identify and analyse architectural characteristics in multi-roomed mastaba tombs in the Unas Cemetery. Nine tombs will be considered in close detail, alongside six other Memphite tombs:

The Unas Cemetery
- The mastaba of Iynefert (figure1.8)
- The mastaba of Unasankh (figure 1.8)
- The mastaba of Seshseshet Idut (figure 1.9)
- The mastaba of Mehu (figure 1.10)
- The mastaba of Nebet (figure 1.11)
- The mastaba of Khenut (figure 1.11)
- The mastaba of Nebkauhor (figure 1.12)
- The mastaba of Niankhba (figure 1.13)
- The mastaba of Kairer (figure 1.14)

South of the Unas Cemetery
- The mastaba of Ptahhotep (LS 31) (figure 1.15)

The Teti Cemetery
- The mastaba of Khentika (figure 1.16)
- The mastaba of Kagemni (figure 1.17)
- The mastaba of Mereruka (figure 1.18)
- The mastaba of Ankhmahor (figure 1.19)

West of the Step Pyramid
- The mastaba of Akhethotep and Ptahhotep (D 64) (figure 1.20)

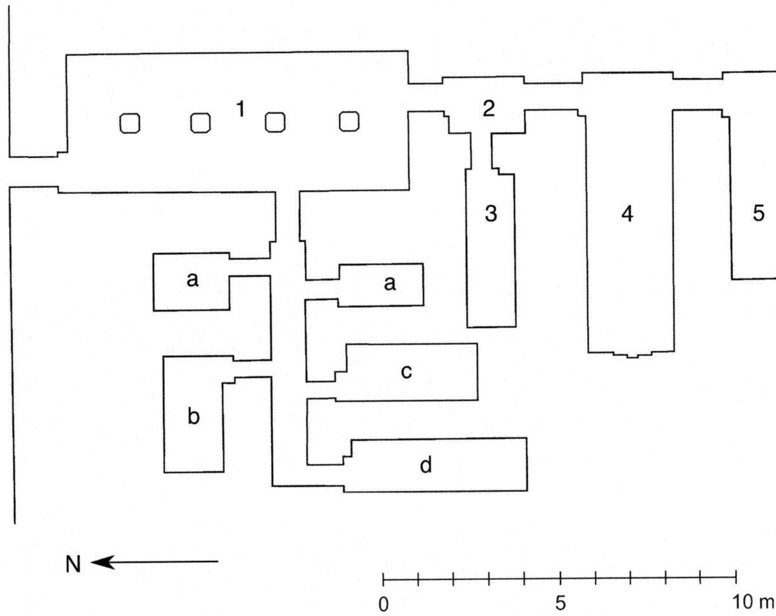

Figure 1.15. The mastaba of Ptahhotep (LS 31).

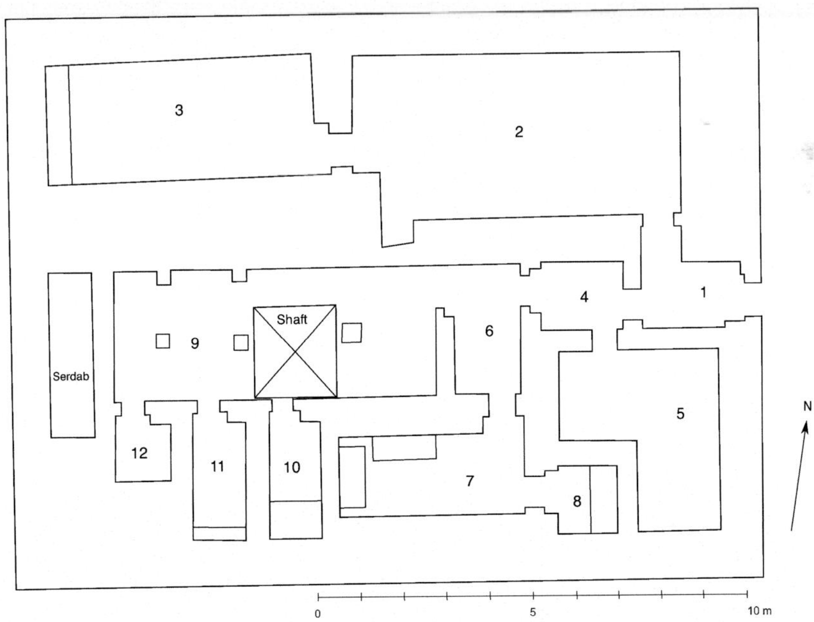

Figure 1.16. The mastaba of Khentika.

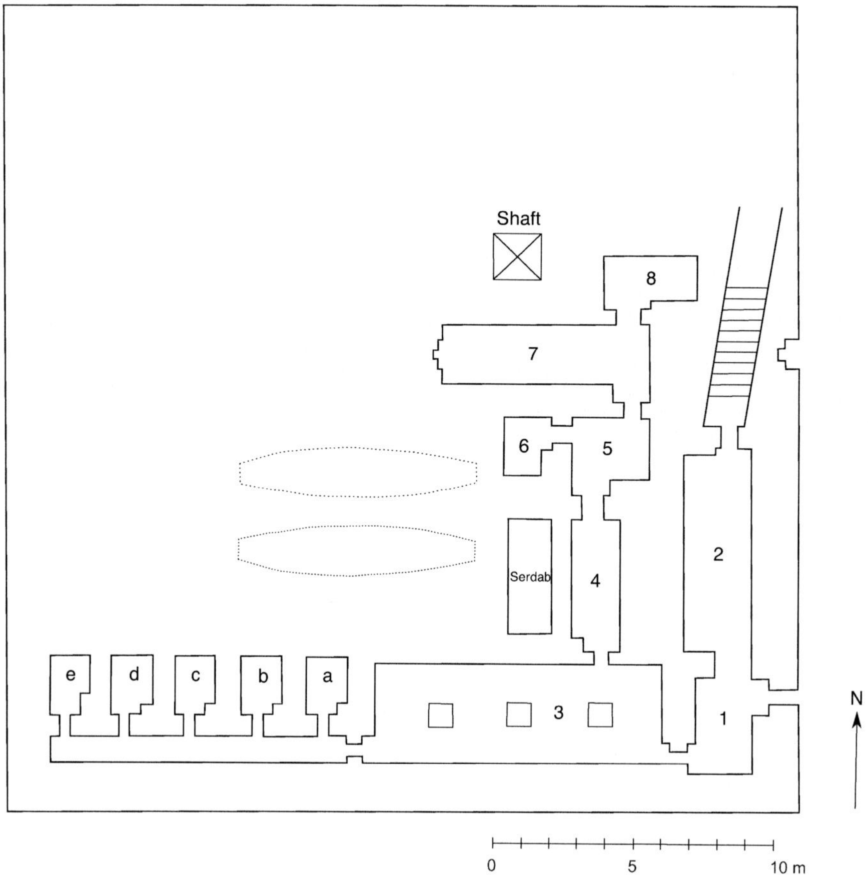

Figure 1.17. The mastaba of Kagemni.

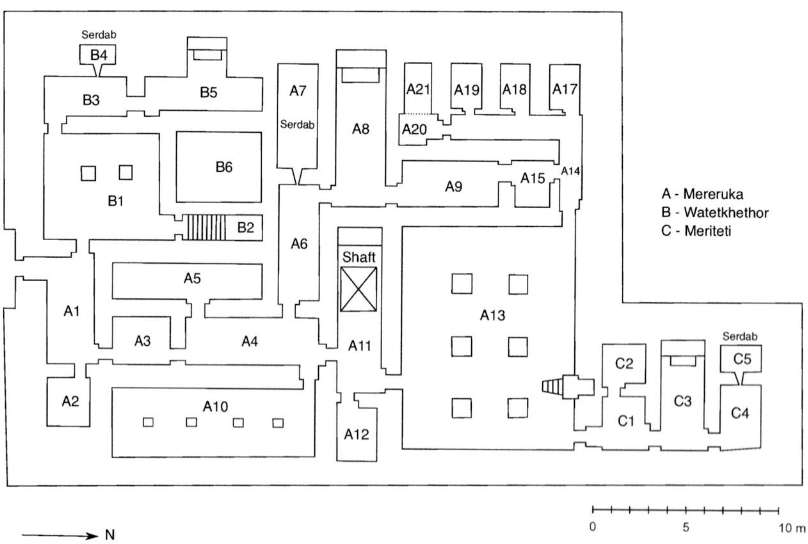

Figure 1.18. The mastaba of Mereruka (including Watetkhethor and Meriteti).

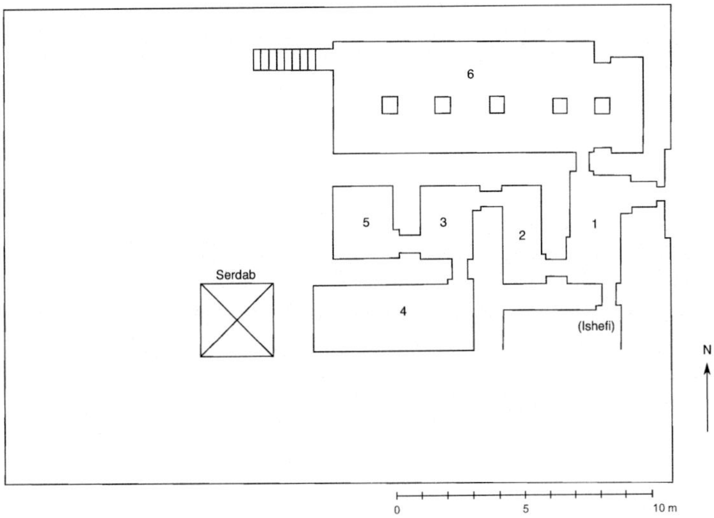

Figure 1.19. The mastaba of Ankhmahor.

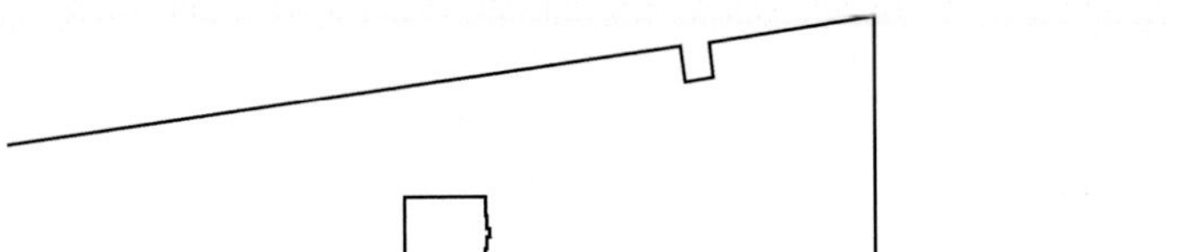

Figure 1.20. The mastaba of Akhethotep and Ptahhotep (D 64).

2. Sources of Stone at Saqqara

"The appearance of white limestone above the sand of an Egyptian cemetery is the signal for prompt theft" Davies (1901: 2).

2.1. Pyramid Cemeteries

Local quarries were the chief source of stone for pyramids, a requirement which influenced the choice where to build (Edwards, 1993: 251; Lehner, 1997: 206; Lucas & Harris,1963: 52). Whilst high-quality limestone from Tura and Ma'sara was used for the casing of pyramids, the smaller-sized core stones would have come from the local vicinity (Traunecker, 1980: cols. 301-303). The Old Kingdom topography of the Giza plateau was transformed by the immense quarrying activity of local limestone to construct the pyramid complexes of 4th Dynasty rulers.[8] Archaeological clearance of the cemetery has revealed that vast areas of the plateau had been stripped by successive pyramid builders. Archaeologists have assigned different quarries to Khufu, Khafra and Menkaura because of the relative proximity to pyramid complexes and other evidence (figure 2.1) (Lehner, 1997: 206; Reisner, 1942: 10-13; Klemm & Klemm, 1993: 53-59; Aston *et al.*, 2000: 40-41). Stone was removed by an open-quarrying method, as revealed by Uvo Hölscher's excavations of a quarry at the north side of the pyramid of Khufu, consisting of a grid of square stumps separated by grooves about 0.50 m. apart (figures 2.2-2.3) (Hölsher, 1912: 33, abb. 19; see also Arnold, 1999: 31-32, fig. 2.4; contra Edwards, 1993: 246, who believes the grooves to be "canals" cut to hold water to establish a level foundation platform).

The limestone at Giza is of the Middle Eocene Mokattam Formation and has a high fossil and nummulite content (giving the term nummulitic limestone) that is visible to the eye (Aigner, 1983a: 314, fig. 1; Klemm & Klemm, 1993: 53-59, fig. 51, pls. 1.3-1.4). The stone used to build the cores of the Giza pyramids is characteristic of the nummulitic limestone at the quarry sites. Because of its distinctive nature George Reisner (1942: 37-38) was able to identify the specific quarry where stone blocks were extracted, and consider the productivity of quarries over time: "The stone used in all the cores of these six cemeteries was of local origin. The fine white limestone from the Mokattam Hills was used, however, in the casing, the stone chapel, and the lining of the burial-chamber, which were all constructed after the cores. The local stone is of the two chief varieties of coarse nummulitic limestone, a softer yellow-drab stone, and a harder grey stone, and both of these occur in several qualities. In general the stone blocks used in each core are of fairly uniform quality and obviously from the same quarry. But a number of the massive cores of latter construction contain stones of both yellow-drab and

8 For a discussion of the geomorphology of the Giza Plateau see Aigner (1983a: 313-322; 1983b: 347-368).

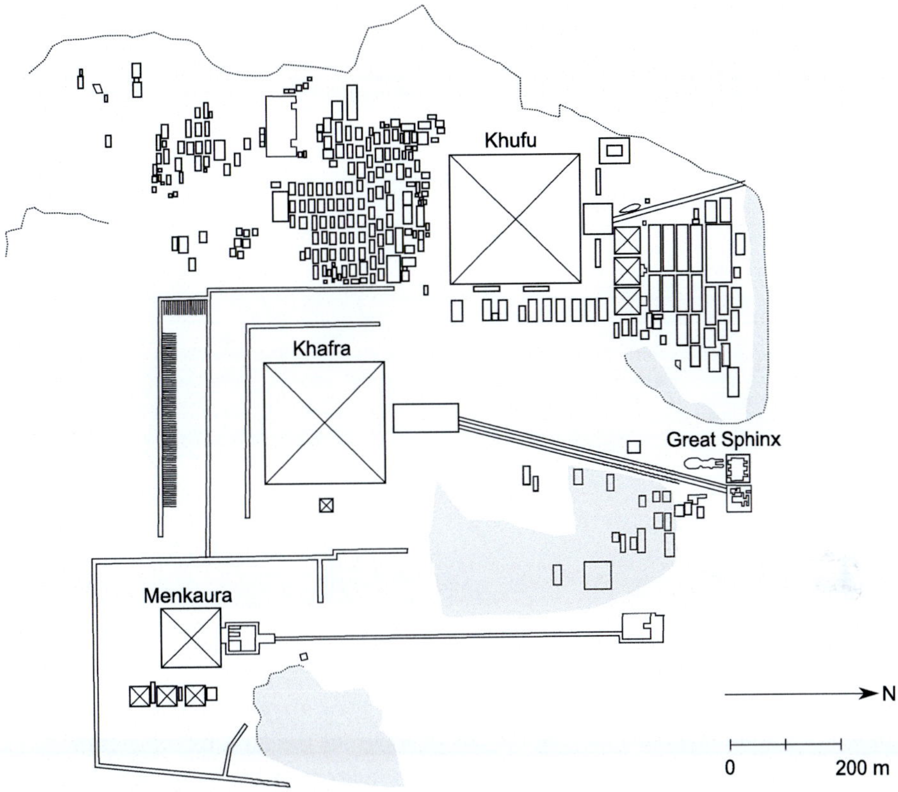

Figure 2.1. Quarries at Giza (marked in gray).

Figure 2.2. Quarry to the north of Khufu's pyramid.

Figure 2.3. Open-quarry floor.

the grey stone ... it is obvious that the various beds of stone were being worked practically simultaneously during the construction of the nucleus cemeteries."

In contrast we know much less about local quarries at the Saqqara necropolis. This is not surprising considering the more systematic and continued excavation and survey of the Giza necropolis and its surrounding area (Reisner, 1942: 20-26). Saqqara, by comparison, remains untouched in vast areas and is seriously in need of a methodical and detailed survey of excavated and unexcavated parts of the site (Spencer, 1974: 1-11). The difference in scale between the monuments at Saqqara and Giza is marked and the sheer volume of stone used to build just three pyramids at Giza dwarfs the figure used for five pyramids at Saqqara by eight times the amount.[9] Limestone at Saqqara would not have been quarried on such a great scale and subsequently quarries will be less obvious features on the landscape. The quarries at Giza were also intensively developed during a short period of time compared to Saqqara where building intensity was spread over a much greater period of time and consequently quarries, smaller in scale, spread further apart and were more likely to have been built over.

9 Based on Lehner's estimation of 5,029,562 m^3 for the pyramids of Khufu, Khafre and Menkaure, and 607,131.m^3 for the pyramids of Djoser, Sekehemkhet, Userkaf, Unas and Teti (1997: 15-17); it should be noted that this does not account for the pyramid complexes as a whole, nor the mastabas and the Gisa el-Mudir at Saqqara.

2.2. Geology

The limestone at Saqqara is also part of the Mokattam Formation that begins just north of Cairo and occupies c. 160 km of Middle Egypt (Harrell, 2016). But, unlike at the Giza plateau, the horizon of limestone at Saqqara does not have a high fossil content (Klemm & Klemm, 1993: pls. 1.3-1.4, 2.4-2.6). The upper stratum of the Saqqara Plateau consists of alternating layers of hard limestones and soft marls (part of the Upper Calcareous Beds) and this distinctive rock structure is known as the Saqqara Member of the Maadi Formation. This rock formation is often topped by gravel and sands from the Quaternary and modern eras, and it is upon this layer that pharaonic monuments were built, using local limestone of the Saqqara Member of the Maadi Formation extracted from the immediate area (Klemm & Klemm, 1993: 72; Mathieson *et al.*, 1999: 21-43, pls. IV-V; Youssef *et al.*, 1984: 137, fig. 4).

2.2.1. Limestone Quarries in Egypt

Rosemarie Klemm made the first comprehensive listing of limestone quarries in Egypt, including Saqqara as one of the forty locations listed within the Nile valley (Klemm, 1984: cols. 1277-1278). Fine white limestone (*inr ḥḏ nfr, ꜥnw, ꜥin*) was considered separately in the Lexikon der Ägyptologie, with the nearest sources to Saqqara being listed as Tura and Ma'sara (Traunecker, 1980: cols. 301-303). Tura was also given its own detailed entry (Meyer, 1986: cols. 807-809). In 1989 James Harrell made a more detailed inventory of ancient quarries (Pharaonic-Roman Period) and extended the list of limestone quarries to 48 (Harrell, 1989: 1-7; 1992: 195-211). Harrell only included quarries that had, "credible published accounts or which have been verified in the field by the author" (Harrell, 1992: 200). Harrell's investigations have been ongoing and the number of mapped quarries stood at 88 in 2000 (Aston *et al.*, 2000: table 2.1), and in 2016 the figure had risen to 95 (Harrell, 2016). Originally Harrell had identified only one quarry at the Saqqara Plateau, located near the Step Pyramid Complex [29° 52.15' N, 31° 12.9' E]. He provides a quarry date belonging to the 3rd Dynasty, making this quarry contemporary to the construction of Djoser's pyramid complex. In 2003 Harrell resumed an ongoing survey of ancient stone quarries supported by the University of Toledo and the Egyptian Geological Survey and Mining Authority. In 2004 Harrell announced the results of this seasons work that included the discovery of a "previously unknown Third Dynasty limestone quarry at Saqqara"; this quarry is further to the west, "in the hills west of Saqqara", [29° 50.9' N, 31° 9.9' E] (Harrell 2004: 26). However, after consulting a high-resolution satellite photograph of the area and taking another visit to the site in June 2004 Harrell concluded that this site was a limestone outcrop misidentified as a quarry in a 1929 soil mapping survey of the eastern Faiyum (Personal Communication Harrell, 2004). Harrell does not know why the map makers thought the site was of a 3rd Dynasty date and the recent survey work has provided a Middle Kingdom date. Inscribed stone blocks and pottery remain at what Harrell believes to be a Middle Kingdom 'shrine' with associated low-status burials. The pit that at once appeared to be a sand filled quarry was most likely created by tomb robbers. Harrell has since removed this site from his list of ancient Egyptian soft stone quarries. Therefore only one Old Kingdom quarry has been confidently identified at the Saqqara necropolis. This recent misunderstanding, however, expresses the problem of locating quarries at Saqqara.

2.2.2. Likely Sources of Limestone at Saqqara

Sources of good limestone will continually be in use as long as demand is high enough to make sites still practical. Fortunately pharaonic quarries are usually easily distinguishable from quarries of the modern era, as Petrie (1938: 26) noted: "The essential principle in Egyptian quarrying was the cutting out of the stone from the rock, carefully avoiding the natural joints. An Egyptian quarry is not a shapeless hole; it is an orderly workshop where fine material is removed as regularly and as evenly as wood taken out of a store." In ancient times stone was carefully removed, with tools often leaving distinctive marks (Arnold, 1991: figs. 2.7-2.11). Rectangular blocks would be detached leaving behind regular lines on the exposed quarry walls and floor (Arnold, 1991: 27-36, fig. 2.1). Modern methods of extraction within the Nile valley are less regular due to the used large machinery and often surfaces are blasted away with explosives (Harrell, 1992: 200). Local quarries on the Saqqara Plateau would have served the building projects of the Early Dynastic Period and the Old Kingdom (Shaw, 2000: 99; Klemm & Klemm 1993: 72). However, as yet it does not seem that they are as distinctive as those at Giza. The necropolis is a site that has been used throughout history and traces of Old Kingdom activity at quarry sites will have often been obliterated by later use and indeed exhaustion of the quarry (Aston *et al.*, 2000: 99-104; Eyre, 1987: 10). Quarry sites further out in the desert are often buried by extensive sand drifts and the same fate is also true for those closer to monuments that have been buried under excavation spoil heaps (Aston *et al.*, 2000: 40; Smith, 1997: 383). James Harrell (1992: 200) maintains that many quarries are not reported because they are of no archaeological interest or destroyed or buried and therefore go unnoticed.

Klemm and Klemm (1993: 72) find the lack of known quarry sites at Saqqara puzzling; especially considering that the core masonry came from the cemetery, just like at Giza. Whilst they have positively identified quarries at Giza they speculate that one searches in vain for comparable quarry locations at Saqqara. The reason for this lies in the different limestone geologic sequence at Saqqara. The hard limestone beds lie in layers between thinner strata of softer marlstone. This allows the limestone to be rapidly dismantled and gives stone blocks of a desirable size. Indeed, these stone blocks are noticeably smaller that those used in the masonry at Giza, and the method of removal is still noticeable at worked rock outcrops.

The rectangular ditch structures found at the Saqqara Plateau undoubtedly provided building stone; the trench associated with the Djoser Step Pyramid Complex is still visible in parts (to the south of the enclosure wall) and the walls appear to be artificially formed (Swelim, 1991: 389-402). However, Klemm and Klemm (1993: 72) argue that these possibilities are not of sufficient volume to have supplied stone for all of the monuments at Saqqara. They propose that the ditch also served as a delivery route for blocks used in the masonry of pyramids and tombs high on the plateau, before the construction of the Unas pyramid complex. This is only understandable if stone is being brought up to the plateau from the lower (east) part of the necropolis; this would be stone delivered by canal and from the worked outcrops here. However, the sheer dimensions of this deep ditch seem too overwhelming to be just part of a delivery route. In Zaki Saad's unfinished exploration of the trench he reached a depth of 27.50 m. and cleared 235 m. to the north of the pyramid of Unas (Saad, 1947: 66-67, pl. XXXV illustrates the extraordinary dimensions of this feature). Klemm and Klemm (1993: 72) believe the exposed escarpments in this area (visible on the modern approach road to the site) are remnants of early quarries. Their inspection of the exposed escarpment beneath the site of the old Egypt Exploration Society house concluded that the rock outcrop had once been worked on a moderate scale. By association Klemm and Klemm (1993: 72) concur that the large steep sided knoll ('*Gebirgsabbruch*') to the north of the valley temple of Unas was also most likely to have been a quarry (figure 2.4). The knoll has a steep eastern escarpment 500 m. long and its steepness reveals that this is potentially a relic of former quarrying activities; much the same as the steep escarpment on the south side of the Unas causeway. The escarpment here has been utilised for quarrying and later terraced to form several levels of rock-cut tombs during the 5th Dynasty (McFarlane, 2000; de Rachewiltz, 1960; Moussa & Altenmüller, 1971; 1977; Moussa & Junge, 1975).

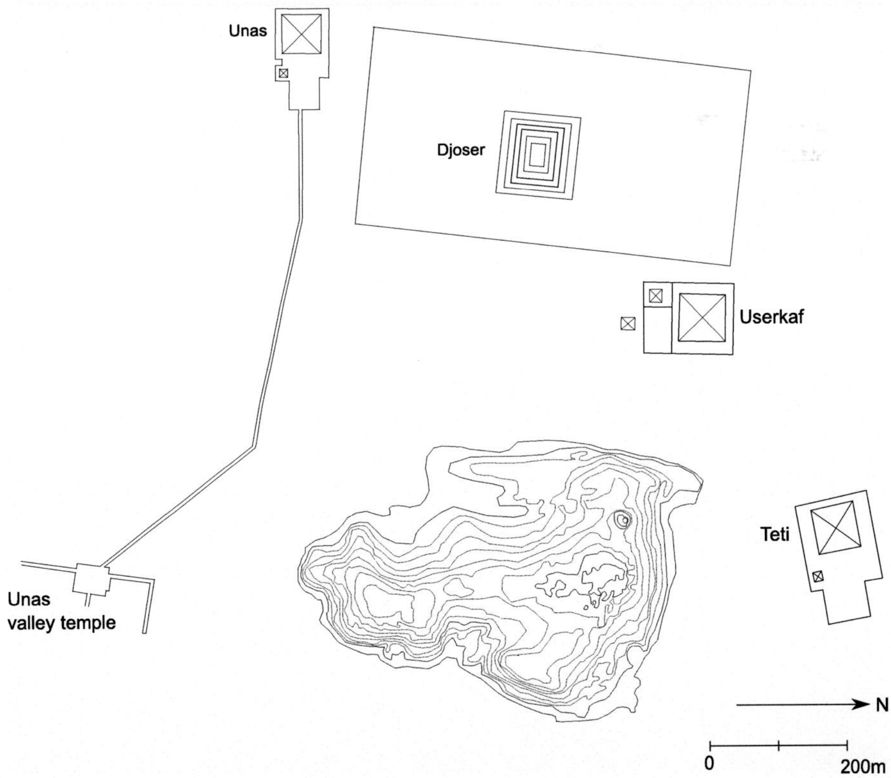

Figure 2.4. Steep sided knoll to the north of the Unas valley temple.

There are some New Kingdom tombs hewn into the east face of the knoll, LS 24 and LS 23 (fig. 2.5) (Porter and Moss, 1981: 588-591). These could be re-used Old Kingdom tombs, and with much of the escarpment being covered over by wind-blown sand, we know very little about the use of this area. Indeed, during the Old Kingdom many tombs were undoubtedly cut into the eastern escarpment of the Saqqara Plateau and at the northern apex that overlooks the modern village of Abusir (Jeffreys & Tavares, 1995: 147, fig. 8; Smith, 1997: 383-384). At Abu Sir and Dahshur Harrell has identified open pits on top of limestone plateaus that are likely to be remnants of ancient quarries and he suggests the best way to identify quarries at the eastern cliffs of Saqqara would be by high resolution satellite images (Personal Communication Harrell, 2004). Clearance at the Giza necropolis has revealed escarpments from former quarry activities were utilized for rock-cut tombs of the same period (figure 2.6), *e.g.*, the rock-cut tomb of Debehen (Hassan, 1943: 159-184).

2.3. Delivery Routes of Building Materials

The EES Survey of Memphis has investigated access routes to the Saqqara Necropolis as part of the wider study on the historic landscape of Early Dynastic Memphis (Jeffreys & Tavares, 1994: 147-151). The study at North and Middle Saqqara has considered the approach routes to the cemetery, which includes that of work crews bringing in quarried stone to the Early Dynastic cemeteries. This has included further consideration on the use of the rock-cut trench that runs parallel to the south enclosure wall of the Step Pyramid Complex; and complements with the hypothesis of Klemm and Klemm (1993). David Jeffreys and Ana Tavares have proposed that this trench was cut to extend the west end of the small wadi that

Figure 2.5. South-east side of the limestone knoll to the north of the Unas valley temple.

terminates near the Unas Valley Temple (figures 2.7, 2.8). This cutting would have provided a gentler gradient from the wadi to monuments higher up on the Saqqara plateau. The lower (east) end of the causeway is more choked with sand, but if one looks carefully it is possible to see a change in the wadi profile. Jeffreys and Tavares propose that the cutting of the trench would have provided stone for masonry cores of nearby monuments and access to the Gisr el Mudir, suggesting the trench

Figure 2.6. Rock-cut tombs in the Khufu/Khafre quarry.

Figure 2.7. Looking down the Unas causeway towards the valley temple.

was cut during the Second Dynasty alongside earlier Second Dynasty monuments. Unas built upon two Second Dynasty substructures: Tomb A, containing cylinder sealings bearing the names Hetepsekhemui and Raneb (Porter & Moss, 1981: 613); Tomb B, containing cylinder sealings bearing the name Nynetjer (Porter & Moss, 1981: 613). This is contra other interpretations: Nabil Swelim (1988: 12-24) believes the trench is a 3rd Dynasty construction built as a dry-moat around the Step Pyramid Complex; Spencer (1974: 4), however, likens the trench to a "descending ramp of an incomplete pyramid" because of the similarity to the great trench at Zawiyet el-Aryan. Like its purpose the size of the trench is also undecided. Swelim (1988: 13) reports the trench to be a uniform width of c. 40.00 m., whilst Spencer's (1974: pl. 1) plan indicates an approximate width of 10.00 m. Both plans share the same southern edge of the trench that ends just behind the tombs of Nebkauhor and Niankhba (figure 2.8). This southern face of the trench is also indicated on the plan of the cemetery made by Hassan (1975a: pl. I) who also marks a ridge on the opposite side that provides a width of c. 32.00 m., with the northern face of the trench indicated with a line to the west of the mastaba of Unashaishtef Haishtef. However, Hassan indicates the escarpment underneath the temenos wall of the Step Pyramid; the rock face that contains the rock-cut tombs of Iarti, 'Ankhi, Snefruhotep and Nengem. Swelim (1988: 13) interprets the gap between the two escarpments as a trench associated with the Step Pyramid Complex and disregards the dimensions of the trench given in the report of the excavator and the very different appearance of the two escarpments (figure 2.9). In both maps by Spencer and Swelim the trench runs underneath the tombs of

Figure 2.8. Exposed side of the trench between the tombs of Nebet and Nebkauhor.

Figure 2.9. Rock-cut tomb of Nengem within the escarpment beneath the Step Pyramid enclosure wall.

Khenut and Nebet,[10] suggesting that both its practical or symbolic purpose was out of use by the reign of Unas. If Swelim's vast width of c. 40.00 m. is to be believed then this would also include the tombs of Unashaishtef Haishtef/Neferseshemptah, Iynefert, Unisankh, Idut, Mehu and Kairer, and this is very unlikely. It also does not agree with the section-drawings of the mastaba of Mehu that includes the foundations of the tomb (Altenmüller, 1998; Hussein, 1942: pls. XXIX – XXX). Altenmüller (1998: 17) describes how the southern section of Mehu's tomb is built above the ditch associated with the Step Pyramid Complex ('Djoser trench') but he describes the ditch as gradually sloping downwards, as can be seen in the plans of this tomb and when in this part of the cemetery. In Swelim (1991: 390, 392-393, figs. C-G) published a map of the Step Pyramid Complex and indicated that the 'dry moat' of Djoser has a further southern arm, like the ⊓⊔ hieroglyph, that runs parallel to the inner east-west arm, and passes beneath many tombs of the cemetery – effectively the two trenches run underneath all of the tombs (figure 2.10). The dimensions for this trench do not correlate with the appearance of the cemetery or the construction of tombs. This new addition to the dry moat passes beneath the tombs of Nebkauhor and Niankhba where the rock of the plateau is visible in the floors and walls of some rooms and within the substructure. This has been clearly communicated by Hassan in his excavation reports (Hassan, 1975a, 57; 1975c, 44-45). Taking into consideration the excavation results of Saad, who

10 The trench does pass underneath the front of the twin-mastaba; see Munro (1993a: 2-3).

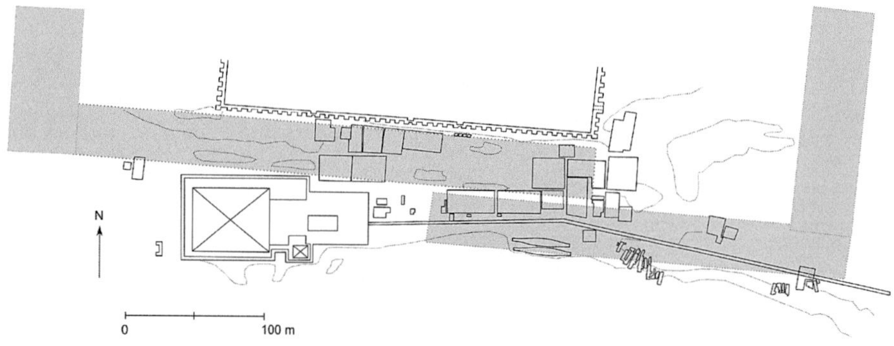

Figure 2.10. Swelim's interpretation of the trench. After: Swelim (1991: figs. C-G).

partially cleared the western section of the narrow trench, it is the proposal put forward by Spencer, that the trench is a feature of a monumental burial, which is most convincing.

The more obvious route to the Saqqara necropolis is via the Abusir valley. The approach to the plateau is gentle and the great concentration of Early Dynastic burials in the north of the necropolis seem to confirm that access was from the north. Access to the cemeteries would have changed in favour of routes across the eastern escarpment as Memphis moved from its earlier more northerly position, but for the hauling of large amounts of stone, the Abusir valley approach would still have its benefits. Stone could be brought in to the valley via the Abusir lake (Birket Mukhtar Pasha or Birket Timsah). Lehner (1997: 82) likens the Abusir valley to a "natural causeway connecting the floodplain below the northern point of the Saqqara Plateau to the front of the Djoser and Sekhemkhet enclosures." The National Museums of Scotland Saqqara Survey Project traced the ancient shoreline of Abusir lake, exploring the Abusir valley for any evidence of an access route. Fossil evidence and other material has confirmed the ancient shoreline of Wadi Abusir and revealed that the height of the lake remained fairly constant for long periods of time (Mathieson, 2000: 35; Mathieson & Tavares, 1993: 24). Mudbrick buildings within the lakes boundaries might be associated with a harbour (Mathieson, 2004: 27); Lehner (1997: 82) proposed that a harbour might be located near the mouth of the wadi. The survey area included the Abusir valley, beginning near the modern town of Abusir and ending at the Gisr el-Mudir at the south (Mathieson, 1999: fig. 1; 2000: 34). This stretch of lower lying desert, between the two plateaus, lies behind the Djoser and Sekhemkhet pyramid enclosures. The whole area has been stripped of the natural surface of gravel, flint and sand, leaving at the edges of the valley undisturbed mounds of the former surface. Mathieson (2000: 36) believes that the surface of the valley was open quarried for tafl, limestone and fill material used in the building of 2nd and 3rd Dynasty monuments. The same is true for the narrower valley between the Gisr el-Mudir and the Sekhemkhet pyramid complex. Excavation near the east wall of the Gisr el-Mudir has revealed a cutting of c. 2.00-3.00 m. passing through the bedrock indicating the quarrying of local limestone (Mathieson, 2000: 36). Utilisation of local stone from the Abusir valley as building material is similar to the practice of open quarrying at pyramid sites elsewhere. The local stone would have served the purpose of core building material and stone for simpler tombs not using finer imported limestone. The natural surface of gravel, flint and sand that Mathieson describes matches the type of material used abundantly to fill the gaps in the 'panelling' masonry technique used in tomb construction (discussed in Chapter 3). The valley would also have provided an access road for the delivery of imported stone brought to the necropolis by boat from the quarries of Tura and Ma'sara. Blocks cut from the bedrock would be of a roughly square shape suitable for transporting to the construction site (Arnold, 1991: 43; Clarke & Engelbach, 1990: 107). Once at the destination it is probable that blocks from the quarry would be first kept at one or a small number of storage areas, depending on how many building projects were taking place/distance between concurrent projects (Arnold, 1991: 43). It may not have been desirable to leave stone stored for too long a time as freshly quarried limestone is easier to dress and the longer it is stored the harder it becomes as it dries out (Arnold, 1991: 43; Duell, 1938: 13-14). However, not all stone used in Egyptian masonry came directly from the quarry; often blocks were taken from older structures and reused. Indeed, whole tombs were usurped and redecorated to suit their new purpose.

2.4. Archaeological Observations Relating to Masonry Materials

Selim Hassan's 1937-1938 excavations in the Unas cemetery uncovered twelve tombs of the late Old Kingdom. Six tombs were published in the three volume series *Excavations at Saqqara, 1937-1938*, including ten others to the west of the Step Pyramid Complex. In this publication series Hassan often makes specific reference to the type of limestone that is used within the masonry.[11] In the description of the tomb of Nebkauhor (1975a) the author provides the limestone composition of each wall within the tomb using the terms 'local' and 'white' for imported limestone from Tura/Ma'sara. At the beginning of the description of each room Hassan provides the dimensions of it, including the maximum surviving height. These details give a general understanding of the planned construction of this tomb with a noticeable preference for local limestone blocks for the lowest courses (figure 2.11). The first courses of masonry on the four walls of the entrance chamber (referred to as 'court' by Hassan) use local limestone topped by courses of white limestone. Within the columned hall (referred to as 'pillared hall' by Hassan) two courses of local limestone at the bottom are topped by several courses of white limestone above, with five courses on the west wall being the maximum surviving number. It is this pattern throughout the rest of the main rooms of the mastaba, with just one exception: the north wall of the 'antechamber' is composed of one course of local limestone topped by three courses of white limestone masonry). This technique does not waste finer white limestone on the bottom courses and

11 However, this detail might be the work of Zaki Iskander who re-edited the publication following the death of the author. Iskander states that the unprepared pages most often lacked descriptions of the tomb and that he visited the sites to obtain missing data (Hassan, 1975a: iii).

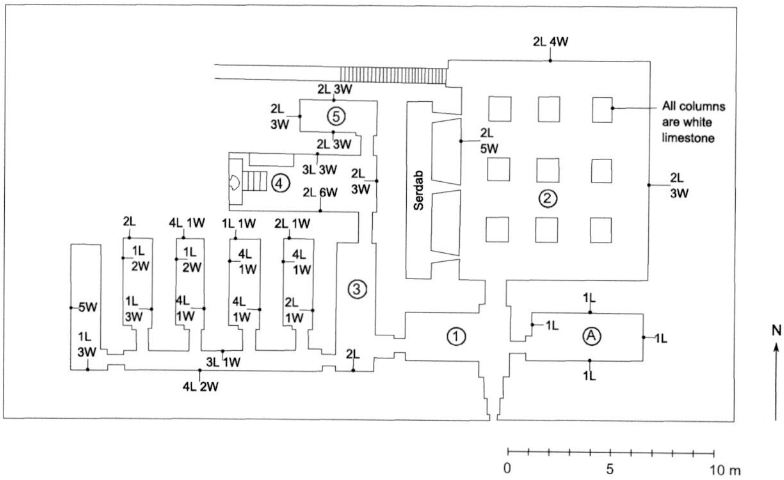

Figure 2.11. Quantities of local limestone (L) and imported white limestone (W) courses within surviving walls in the tomb of Nebkauhor.

utilises the stone in the position where the wall is carved with relief decoration. The lowest courses of local limestone appear to have all been painted black as a dado that was used throughout the main rooms of the mastaba. In six places (Hassan, 1975a: 7, 8, 37, 44 the decoration on the bottom of the walls has survived and is of a constant pattern: "Below this scene is a black dado relieved at its upper edge by two superposed bands of red and yellow separated by narrow black stripes." (Hassan, 1975a: 8; this pattern can be seen most clearly in pls. IV B, V C and XIII B). With the lowest courses being painted black it is more economic and practical to use the local limestone and reserve the finer white limestone for areas that were to be carved. Indeed this is definitely the case with the masonry within the mastaba of Userneter (D1), as Murray (1905: 19) describes: "As in the tomb of Ptahhetep II, the lowest courses of stone are left rough and are painted red, the upper courses being of dressed stone and sculptured."

The use of different courses within the storerooms and the serdab is less regular. In the storerooms the predominant pattern is to use four courses of local limestone and then upper courses of white limestone. The greatest exception to this is within the largest storeroom at the west end (storeroom 11) of the corridor. The surviving west wall of this storeroom is composed entirely of white limestone and the surviving east and south walls use just one bottom course of local limestone and then upper courses of white limestone. Roth (1991: 112) has suggested that the larger storeroom within storeroom complexes used by cult personnel organised into phyles in private mortuary cults would normally belong to the *imi-wrt*. This phyle name imitates the first phyle of a royal cult, the *wr* phyle, which was used exclusively in royal cults, and most often occupied the largest storeroom. If this is accurate then the different status of the phyle using this room could be reflected in the construction of the storeroom that uses finer limestone of a better appearance.

The neighbouring mastaba of Niankhba is not so well preserved and lacks decorated walls within the superstructure. Consequently the publication lacks the same detail applied to that of Nebkauhor. The exterior of the mastaba is described as being constructed of 'white' limestone blocks but from there on the description of what type of limestone is used within the courses of masonry stops, except for the odd occasion.

Macramallah (1935: 1) only briefly describes the exterior masonry of the superstructure of the mastaba of Idut. He states that the walls are constructed from local limestone rubble with a facing of white Tura limestone arranged in irregular courses. This seems to be a general pattern for comments on the masonry within mastabas. Firth and Gunn (1926: 20) only describe the type of stone used on the exterior of the mastaba of Kagemni: "It was cased with fine white limestone except the doorway and the lowest foundation course which are of the local greyish yellow limestone". Duell (1938: 7, no. 40) makes a comment on the exterior of the mastaba of Mereruka: "Like others in this group, Mereruka's mastaba is faced within and without with limestone, that used inside being of a finer texture than the rest. Limestone of the fine quality used for lining mastabas was quarried across the Nile just south of Cairo." It would seem Duell distinguishes the limestone on the outside as being local and that used within the tomb as being imported limestone form Tura/Ma'sara. In the publication of the mastaba of Akhethotep and Ptahhotep (D 64) N. de Garis Davies (1901: 3) comments that the masonry within the superstructure generally consists of lower courses of local limestone ('coarser stone') and 'fine' white limestone for the upper courses. Indeed in the offering room he provides dimensions for this arrangement: the lower courses of local limestone are 1.02 m. (c. 2 cubits) in height and the upper courses of white limestone provide a total height of 3.76 m. These observations were also recorded by Murray (1905: 18-19) in her publication of mastabas in this complex. She (Murray, 1905: 26) also attempts to categorise the stone used within the mastaba of Ptahhotep (D 62) referring to "fine limestone from Mokattam" being used to build the tomb, though she does also make reference to a 'rougher' non-white limestone being used for the lower courses. The exterior walls are apparently built from a different type of limestone that Mariette described as being a "silicious limestone".

The *Giza Mastabas* series published by the Museum of Fine Arts, Boston, includes more than adequate detail about the specific types of stone used in the construction of tombs within the Giza Necropolis. For example, in volume 6, A Cemetery of Palace Attendants, Ann Roth (1995: 13) describes in detail the nummulitic limestone that was used to build mastabas in the Western Cemetery and how closer observations of the specific limestone at Giza can illuminate matters such as sourcing quarries used for different phases of building: "Some blocks contain veins of purplish mineral that appear initially to be paint. Other blocks have a distinctive stratum of soft stone that weathers easily and appears as a white streak. This streak runs across several blocks in the final extension of 2088 at the same level, which implies that they were quarried from adjacent areas in a single stratum of stone.". In this cemetery Roth (1995: 21) observes that the finer stone was utilised for masonry within western walls that were carved. She also considers that this was not just to provide a better medium for carving but might have been a matter of prestige as this wall would be the most visible from the outside.

2.4.1. *Imitation of White Stone*

If imported limestone could not be used it seems builders went to some considerable efforts to imitate the appearance of a more prestigious building material. In a season of work between November 1929-April 1930 Cecil Firth directed excavations for the Antiquities Service at Saqqara and investigated a group of Old Kingdom mastabas at the east side of the Step Pyramid Complex (Firth, 1930: 185-189; Porter & Moss, 1981: 575-580). Firth (1930: 188-189) states that the mastabas were built of "very large blocks of yellow local limestone", and dated the tombs to the reign of Userkaf, whose pyramid complex is located to the north of this group. Firth describes a mastaba that has the appearance of a small pyramid but has been altered and includes an additional offering room built from mudbrick that has been plastered and whitewashed. The local limestone masonry has also been encased with a metre thickness of mudbrick that has been coated in plaster and whitewashed. Firth believes that the original plan was to case the structure with white limestone, but a failing to achieve this, builders imitated the appearance of white limestone and increased the dimensions of the superstructure. To good effect Arnold (2002: 115) uses a quote from an American architect, Richard Meier, to capture the impact of white stone architecture in words: "White is the light, the medium of understanding and transformative power. White is the ephemeral emblem of perpetuated movement. The white is always present but never the same." The symbolism, and ultimately the importance of white limestone, is best summarised by Arnold (2002: 115): "When the pyramid complex of Senwosret III was completed, the large, impressive monument must have been a spectacular sight, dazzling the visitor with its white, freshly carved limestone casing and its white enclosure walls. The simple geometrical forms and whiteness must have given the complex an otherworldly, immaterial aspect well suited to the dwelling place of the akhu, or "souls of light," as the deceased were termed."

2.4.2. *Imitation of Stone*

It is rare to find roofing blocks *in situ* in mastabas at Saqqara, though it is possible to appreciate how they were decorated by examining preserved decoration on the underside of door lintels and the ceilings within the burial chambers. A combination of black and white pigments is often used together upon a base of red painted stone to imitate the appearance of granite. The ceiling in the columned hall of the mastaba of Nebkauhor, in the Unas Cemetery, was, according to Hassan (1939: 513) "painted in red to imitate granite." This decoration style was also used in the substructure of tombs: the roof of the burial chamber of Mereruka was dressed in limestone painted red and black that gave the appearance of granite (Firth & Gunn, 1926: 24). This can be seen on the underside of doorways within the mastaba of Mereruka (figure 2.12). This imitation technique is still visible in the tomb of

Iynefert, located in the Unas Cemetery (figure 2.13). In the mastaba of Mehu Hussein (1942: 421) notes that "The ceiling in all parts of the mastaba, excepting that of the serdab, was painted to imitate red granite." This imitation technique used frequently for the roofing within mastabas, such as those of Seshseshet Idut (Macramallah, 1935: 3), Mehu, Ptahhotep [I] (D 62) and other tombs in this complex (Murray, 1905: 6, 17-18, 23, 25). It is also used for roofing within rock-cut tombs, such as the tombs of Khentkaus (Saad, 1947: 62), Neferseshemptah and Nefer and his father Kahay in the Unas Cemetery (Moussa & Altenmüller, 1971: 12). This imitation technique is not just confined to ceilings. False-doors are also decorated with paint to imitate a more expensive stone, such as the false-doors of Iynefert (Saad, 1940: 687), Mehu (Saad, 1940: 690, pl. LXXXI; Altenmüller, 1998: pl. 75), and Ptahhotep (D 62) (Murray, 1905: 26).

2.4.3. Imitation of Organic Material Using Stone

Duell (1938: 8, no. 46) proposes that the underside of the roof in the tomb of Mereruka was carved in a succession of semi-circular units that ran across the widths of the room and represented trunks of palm trees, making reference to other Old Kingdom examples. One such example includes the ceiling within the mastaba of Akhethotep and Ptahhotep (D 64) that was carved in this manner and was painted "warm red" (Davies, 1900: 4, 8, pl. ii.). George Reisner is quoted by Clarke and Engelbach in *Ancient Egyptian Construction and Architecture* (1990: 200-201) about painted decoration in mastabas at Giza: "The imitation

Figure 2.12. Painted ceiling in the tomb of Mereruka.

Figure 2.13. Painted ceiling in the tomb of Iynefert.

of wood graining also occurs, but only on the 'false door', and more often on plastered crude brick than on stone. The imitation of wooden roofing (logs) occurs in both stone and crude-bricks. The two cases on crude brick were both in 'leaning-course' vaults. The wood was painted red (no graining) in all cases.". This imitation of tree logs can also be seen in the 3rd Dynasty tomb of Hetephernebti (Clarke & Engelbach, 1990: 200), and within the architecture of the Step Pyramid Complex of Djoser, which seems to have acted as an influence on later tomb architecture in nearby cemeteries (Lauer, 1936a: 120-122, 150; 1936b: pls. XLI-XLIII, XLV, LXX 2).

2.5. Acquisition of Stone

Officials who performed well in their duties could be rewarded by the king with fine stone, such as white limestone from Tura or granite from Aswan. These prestige materials would have been difficult to acquire without assistance of the royal administration. Officials like Weni made sure such gifts were recorded on their tomb walls, wishing others to know they had been handsomely rewarded by the king more than any other of their contemporaries (Sethe, 1933: 98-110; Simpson, 2003: 402-407). Imported limestone was distinguished from local limestone in the Memphite necropolis, with the nearest source being Tura, the principal fine limestone quarry in northern Egypt, located on the east of the Nile (Harris, 1961: 69). Documents recording royal gifts of imported stone are usually confined to specific elements of the tomb, such as the false-door, sarcophagus or doorjambs.[12] However, there is a larger body of evidence attesting how the owner self financed the construction of his tomb, by means of their own property (Eyre, 1987: 5-47; Roth, 1987: 201-214; 1993: 33-55; 1994: 227-240).The owner asserts his integrity by a declaration that all stonemasons and artisans were rewarded for their work with generous payments of bread, beer and clothing etc. The balance between royal and private contribution to the construction of private tombs is complex and beyond the scope of this study. Violaine Chauvet (2007: 313-322; 2013: 57-71) has collected together a corpus of documents mentioning or referring to tomb construction and evaluated it against its archaeological context to present a more complete understanding of the economy of tomb construction.

Access to skilled craftsmen is just as important. Roth (1987: 203-205) notes the favourable resources made available to holders of the title 'overseer of works'. Indeed, Eyre (1987: 9) remarks upon the more than adequate tomb provision holders of this title and their spouses receive. Recycling of material from older monuments should also not be overlooked. Textual sources suggests the practice was frowned upon but occurred with such frequency that tomb owners made warnings against "every workman, every stonemason, or every man who shall (do) evil things to this tomb of mine of eternity by removing bricks or stone from it" (Strudwick, 2005: 218).

12 For example in the tomb of Sekhetenankh with reference to "two false-doors in stone from Tura" (Sethe, 1933: 38: 11-12).

3. Masonry in Tombs at Saqqara

"The modern architect might assuredly gain some useful inspiration from a study of Egyptian architecture, particularly the architecture of the Old Kingdom, for like his predecessors of that distant epoch he is faced with the problem of how to deal satisfactorily with great rectangular masses of masonry". (Blackman, 1935: 12).

3.1. Introduction

Following the 3rd Dynasty larger stone blocks were employed in masonry and it is apparent that there was no fixed standard for the sizes of blocks (Arnold, 1991: 120-21; Lucas & Harris, 1962: 50-55). Local quarries were used for rough stone while finer stone used for casing blocks came from more specific sources such as the limestone quarries of Tura el-Masara (Clarke & Engelbach, 1990: 10-22; Eyre, 1987: 10; Lucas & Harris, 1962: 63-65, 52-55). Blocks cut from the bedrock would be of a roughly square shape suitable for transporting to the construction site (Arnold, 1991: 43; Clarke & Engelbach 1990: 107). Arnold (1991: 43, no. 44) states that delivery dates on foundation stones within the pyramid complex of Senwosret I were not all of the same date and often blocks with different dates are lying side by side, However, not all stone used in Egyptian masonry came directly from the quarry; often blocks were taken from older structures and reused. The building may have been dismantled much earlier and the stone blocks moved away from the mastaba or the stone might be purposefully stripped away from the building and used as a quarry. A carved block of perhaps the 5th Dynasty was reused as paving stone in Room A9 in the mastaba of Mereruka (see fig. 1.18). The mastaba is believed to have been built and decorated during the reign of Teti, providing a relatively short span between the completion and demolition of the 5th Dynasty tomb that, according to Duell (1938: 5) was "evidently then being demolished and used as a quarry". Indeed, often whole tombs were usurped and redecorated and reconstructed to suit, such as the mastabas of the usurpers Seshseshet Idut and Nebkauhor in the Unas Cemetery. In both these cases it seems unlikely that there was much time span between the completion of the mastaba and the appropriation of the mastaba; what became of the reburial (if any) of the original owners is unknown.

3.2. Masonry Classification

Clarke and Engelbach were the first to provide a detailed technological study of Egyptian construction methods in 1930 with the publication of *Ancient Egyptian Masonry: The Building Craft* (Aston *et al.*, 2000: 63). Clarke and Engelbach split the topic into two groups: small-block masonry, such as that used in most late Old Kingdom mastabas, and megalithic masonry used within temples and pyramids.

Masonry can be classified by its surface appearance or by cross-section (Arnold, 1991: 148) and this chapter will use this approach to discuss masonry walls within tombs in the Unas Cemetery and comparable examples elsewhere.

3.2.1. Masonry by Cross-Section: Freestanding Walls within Mastabas

George Reisner (1942: 38-56) used a system to group types of core mastabas within the Western Mastaba Field at Giza within the Giza Necropolis publication series. Emphasis is placed upon the type of material used to fill the core, the shape of the superstructure and the appearance of the exterior masonry walls. Dieter Arnold (1991: 148-149) has identified four general types of masonry within the cross-section of freestanding walls (figure 3.1). Arnold's Type 3 is similar to the most commonly used technique in mastaba architecture at Saqqara, described as, "a coat of casing slabs that disguises a core built of fieldstones or roughly dressed stones, the joints filled with mortar and chips." (Arnold, 1991: 148). The type of masonry in mastabas differs slightly from Arnold's Type 3 as his classification system is rooted more in the observations of masonry within royal architecture. The walls within mastabas are not (usually) inclined and the gap between the two faces is narrower with a core filling of material smaller than roughly dressed

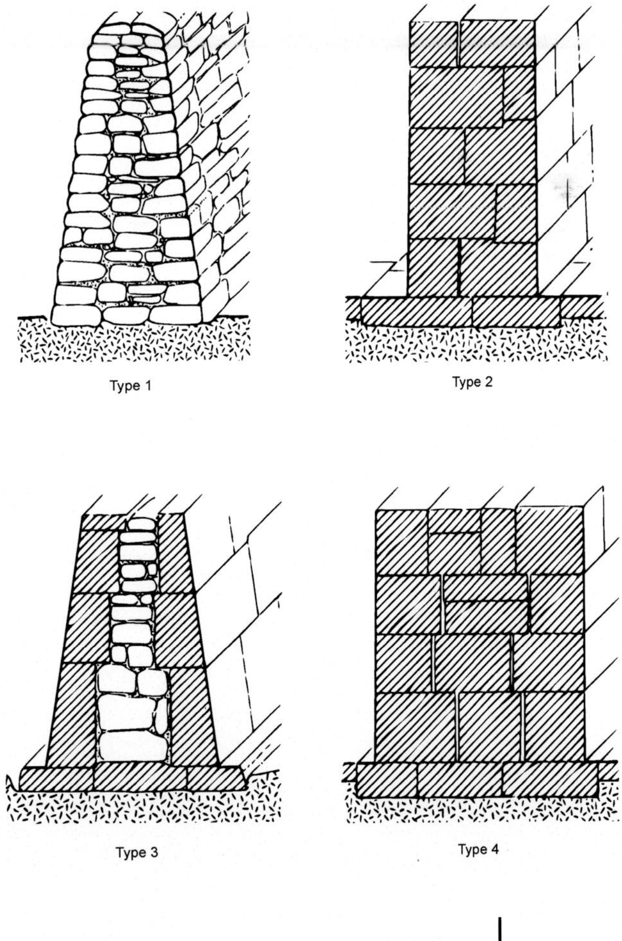

Figure 3.1. Arnold's classification of masonry in freestanding walls. From: Arnold (1991: fig. 4.72).

stones that is more like large flakes of limestone and tafl conglomerate. In parts this type of masonry is used in conjunction with walls consisting of larger blocks of the same thickness as the wall that equals Arnold's Type 2. This is typical of free-standing vertical walls and described by Arnold (2003: 137) as being "[built] using rectangular blocks, only one or two stones thick with headers used as through-stones; often used to separate rooms". This type of masonry is typically used for the walls of doorways that are positioned within freestanding walls.

Internal Masonry in the Tomb of Kairer

Restoration of the tomb of Kairer in 1936-1937 prevents examination of cross-sections of the walls. However, it is possible to establish the bonding used within the end of walls when doorways are built through a wall.

With at least three sides of most blocks exposed on the wall between Rooms 2 and C (the west wall and the east wall of each room respectively; figure 3.2) it is possible to examine the bonding of the blocks in this wall in some detail. The distance between the two walls is 1.10 m. with blocks from each side of the wall meeting near or close at some point in between. The first and second course consists of a general arrangement of blocks, with one being cut at the lower corner to accommodate the threshold that is higher than the paving within Room 2. The third course has a through-block ('stretcher') cut at the right corner to accommodate the inside thickness of the recess on the west side of the doorway.

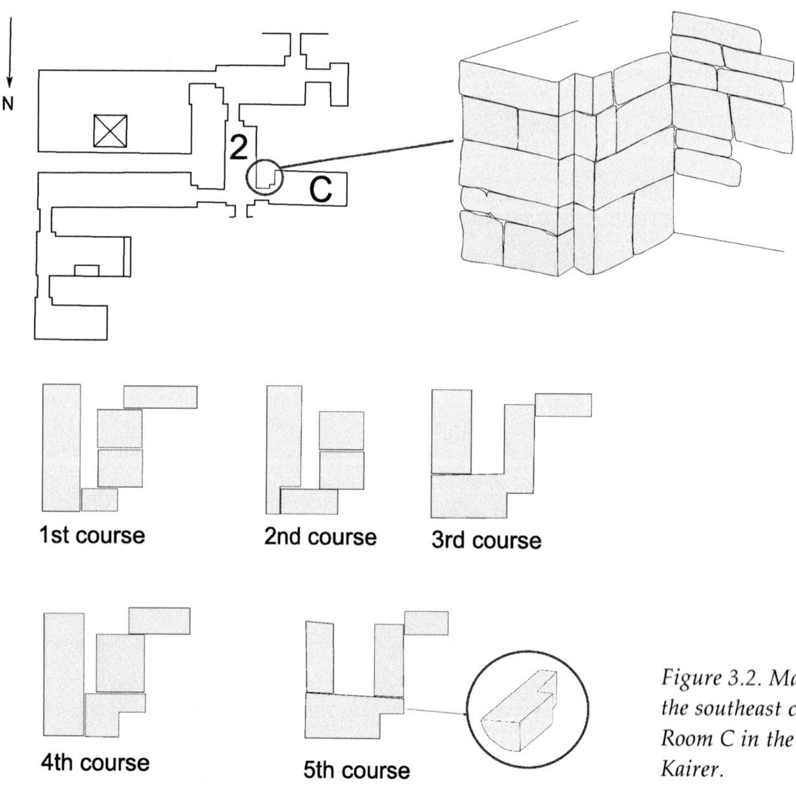

Figure 3.2. Masonry at the southeast corner of Room C in the tomb of Kairer.

This effectively holds the lower blocks of the corner securely in place. The fourth course uses a smaller block that is cut to the shape of the corner, and a block on the east wall is a quoin header that provides more stability. Indeed this quoin header is cut at one end to accommodate a block of the fifth course in its entirety and at one corner to accommodate a small square shaped block. This is another example of a 'locking' block that has been cut to provide stability in a wall, and has been placed here, as a through-block (stretcher) at the top height of this doorway.

Internal Masonry in the Tomb of Niankhba

In 2004 and 2005 the author made a survey of the internal masonry of the mastaba and part of the results is presented here.

The south wall of Room D (pillared hall; figure 3.3) is constructed from two outer skins of limestone blocks and a thickness of rubble. This wall is 12.00 m. in length and separates the columned hall from Rooms B and C, and Room A (the entrance chamber). The east end represents the highest part the wall and consists of four courses of masonry. At the middle of the wall, alongside Room B, the height has been reduced to two courses exposing the cross-section of the wall at this point. The wall is 1.03 m. thick, with at least 0.35 m. being the gap between the two outer casing blocks. Approximately all of these blocks are over 1.00 m. in length and at least 0.30 m. thick. The outer facing of the blocks consists of horizontal bedding joints and vertical rising joints. The cross-section reveals that the fineness of the joints between adjacent blocks does not extend completely inwards. Unlike

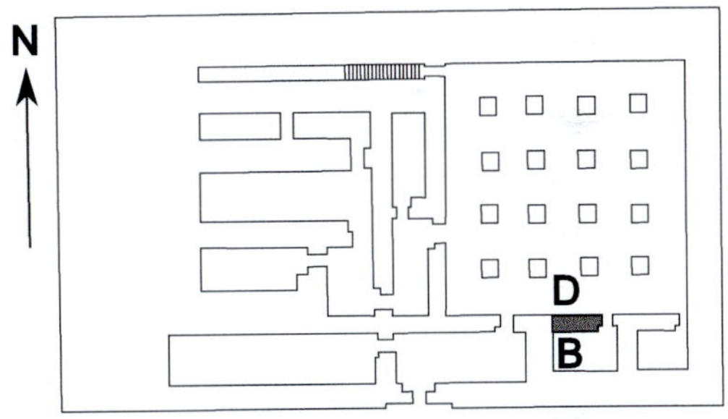

Figure 3.3. The tomb of Niankhba: cross-section of the east end of the wall between Rooms B and D.

the faces of the blocks the backs have been left very roughly dressed, and may not even have been cut since they were delivered at the tomb site. The doorway to Room B is 0.63 m. wide, 0.66 m. in length and opens inwards into a recess 1.02 m. wide and 0.37 m. deep. The casing blocks that form the west wall of the doorway and the inside thickness of the recess meet against each other at the end of the wall. The rising joint between the two second-course blocks of the west wall of the doorway is a close fit, but the cross-section reveals that the joint only extends inwards for 0.05 m. The block on the left side (*i.e.*, forms part of the south wall of Room D) is a large quoin header, being a header within the doorway and a stretcher in the return south wall. This block has maximum dimensions of 1.17 m. x 0.66 m. and is roughly rectangular, except for the southeast corner which is broken off and not dressed. This block is typical of the blocks used to form the end of walls within the mastaba. The end of the wall is constructed of alternate layers of blocks arranged as described above and larger blocks that form the whole corner of the wall with headers used as through-stones.

The same construction technique can be observed in the wall between Room H and Room I, the main offering-room of the mastaba (figure 3.4). The false-door occupied the whole length of the west wall but now only 0.65 m. of the base remains (Hassan, 1975c: 44). The south wall is 7.74 m. in length and contains a doorway, 0.75 m. wide at the eastern end, set within a recess 0.90 m. wide. The wall is 1.04 m. thick and consists of two outer skins of limestone and a rubble core. The casing blocks on the south side of the wall is formed from two courses of masonry whilst on the north side only one course of masonry remains, allowing us to see the back of the second course south casing blocks. The backs have a bulging convex profile that vary in width, with each being at least 0.30 m. wide, suggesting a gap between the blocks of the same width. The exposed first course has less of a gap between the two skins and at the end of the wall (where the doorway is located) a whole block has been used. This through-stone is 0.45 m. wide on the

Figure 3.4. The tomb of Niankhba: east-west wall between Rooms H and I.

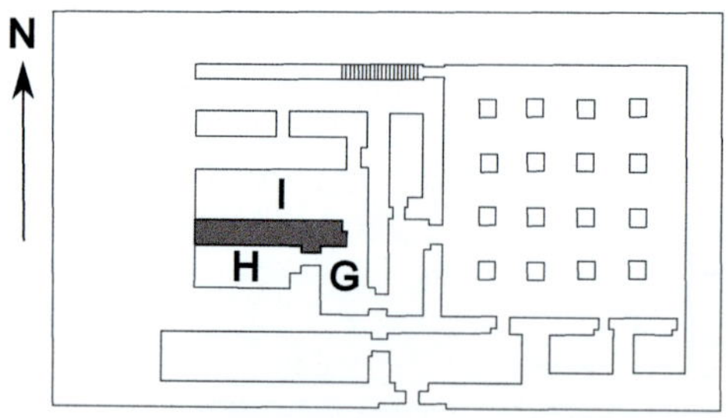

south side, but the north side has had a corner removed to create a recess framing the doorway, with a depth of 0.33 m.

Figure 3.5 illustrates how one larger block has been used to form the east doorframe of the doorway between Room I and J. Throughout the entire mastaba, doorways are constructed in this manner. As discussed above both sides of doorways are constructed by a succession of single through-stones and two blocks that meet against one another with little or no gap between them.

Figure 3.6 illustrates how a doorway between Rooms E and G was constructed. This is the end of the north-south wall that runs between Rooms E and F on the east and Rooms G, I and J on the west. At the northern part of this wall the masonry is exposed and the cross-section reveals the wall is built from two outer skins of limestone and a core filling of rubble, as discussed above. At this final part of the wall the blocks used at the end of the wall close the gap between the two skins. This is done by successive courses of through blocks, with stretchers running across the doorway wall, and two blocks placed against each other with no gap, and thus being two headers running across the doorway wall. This is quite typical of the doorways within this mastaba and the nearby mastaba of Kairer.

A doorway at the northwest corner of room D (pillared hall) gives access to a staircase built alongside the external north wall of the mastaba (figure 3.7). The north wall of the doorway survives to a height of three courses of masonry whilst only two survive on the south side. The second course consists of two blocks placed close to one another with only a slight gap in between them. The cross-section reveals that the rising joint between these two blocks only extends for c. 0.05 m.

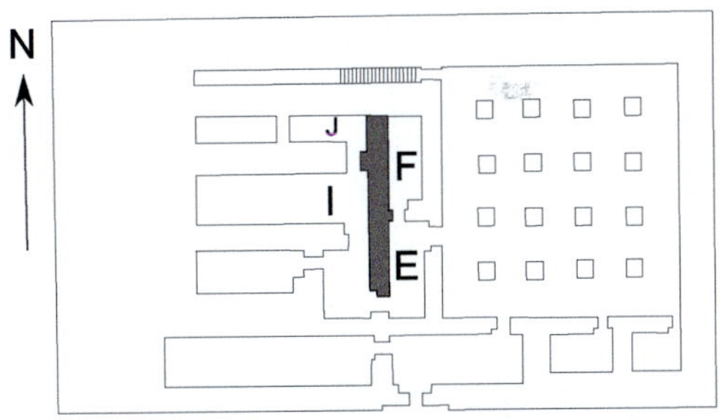

Figure 3.5. The tomb of Niankhba: wall between Rooms E and F on the east side and Rooms I and J on the west.

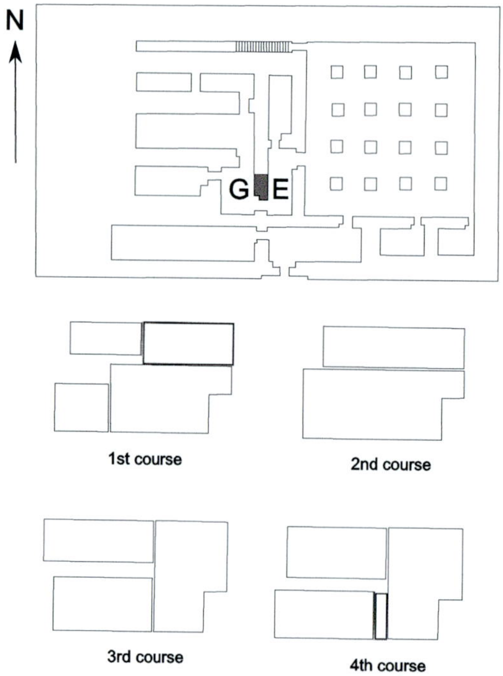

3.6. The tomb of Niankhba: pattern of masonry in the doorway between Rooms E and G.

3.7. The tomb of Niankhba: staircase.

and that the back of the blocks are very roughly dressed with a convex profile, which is in stark contrast to the face of the corner block that is perfectly cut to form the doorframe of the doorway and the inside thickness of the doorway recess.

External Masonry in the Tomb of Niankhba

The front of the mastaba has a length of 32.60 m. The entrance (0.75 m. wide) is situated near the centre and is set within a recess 3.25 m. wide and 0.30 m. deep. The masonry on this side survives to an average of two courses and does not give much information of the external appearance of the mastaba. However, the neighbouring mastaba of Nebkauhor is built in the same style and the exterior survives to a better extent. The south side is 34.00 m. in length and like in the mastaba of Niankhba the doorway is located within a recess of similar dimensions. However, this was part of the original design of the mastaba when it belonged to Akhethotep and remains of the third and fourth course blocks at the very left side of the recess survive and are decorated with a figure of Akhethotep and part of an inscription. When Nebkauhor usurped this tomb the recess was blocked with masonry to conceal these original inscriptions and new reliefs were positioned above the doorway at a greater height; these were repositioned within the doorway during the restoration by the Antiquities Service (Hassan, 1975a: 6, pls. III, IV A). One can expect that if higher courses had survived within the door recess in the mastaba of Niankhba there would be decoration in the same style. In both mastabas it is expected that, just like other tomb facades in the cemetery, the vast exterior of the tomb was left as clean dressed stone with decoration kept to within the entrance recess (*i.e.*, the walls to the sides of the doorway, the doorframe and lintel).

The external masonry of the tomb has a slight batter and at the back of the tomb the masonry overall survives to two courses (figures 3.8-3.9), with the odd exception of a third course block surviving in places and the northeast corner where four courses survive and best illustrate the sloped profile of the mastaba walls. The external walls are constructed in the same manner as the internal walls, with the only exception being the slightly sloped profile of the block faces. Furthermore, the gap that separated the two skin walls is larger, being on average approximately 0.60 m. wide.

Internal Masonry in the Tombs of Khenut and Nebet

In September 2004 the present author made a short survey was made of the internal masonry within this tomb. The adjoining mastaba of Nebet has been restored and was not open to the public, but the 1993 publication of these two tombs by Peter Munro recorded the masonry in great detail, enabling a consideration of the construction techniques in both of these tombs (Munro, 1993a). The blocks in both tombs vary in thickness c. 0.35 -0.50 m. and have an average height of 0.80 m. The internal masonry is constructed with the same method used in the mastaba

Figure 3.8. The tomb of Niankhba: external wall, west of the entrance.

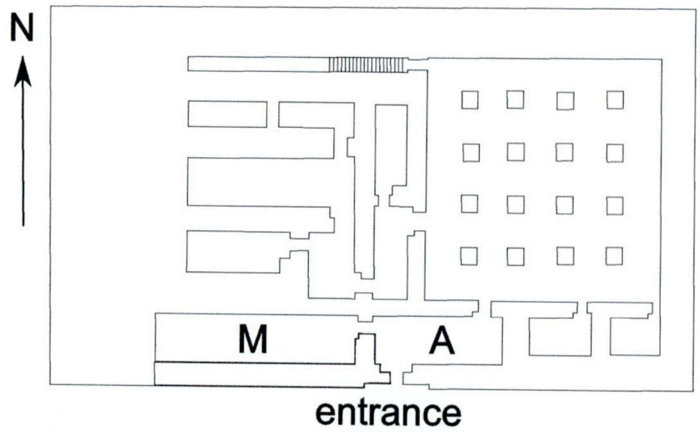

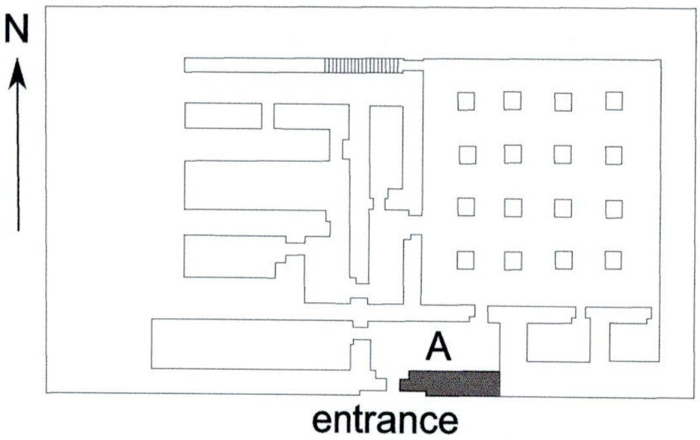

3.9. The tomb of Niankhba: external wall, east of the entrance.

of Niankhba, a technique similar to Arnold's Type 3. In general the internal walls have two thicknesses: the north and west walls of the open courtyard are 1.60 m. in width and all other walls are 1.10-1.25 m. in width.

The construction of walls at doorways in the tomb uses the same method as in the mastaba of Niankhba (figure 3.10). The east end of the wall runs east-west between Rooms M1 and M2 and Room B and C; it is at this point that there is a doorway, 0.75 m. wide, which connects Rooms B and M1. The end of the wall is constructed from single through-stones and two blocks that meet against one another with little or no gap between them.

Exposed walls between Rooms M1-M3 (three magazines) in the mastaba of Khenut reveal blocks are 0.30-0.35 m. thick with roughly dressed backs (figure 3.11). The bottoms of the blocks are not cut flat all the way to the back and this is also true for some of the exposed tops. The gap between the two rows of outer casing blocks is approximately 0.30 m. in width throughout and is filled with rubble (rough stones much larger than in the mastaba of Niankhba).

External Masonry in the Tombs of Khenut and Nebet

The external walls of the tombs of Khenut and Nebet are much thicker than those within the mastaba and vary in thickness (Munro, 1993a: pls. 1, 5). The south wall in both tombs is 2.00 m. thick and the incomplete state of the wall within the mastaba of Khenut reveals a cross-section that demonstrates the external walls are constructed using the same technique as the internal walls. The outer casing blocks on the north side are 0.40 m. thick and those on the south are 0.50 m. thick. The gap between the two skins is much wider than that within the internal walls, being 1.15 m. in width. The north wall of both tombs is 2.60 m. thick and it would seem the gap between the two skins is approximately 1.50 m. thick. The east wall of the mastaba of Nebet is 2.80 m. thick and the wall between the two tombs is 4.00 m. at its thickest and 1.80 m. at the thinnest point, behind the false-door of Nebet in the offering-room. The upper section has been restored with modern bricks, but the lower part reveals a skin of large limestone blocks and a core of rubble and tafl. The slight batter of the walls can also be seen.

Internal Masonry in the Tomb of Mehu

Although Hartwig Altenmüller's publication of this tomb is primarily concerned with the wall decoration (and states so in the first chapter) the plans and architectural details are admirable and very useful (Altenmüller, 1998: 17, no. 1). A detailed report on the restoration of this tomb carried out in 1940 also contains valuable architectural data (Hussein, 1942: 417-55, pls. XXIX-XXXV). The walls within the mastaba are built using the same technique as in the mastabas described above, as Hussein (1942: 420) notes: "The walls consisted of two outer casings in dressed stones and the space in between was filled with rubble of 15 to 40 cm. in diameter." The internal walls are all of an average thickness of c. 1.00 m, except for the wall between the offering-room of Mehu (the main offering-room) which is 1.25 m. thick (Altenmüller, 1998: 18). The casing blocks vary in thickness

Figure 3.10. *The tomb of Khenut: wall between Room B and M1. From: Munro (1993a: pl. 2).*

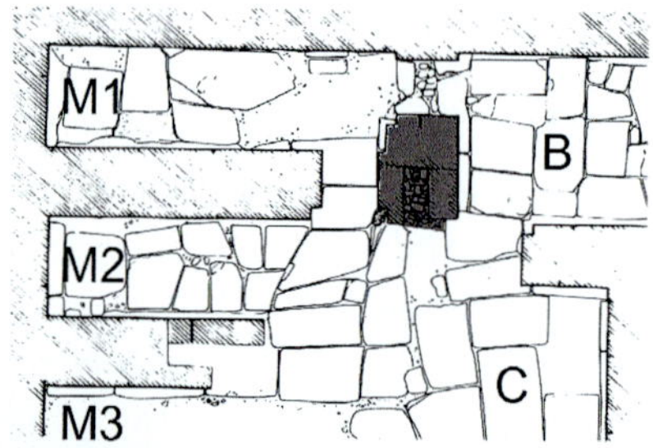

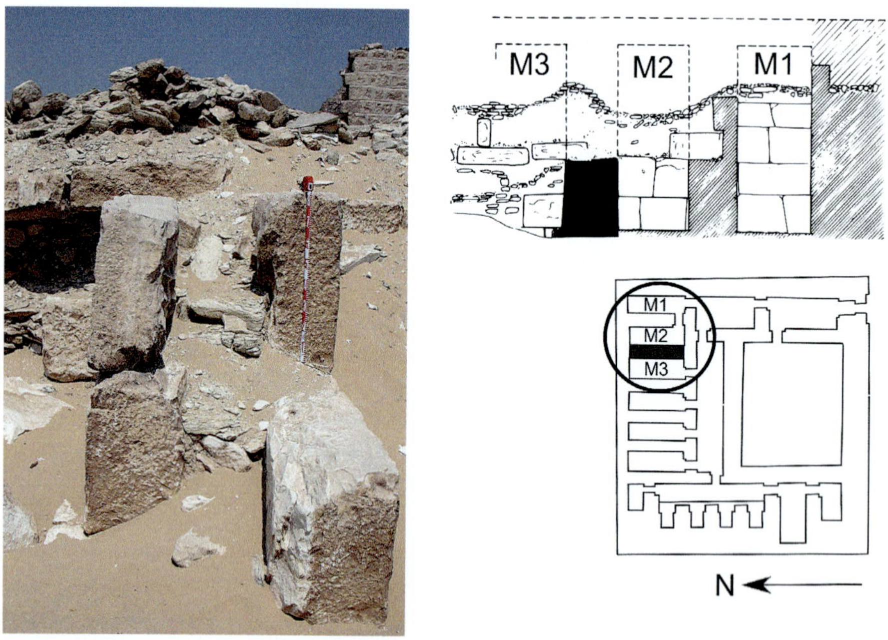

Figure 3.11. The tomb of Khenut: wall between M2 and M3. After: Munro (1993a: pl. 4).

between 0.40-0.50 m., and have the same height. The gap between the skins does vary between 0.15-0.40 m., as Hussein states, with the average being 0.30 m. The plan of the tomb in the publication by Altenmüller (1998: plan A) demonstrates that the same construction techniques as used in the mastabas described above are used to build the end of walls/doorway walls. The north wall of the serdab uses the same masonry style but instead of using two skins of limestone blocks to contain the rubble core, the cut rock face that the mastaba is built against forms the outer skin. The thickness of the gap varies between 0.50-0.60 m.

External Masonry in the Tomb of Mehu

The external masonry of this tomb is quite exceptional and reflects certain difficulties the architect had to overcome because of the site topography. The mastaba is built on an east-west axis, with the north wall of the tomb abutting the vertical face of the rock that forms the base of the enclosure wall of the Step Pyramid Complex. From this point the rock floor slopes downwards for some distance and the southern half of the mastaba is built upon this quite steeply sloping ground (Altenmüller, 1998: plan D; Hussein, 1942: pls. XXIX, XXX). The space between the paving of the tomb and the rock face was filled with accumulation of sand and rock debris (c. 1.50 m. at its thickest) (Hussein, 1942: 417). The external wall is constructed in the same manner as the internal walls. The east and south walls are 1.25 m. thick with a gap between the two skins that vary between 0.50-0.60 m. in thickness, which is filled with rubble. The south wall extends the complete distance between the front of the mastaba and the east wall of the mastaba of Seshseshet Idut. The north wall is 26.50 m. in length and behind the 7.50 m. on the east side is a thickness of sand and rubble filling the space between the south wall and the rock face against which the mastaba is built. The external wall on the northern side of the mastaba is built upon a higher level of the rock face and consequently begins just beneath the ceiling height of the rooms within the superstructure. This wall is 3.00 m. in thickness and like the east and south walls the top of the wall has been capped with horizontal top stones. Because of the uneven nature of the foundations the mastaba has suffered from the effects of the southern side subsiding. This, it would seem, manifested itself as a problem quite early after the mastaba was completed, perhaps at the same time as the completion of the building measures were carried out to support the slumping southern side of the mastaba and prevent damage to the whole structure; the brick wall on the north side also contains a gap filled with rubble (Altenmüller, 1998: 17-18, plans A-E). A brick wall was built against the south and east limestone masonry walls, and also on top of the rock slope against the parapet wall on the north side. The brickwork is bonded using type A2 of Spencer's corpus of brick bonds and consists entirely of tafl-bricks measuring 0.30-0.31 m. x 0.145 m. x 0.09 m. (Spencer, 1979: 27, 34, pl.1; see also Altenmüller, 1998: 18). This brick wall is 2.00 m. thick and has been supported by a 2.20 m. thickness of laminated rock debris and sand; it is unclear if this wall was erected at the same time as the brick wall (Altenmüller, 1998: 17-18, plans A-E).

Internal Masonry in the Tomb of Khentika

The restoration of the tomb of Khentika within the Teti Cemetery did not reconstruct walls to the height of the roofing and allows one to observe cross-sections of the walls.

The walls are constructed in the same manner as in the tombs of the Unas Cemetery described above, similar to Arnold's Type 3 (figure 3.12). Indeed, this is typical for the construction of other mastabas in the Teti Cemetery; for example, the columned hall of the mastaba of Ihy, where the cross-section of masonry is visible (Firth & Gunn, 1926b: pl. 16). The thicknesses of the walls vary within the superstructure with some walls being 0.50 m. in width and others 0.90 m. The wall between Room 9 (courtyard) and Room 3 (offering-room) is the thickest internal wall (c. 2.00 m.) as this was originally an external wall of an earlier building that was incorporated into the mastaba superstructure (James, 1953: 16-18, fig. 7). Further modifications to the superstructure can be observed in the masonry, including the unusual construction of the doorways (see Chapter 5). The construction of the doorway between Room 4 and Room 5 is unusual compared to the doorways discussed in other tombs above. Rather than using single through-

Figure 3.12. The tomb of Khentika: south-west corner in Room 5. Courtesy of The Egypt Exploration Society.

blocks or two blocks positioned close together with no gap, the builders have continued the same method of using two skins all along the wall and closed the gap at the end of the wall with a narrow strip of stone that is c. 0.10-0.14 m. thick.

External Masonry in the Tomb of Khentika

The exterior walls in the tomb of Khentika vary in thickness between 0.90-1.10 m., except for the wall at the north side of the entrance that is 2.00 m. in width. The walls are formed using the same construction technique with a larger gap between the two skins of masonry. The entire facade of the mastaba masonry has large inscriptions and figures of the owner in raised relief (James, 1953: 19-20, 37-42, pls. I, V-VIII).

3.2.2. Surface Appearance

Internal masonry was merely part of a building structure, usually a canvas for relief carving and painting. It could be argued that the detailed appearance of Egyptian masonry was unlike the isodomic masonry of Classical Greece and not of any aesthetic importance if the wall was to be smoothed over and decorated. Smith (1949: 245) considers the technical methods employed in Old Kingdom reliefs and paintings in some detail and summarises the liberal use of plaster in all types of tombs: "The preparation of the surface was also accompanied by a certain amount of mending and patching in plaster, depending upon the quality of the stone of which the wall was composed. In work in fine limestone, where the joints of the masonry are accurate, this was almost entirely unnecessary. Ordinarily the same coarse plaster that was used to float the stone into place was employed to fill the interstices remaining between the stones, and to conceal flaws and breaks in the wall surface. This was necessary sometimes even in chapels of the best workmanship…". Other authors of works concerning Egyptian masonry have made reference to the use of plaster on dressed stone wall (Lucas & Harris, 1962: 77), and publications of Old Kingdom tombs often include details on plaster being used to cover a wall after it was dressed and after relief carving (Smith, 1949: 244-245; Williams, 1932). In her publication of the core mastabas within the cemetery of palace attendants within the Western Cemetery' at Giza, Roth (1995: 14) comments on the final treatment of the external limestone masonry: "Both horizontal and vertical joints of even the most roughly finished walls were often filled with plaster, down the centre of which a single line was scored. These lines appear to have been made with a sharp point while the plaster was still wet. They perhaps intended to mimic the hairline joints of finer masonry." This treatment refers to external masonry and Roth found that overall the same technique was not used for internal walls but rather that for internal masonry poorer quality limestone would be covered with a layer of plaster before carving. According to Roth (1995: 20) similar techniques were used for other masonry: "decoration was carved directly into the limestone, although the gaps between blocks were often filled with plaster and decorated using the same technique used to decorate poor stone. The harder stone surfaces were also generally smoothed with a film of plaster that would have served as a base for paint. In some cases, this plaster film seems to have been applied after the decoration was carved, to smooth out any mistakes in the carving as well as flaws in the stone.". This practice is not just specific to the Western Cemetery at Giza and must have been used throughout the Memphite Necropolis. In the mastaba of Mereruka, Duell (1938: 7) notes that a mortar probably made from gypsum was used as a plaster to fill in any gaps between blocks and any chips in the stone block faces. In the mastaba of Khentika large areas of the wall were plastered to smooth the surface before the walls were carved and painted (James, 1953: 17). In the mastaba of Seshseshet Idut the limestone walls were covered with a thick layer of plaster that was then carved and painted (Macramallah, 1935: 2-3, pls. IV, VI, XXVII). With so much of the internal masonry within mastabas being plastered and/or painted over Arnold (1991: 148) believes this is why the Egyptians often employed several 'types' of masonry in one building, and why little has been done to classify types of Egyptian masonry. In their classification study Clarke and Engelbach (1990: 100) focussed on the use of oblique joints to determine masonry types (figure 3.13). The authors were keen on questioning why the ancient Egyptians used so many oblique joints in their masonry; something they thought was a peculiarity of fine megalithic masonry with no modern parallel. Often a wall appears to use rectangular blocks if the bedding joints and rising joints are at right-angles to one another. However, in Egyptian masonry the blocks are often odd shaped and the bedding joint is not always at a right-angle with the side joint; this type of masonry was classified by Clarke and Engelbach as 'Type A'. Masonry with a more visible use of oblique joints (*i.e.*, when the bedding joint was at an acute or obtuse angle with the rising joint and the bedding joint was at right-angles with the side joint) was classified by Clarke and Engelbach as 'Type B'. They found both types were common in Old Kingdom masonry, occasionally together in one wall, but it was only Type B that was used afterwards (Clarke & Engelbach, 1990: 103-104). They also noted the frequent use of stepped masonry, where the height of a course is not level. This was assumed to be a deliberate style, rather than a method of minimising the cutting of stone. If stone was arriving from the quarry in a fairly uniform size (at

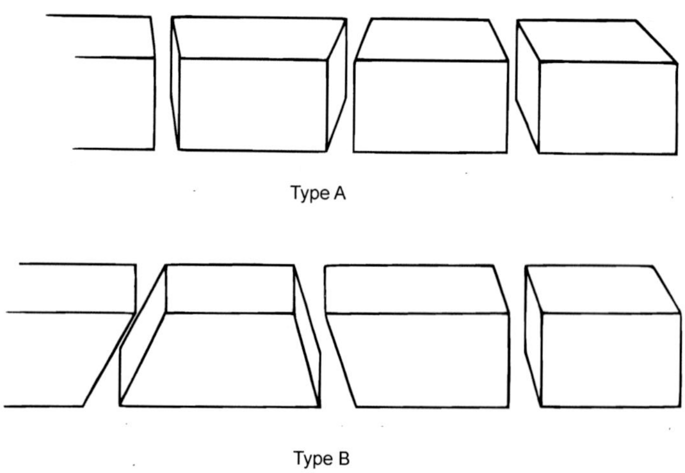

Figure 3.13. Clarke and Engelbach's masonry types. From: Clarke & Engelbach (1990: figs. 105-106).

least in height), and dressed in one go, then a wall would inevitably be composed of straight joints. They argued that an inordinate number of straight joints meant a lack of solidity in the structure. Rather than being a method of economisation, the stone was actually deliberately cut smaller to form stepped bedding joints. This would all take place on site, in front of the wall that was to be laid. This proposal may be influenced by Clarke and Engelbach's determination to assert that blocks were dressed as an individual group on site, rather than blindly as a whole at some intermediate work place between quarry and building site.

Reisner devised a system of categorising the different types of exterior masonry used in the construction of mastabas at Giza by distinguishing between the surface appearances (Reisner, 1942: 39-56; Roth, 1995: 14). He named each type after a letter and used this with a combination of other category codes to label mastabas and arrange them into an order. Many of the mastabas at Giza have external walls that have a stepped profile, with each block being set back about 0.05 m. from the block below it. The face of each block has been cut at a slight angle to give a batter. The blocks are positioned with horizontal bedding joints and each course is of a uniform height. The type of joints used can also vary. U-masonry is less regular and the heights of courses can vary and so does the finished dressing on the block faces. W-masonry does not have a stepped profile and is a battered façade with very roughly finished block faces. This system can be applied to some of the mastabas within the Unas Cemetery.

In his study of Egyptian masonry Arnold (1991: 148) observed three distinctive features:

- frequent use of mixed types of masonry in single structures.
- regular re-use of building materials.
- use of poorer materials in building cores.

Arnold's classification of masonry approaches the cross-section of walls separately from the surface appearance of buildings, which he divides into five types (1991: 148-153) (figure 3.14).

Type 1 - 'Stepped' masonry (or 'broken' masonry) where a horizontal course has blocks of different heights. This is explained by the Egyptians "apparent economy in the use of material" (Arnold, 1991: 148), rather than being deliberately purposeful as Clarke and Engelbach believe (1990: 107). Arnold states that the Egyptians did not produce blocks of a uniform size and in order not to waste material blocks of different sizes (heights) would be minimally cut neat and used alongside one another. Like Clarke and Engelbach Arnold believes that masons would lay one course and then, if needs be, steps would be cut into this course to accommodate taller blocks of the next course. This process would create a horizontal bedding joint on the top course. However, if odd height blocks were to be laid upon this row then steps would have to be cut again. It is easier to accept this as being the mode of production rather than the other way, *i.e.*, cutting steps into blocks before they were laid; this would require more handling and measurements.

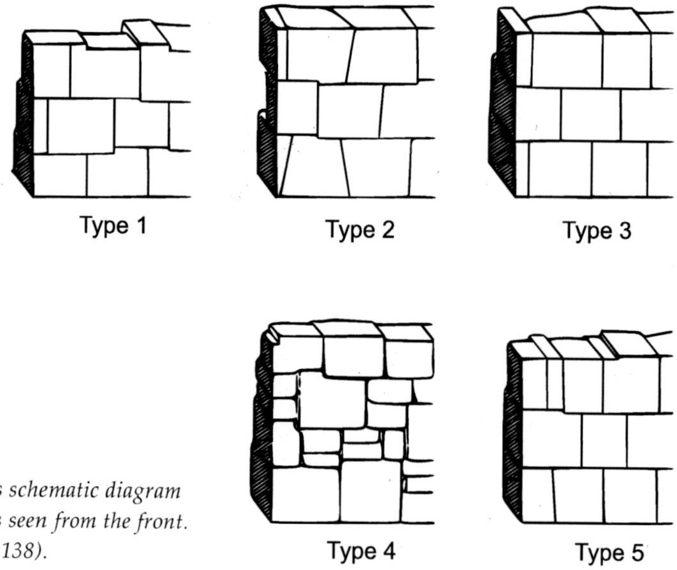

Figure 3.14. Arnold's schematic diagram of free-standing walls seen from the front. From: Arnold (2003: 138).

Type 2 - 'Trapezoidal' masonry, where oblique angle rising joints and side joints are used. Clarke and Engelbach (1990: 106-107) argued that there must have been some structural reason for using trapezoidal joints because of their great frequency. Arnold (1991: 151) disagrees that they were used consistently and therefore rejects their presence being structural, or decorative, but rather another example of masons' "stone-saving mentality". Arnold (2003: 117) states that trapezoidal masonry is more common in the Old Kingdom and less so in later periods. The frequency of trapezoidal masonry in buildings is obviously a construction technique that needs accurate quantifying.

Type 3 - Isodomic masonry that resembles brickwork. Often in Egyptian masonry the courses of a wall can appear to be of a pattern, alm ost ashlar, with some courses being composed of stretchers and other that appear to be headers. But as Arnold (1991: 153) observes, this pattern is almost always interrupted by the use of stepped joints and trapezoidal joints; his reason being that courses were not laid for appearance.

Type 4 - Extremely irregular masonry. Not merely a mixture of all the above, but a complete random use of many different sizes of blocks that are packed together, rather than laid as a unit. Arnold (1991: 153) believes this type to be rare because masons respected structural stability over economy, and that examples of this type typify severe shortage of material. A lack of time may also be factor that accounts of examples of this type.

Type 5 - Mixed masonry, is most common method used in Egyptian monuments.

Arnold's study is primarily concerned with royal monumental architecture. Similar principles, however, can be used to discuss the masonry within mastabas in the Memphite Necropolis. This study will consider three aspects of masonry classification:

- vertical joints
- horizontal joints
- bossed masonry and corner construction

Vertical Joints in Masonry

The most straightforward means of assembling blocks is to use vertical rising joints. With this system all corners of the block are at right angles and can be fitted against another block with the ease of a mason's square. In Egyptian masonry there is a popular use of oblique angled rising joints alongside regular vertical rising joints. Greater stone-cutting skill is required when using oblique joints, as the rising plane of each partnering block needs to mirror one another for a close-fit. Clarke and Engelbach (1990: 106) have questioned why the Egyptians used so many oblique angles in their masonry. We do not know the methods that the Egyptians used in preparing blocks of oblique angles. Clarke and Engelbach (1990: 100-111, figs. 104-109; *cf.*, Arnold, 1991: 122-123, figs. 4.19-4.20) proposed a number of methods that involve taking measurements and lining blocks up against one another. This preparation would have taken place within the mastaba, rather than at some intermediary site. As noted above, not all blocks from the quarry would be rectangular. The presence of oblique joints in Egyptian masonry could be a reflection of quarrying practices. Arnold (1991: 122) believes the only reason for the large use of oblique joints is a maximisation of stone resources. However, using irregularly shaped quarry stones would have required more effort, with masons having to take a variety of measurements to fit blocks together. Did the economy of stone therefore override work and time expended in construction? Another possibility could be for greater structural stability within a wall. The masonry within the mastaba of Mehu features courses of different heights and a large amount of oblique rising joints leading Hussein (1942: 420) to the conclusion that this was an intentional method to promote solidity within the masonry. Duell (1938: 7) regards the oblique rising joints in the masonry of the mastaba of Mereruka to be result of possible labour saving. However, in decorated tombs, joints within the wall would not be visible in a finished tomb. This obviously eliminates any notion that oblique joints were used for aesthetic reasons. It also indicates that the appearance of the masonry was not an over-riding factor, and that as long as the wall was structurally sound it did not matter if irregular shaped blocks had been used.

Vertical Joints in the Tomb of Kairer

Within Room 1 (figure 3.15) there is a block on the third course of the south wall that has an upright angle of 104 degrees. The adjoining block has an almost parallel plane, though the cut of the stone is not clean. In Room 2 (figure 3.15)

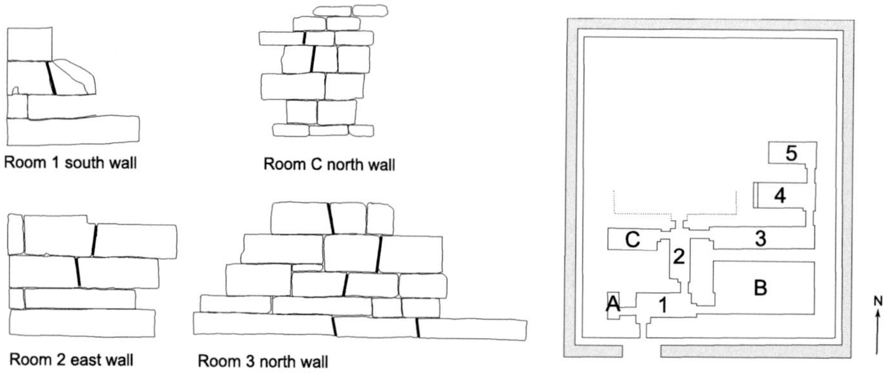

Figure 3.15. Oblique masonry joints in the tomb of Kairer (emphasized in black).

on the east wall there is an oblique joint on the third course (97 degrees) and one other on the 4th course (100 degrees), both have corresponding adjoining blocks, though there is a slight gap between them. Room C (figure 3.15) is a storeroom with undecorated walls and the masonry is more irregular than other rooms in the tomb. On the north wall there is only one real example of an oblique joint and this is on the 5th course of the north wall. The angle is 111 degrees and the joint is very neat with the two blocks fitting closely. In Room 3 (figure 3.15) on the north wall are five examples of oblique joints can be seen on this wall: first course (102 degrees), third course (102 degrees), 4th course (97 degrees) and the 5th course (98 degrees); all of these oblique joints are neat with blocks being close-fitted.

Summary of Vertical Joints in Masonry

All angles of oblique joints are obtuse with both stones meeting closely, indicating that both have been well cut to fit together. Just how frequent trapezoidal masonry was used in Old Kingdom monuments needs quantifying. It cannot really have been appreciated for its structural support in the tomb of Kairer because it is not used to any great degree. However, some walls are missing; the long north wall of Room 3 had several oblique joints, perhaps if the opposing wall had survived to the same height, more could be seen. It is interesting that it is in this long wall that we see it employed most; a wall that perhaps requires more structural support than most.

Horizontal Joints in Masonry

It is likely that the tops of blocks would not be levelled until a whole row had been completed (Arnold, 1991: 44, 122). Indeed, Clarke and Engelbach (1990: 108) state that this was the normal way in Egyptian masonry and that ancient builders were "bound by convention and worked by rule of thumb". With this being the established process of building a wall, the dressing of the top of the block would have been most usually the penultimate dressing. Before this took place the base of the block would have to be dressed and so would the sides of the block. The front of the block was almost always left with extra stock and the rear of the block was often just left roughly cut (Arnold, 1991: 44; Smith, 1949: 244). However, in mastabas some blocks in a wall are exposed on three sides, if the wall is only as thick as the block is wide. Once all the blocks in a row had been positioned alongside one another the tops of the (bossed) blocks would be levelled in one process. A cord would have been used to mark a level line near the top of the blocks, and excess stone above this line would be chipped away (Arnold, 1991: 44). This is, of course, an easier single process than measuring the height of each block and cutting it individually before laying it - this process Clarke and Engelbach (1990: 108) believe to be "contrary to the practice of the ancient builders". Slanted horizontal joints in masonry certainly indicated that this was a favoured method of construction. Using examples from the columns of the cross-hall of the western colonnade in the Djoser Step Pyramid Complex and slanting beds within the temple of Amenhotep III at el-Kâb, Clarke and Engelbach (1990: 98) contend that flat bedding joints that are not parallel with those of other courses within a wall could have only been achieved if the top of a course was levelled in one process, once all blocks had been laid. Arnold (2003: 117) states that the only time purposeful sloping bedding joints are used is downward sloping corridors and walls along staircases and in the inward sloping casing of pyramids of the 3rd Dynasty. Often the height of bedding joints within rooms will be the same for each wall; indeed Clarke and Engelbach (1990: 107) see that this pattern was a desired standard: "...the rule seems to have been an attempt to keep the beds of a certain number of successive blocks at one level.". How this was achieved we do not exactly know. For this to be done the foundations must have been flat. However, masonry does not always use horizontal bedding joints. As discussed above, stepped masonry is a common feature in Egyptian architecture. Clarke and Engelbach (1990: 107) believe it was used purposefully to promote constructional stability; and Arnold (1991: 122, 151) states it is a process of utilising different sizes of blocks. Either way, both agree that the step was cut into the laid course and the block of the next course was placed within this step 'frame'.

Horizontal Joints in the Tomb of Kairer

Room 1 (figure 3.16). The top of the first course of the north wall has not been levelled flat. The central block of the course has a curved top that rises 0.06 m. from the height of the corners. The bedding joints of the above blocks of the second course fit closely to irregular first course, but the top bedding joints are cut horizontally. The first and second course blocks are of a good length and a narrow height. Larger blocks are used within the third course (one of which is c.1.20 m. x 0.55 m.). One surviving block of the fourth course suggests that blocks of a similar size to the third course were used. Indeed, this block that forms part of the wall of the passage between Rooms 1 and 2, has a step cut into its left corner, indicating that there was a fifth course. The block at the other side of the wall, on the fourth course, is also cut with a step. The true height of this block is the same as the 'stepped' height of the other block. Daoud (1995: 37) believes this block, decorated with part of a funeral scene, is incorrectly positioned. It makes little sense for the step-cut to be positioned against the west wall. In respect of building

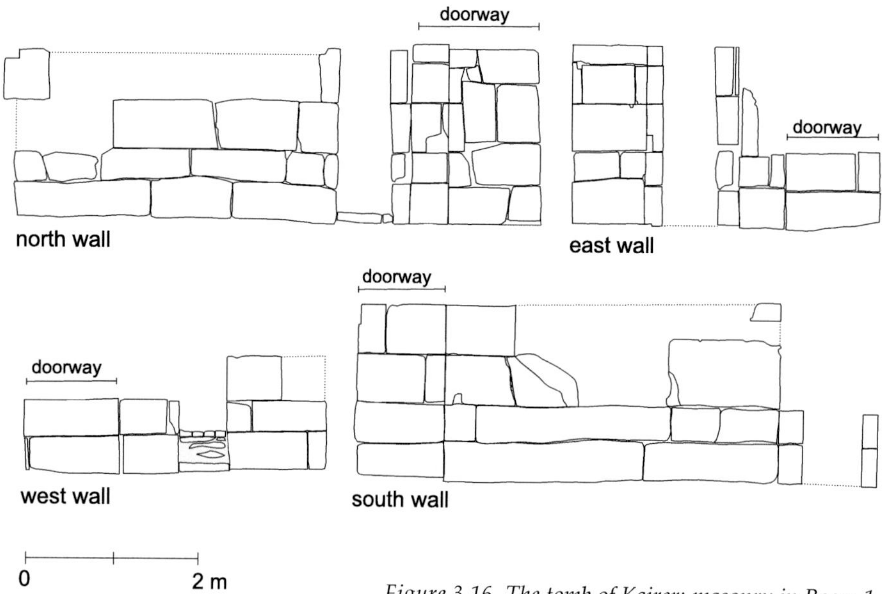

Figure 3.16. The tomb of Kairer: masonry in Room 1.

'sense', this block needs to be much further along from the wall edge. The height of bedding levels on the south wall is parallel with those on the north wall. Like at the north wall long and narrow blocks have been used on the first and second course (indeed, one block measures 2.40 m. x 0.50 m.). Again, as at the north wall, very large blocks have been used for the third course (one being 1.33 m. x 0.78 m.) and the fourth course (very little survives). The west wall contains a narrow (0.60 m. wide) doorway to Room A, and little remains beyond the second course. All bedding joints here are horizontal and parallel in height with the other course in the room. Very little remains of Room A and at present the room is full with a thick layer of debris to the height of the later wall that blocks the doorway. The east wall contains a doorway to Room B set within a recess, which is now sealed off with a modern wall. Most of this wall is composed of corners and is discussed in the separate section on corners.

Room 2 (figure 3.17). The two long parallel walls of Room 2 are the east and west walls. The height of corresponding bedding levels on either wall is roughly parallel. The first course of the east wall uses an incredibly long block (2.64 m. x 0.50 m.), which almost stretches the entire length of the wall. The west wall has three blocks of a similar height. On both walls the second course is composed of generally long thin blocks (0.30-0.35 m. in height). The narrow second course blocks on the west wall are slightly taller at the south end of the wall (0.10 m. taller), making up for the slightly uneven floor of the room (distance from baseline to ground at north end and south end is 1.50 m. and 1.40 m. respectively). The third and fourth courses have blocks of a more substantial size, better suited for relief carving. There is a gradual increase in the height of blocks in the third course (a rise of 0.08 m. from south to east, over the 3.53 m. distance), giving a slightly sloping top bedding plain and supports the understanding that blocks were dressed together after laying (Clarke & Engelbach, 1990: 100). On the fourth course of

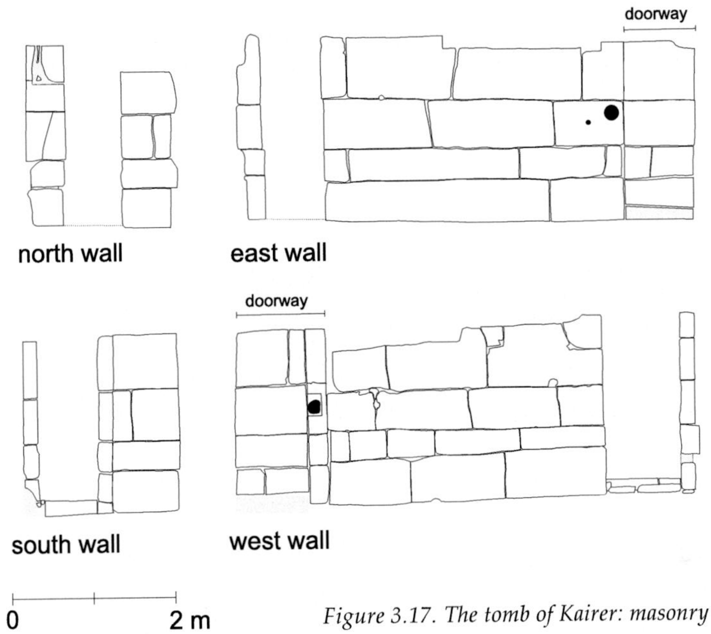

Figure 3.17. The tomb of Kairer: masonry in Room 2.

the east wall, steps have been cut into two blocks to form a 'frame' 0.15 m. deep by 1.90 m. wide. The shorter block between the two was either already of this height or was cut to this height. In this case it depends on what was the deciding factor in this part of the wall –width or height? Indeed, this is a considerable width that probably accommodated more than one block; if so, both must have been the same height. Whatever blocks were positioned in the fifth course must have formed the uppermost part of the wall, or possibly the ceiling. Clarke and Engelbach (1990: 107), and Arnold (1990: 151) have discussed how stepped masonry was used to accommodate 'taller' blocks into a course. In this case, very near the ceiling height, taller blocks may have been the reason for the stepped masonry. It could be to allow greater stability through bonding in the wall; something that would be important higher up in the wall where a ceiling would be supported. On the fourth course of the opposite wall, on the west there is one block cut with a step. This block of considerable length (1.85 m.) does not have a partnering/parallel step. Instead there is just a 1.55 m. span before the corner of the south wall. However, the fifth course block of the south wall is missing; it may be that this was a corner block that spanned both walls and may have had a partnering step cut into its corner to form a frame to accommodate a block of the fifth course. The present author is, however, inclined to think that this stepped masonry, at such a height, has some purpose concerning the ceiling of the room. The tops of both walls are not flat and the stepped levels perhaps represent the presence of interlocking blocks or masonry associated with the roofing of the room. With no roofing surviving in the mastaba the height of the ceiling is unknown. The passageway between Rooms 2 and 3 has bedding joints on both sides that are parallel and horizontal. Long thin blocks are

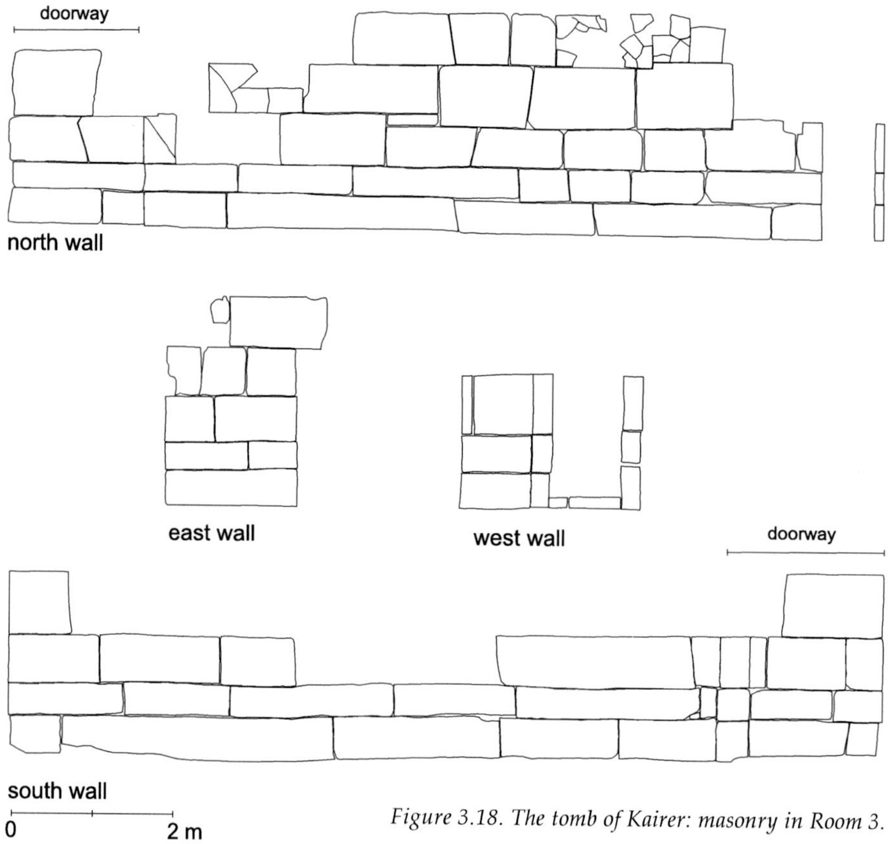

Figure 3.18. The tomb of Kairer: masonry in Room 3.

used for the first and second course, and much larger blocks (*e.g.*, 0.78 m. x 1.20 m.) are used for the third and fourth course.

Room 3 (figure 3.18). The levels of the first and second course top heights are the same on the north and south wall. The first course employs exceedingly long blocks (one being 2.80 m.) that are narrow in height (c. 0.40 m.). The second course blocks are slightly narrower and much shorter. This is a very large room and the use of long blocks of the first course must have been the quickest method of defining the size of the room, using blocks all cut to the same size, and presumably from the same quarry. The third course is slightly different on the north wall as it is stepped in three places. As a rule, the north and south wall follows the same height (c. 0.48 m.), however, the height of the third course changes in places where stepped masonry has been used, to allow for better quality larger blocks at eyelevel. The block at the far west end has had both corners cut: one to accommodate a large block above, and the other to form a small 'frame' with the adjoining final block of this wall. In this later case the 'frame' created is only 0.25 m. wide. With the blocks of the above course now missing it is not possible to see what above block would have required this cutting. Indeed, it is hard to understand why such effort was made to accommodate the odd shape of an overlying block. It is more reasonable to assume that this is a stepped cutting to provide a cavity, perhaps for scaffolding, rather than to accommodate a block. Further along on the third course a large block has been used, raising the level of the bedding joint (interestingly this block is of the same height of the latter stepped block on the same course). This block is accommodated into the top course without any stepped joints. Instead a slightly narrower block has been placed above it (*i.e.*, narrower in height than the adjoining blocks of the same row) and a small thin block has been used to fill the gap between the two courses. This is an example of how bedding levels can be broken without using stepped masonry: the method requires less cutting, and is perhaps more economical, though there is less structural bonding between the courses. Also, stepped masonry is seen as being used to accommodate blocks of an above course, *i.e.*, the block of the next course dictates where the cuttings are to be made in the below course. But this example shows that the lower block dictated the shape of the above block, not the other way round. The last block of the fourth course, on the right hand side of the north wall, has a small step cut into its top left corner. In this case the block is only slightly taller than the rest of the course. Rather than trim it down, a small step has been cut so that the above block (that also lies on top of the adjoining block of the fourth course) can sit above it horizontally for just a small distance. Two smaller blocks are then used to fill the gap of the fifth course. The third course on the south wall has a large part missing; indeed, only one block of the above fourth course survives. By comparison with the north wall, the missing blocks on the fourth course of the south wall must have been large blocks that were most suitable for relief carving.

Room 4 (figure 3.19). The bedding levels on both sides of the doorway between Rooms 3 and 4 are identical. The first and second courses consist of small blocks and the third and fourth course use much larger blocks. The north and west walls

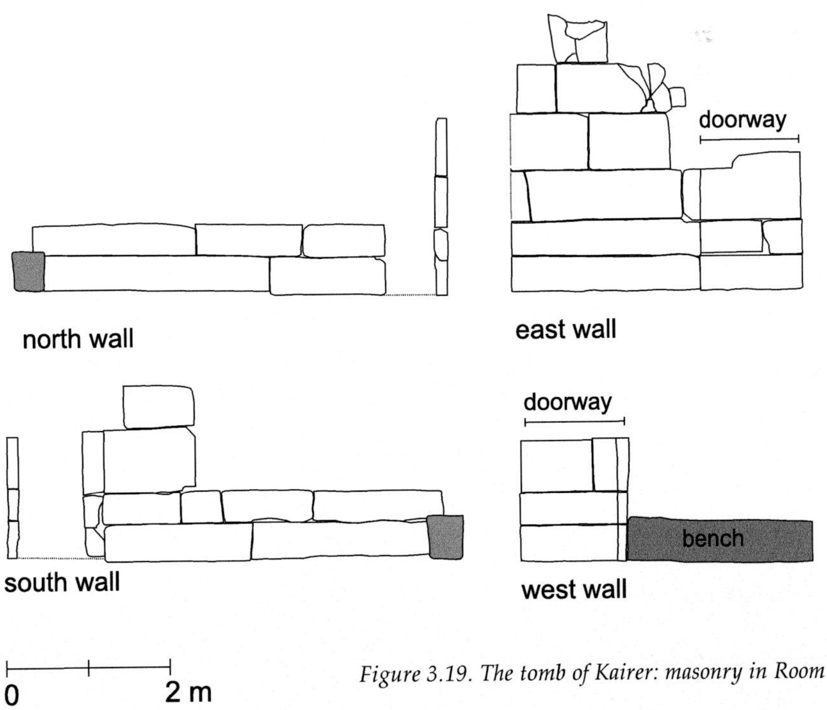

Figure 3.19. The tomb of Kairer: masonry in Room 4.

of Room 4 have identical heights for the top of the first and second course. The same height of blocks was also used on the south wall where six courses survive, all with horizontal bedding joints. Of the west wall, where the false-door would have been positioned, only one protruding block remains.

Room 5 (figure 3.20). The first course blocks are of the same size but with near-horizontal bedding joints. There is a gap beneath the first course block on the west wall; not all the paving stones have survived and the 0.10 m. gap is created by a paving stone(s) that underlay the wall now missing. The second course on the north wall is quite disordered. None of the blocks appear to have well dressed joints and they are packed together to suit the size of the blocks rather than to fit within defined course. Above this course in the room there is an overall impression of having level bedding joints but this has not been rigorously enforced, *e.g.*, stones that perhaps just required only 0.05 m. to be removed to make them flush with the rest of the bedding level have been left and blocks above are slotted into shape. In some places stepped masonry is used, but it is of a style unlike that seen in the rest of the tomb; the joints are more natural in appearance –perhaps not even purposefully cut at all. Like in Room 3 very narrow blocks have been used, with ease, to raise the height of a course on the south wall, rather than use stepped masonry. The top courses of the room are all alike, using small blocks of quickly dressed appearance (*i.e.*, the sides are not horizontal and the corners are curved). The irregular masonry in this room may be explained by there being no intention to decorate the room, especially so if it merely served as a storage room for equipment used in the adjacent offering room. Admittedly, joints within masonry can be filled

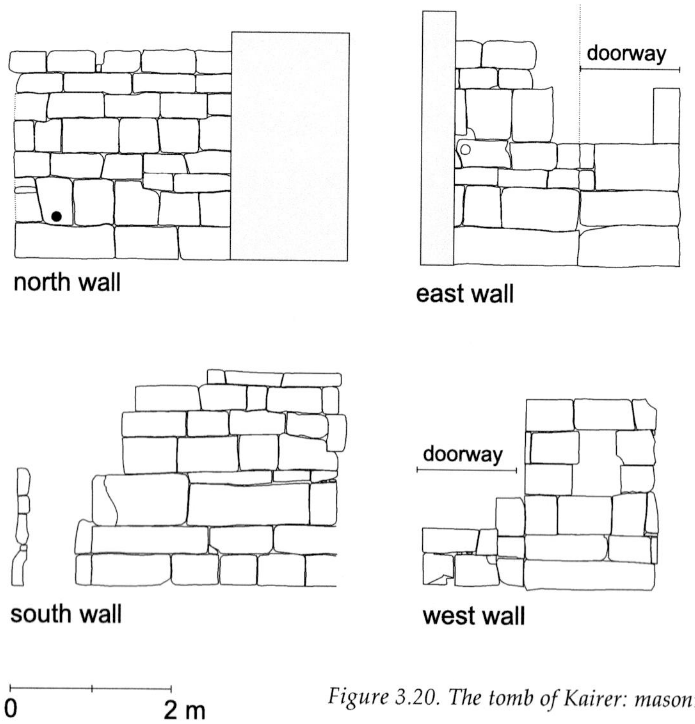

Figure 3.20. The tomb of Kairer: masonry in Room 5.

in to give a smooth appearance, but if a lot of relief carving was to be applied it would be wiser to use regular large shaped blocks to avoid too much carving into the plaster, that could more easily break away. Another hypothesis is that this room was intended to be decorated but the owner died before its completion and it was decided to leave the room bare of decoration. The room is annexed to the north of the offering-room, in a layout similar to other multi-roomed mastabas. This type of side room is usually decorated with scenes of offerings, especially oils (discussed in Chapter 6).

Summary of Horizontal Joints in Masonry

It has been noted in other mastabas that the builders would try and achieve level heights of courses throughout a room and the masonry in the mastaba of Kairer is no exception. The use of blocks of the same height implies that blocks of roughly the same size were being delivered to the tomb and processed in groups corresponding to the course of each room. Long and narrow blocks are favoured for the first course and this would allow the layout of the tomb to be quickly established. An even line of courses would be advantageous for the artists whose job it was to carve the stone. If all the joints are in one place it is easier to arrange scenes in places where there are fewer joints, especially if the joints are not flush and gaps have been filled with mortar or plaster.

Bossed Masonry and Corner Construction

The outer face of Egyptian masonry was generally laid undressed, with a convex face sometimes referred to as 'bossed' or 'pulvinated' masonry (Arnold, 1991: 132-141; Clarke & Engelbach, 1990: 192-193). Several incomplete building works reveal this method of construction and a closer inspection of completed structures also reveals this practice. Old Kingdom examples in royal mortuary architecture include the undressed blocks on the lowest courses of the Step Pyramid Complex (Clarke & Engelbach, 1990: fig. 95), the pyramid of Menkaure (Arnold, 1991: fig. 4.51) and the pyramid of Meidum (Arnold, 1991: fig. 4.52). A non-royal example is the decorated rock-cut tomb MQ2 in the Menkaure quarry that has undressed lower courses of masonry (Smith, 1949: 244-245). There are different reasons for the Egyptians using bossed masonry, one of which is to protect the stone during transport from the quarry to the building site. Blocks may also be left with a convex profile and protrusions for ease of handling (grip) during the transport phase (Arnold, 1991: 135-37, fig. 4.53). Once at the building site the blocks may receive some preliminary dressing to perhaps cut the block to a rough shape or they may be positioned within the wall with only the underneath being dressed. It was common practice to lay blocks with a minimum number of dressed sides, making it easier to dress a complete wall down to one level than to do each block individually (Arnold, 1991: 44). Petrie (1938: 47) regarded dressing a masonry wall within a mastaba and dressing a rock face in a rock-cut tomb as being similar and considered stonemasons undoubtedly performed both activities and kept the same technique for both. Egyptian masonry was rarely ever left with bossed front faces (Arnold, 1991: 132). Once a complete wall was dressed it is only at the inner corners of a room that this construction method can occasionally be detected. This is because quite often the rising joint between two blocks does not occur at the corner; the front faces of the blocks have been cut back after they were laid and often one of the blocks is cut back further than the other, creating an L-shaped corner stone (Arnold, 1991: 139, fig. 4.58; Clarke & Engelbach, 1990: 193-94, fig. 230). The shorter branch of one side of this L-shaped block represents the original thickness of the block, *i.e.*, the amount of stone that was cut back during the dressing process. In this study reference to this element is made as 'stock'. The amount of stock left on a block varies and Arnold (1991: 139) believes 0.12 m. to be the maximum thickness. The evidence for bossed masonry comes from the corners of a room and consequently recording details of stock in corners can reveal information about how the corner of a room was constructed. Using a quoin block to span a complete corner ('quoining') gives greater stability to a corner because of the better distributed internal bonding; this is especially the case when positioned in higher courses so to exert force downwards through the lower bonds. This understanding of masonry construction was still in its formative years in the early Old Kingdom as Lauer (1962: 254; see also Arnold, 1991: 128, fig. 4.43) found quoining to be a weakness in the construction of Djoser's Step Pyramid Complex. In most cases he found that a corner block only penetrated the opposing wall by a few centimetres or made no contact at all. However, later in the Old Kingdom, where the shorter branch of the 'L' is only a few centimetres long, this is most likely the result of bossed masonry being dressed after the blocks had been laid creating an L-shaped block at the corner. The thickness of stock can be around 0.12 m., so any L-shaped block with a short branch greater than this amount should be considered a crafted corner block; indeed, with respect to less megalithic architecture, the thickness of stock would be smaller, perhaps half this amount (Arnold, 1991: 139). Parallel to studying the corner blocks is the use of blocks cut with a 'locking' mechanism. Lauer (1962: 253, figs. 70-71) found an uncommon use of stone blocks that had been cut with grooves to accommodate adjacent blocks so as to lock the whole into position (see also Arnold, 1991: 127, fig. 4.36). The purpose of this is parallel to quoining with both increasing the situational stability of blocks in a wall. It may also have been more aesthetically pleasing to use complete L-shaped blocks to achieve a neat corner; though if joints were to be filled in with plaster, this may not have been a real concern. Quoining and the employment of similar 'locking' mechanisms are seen in the tomb of Kairer.

Bossed Masonry in the Tomb of Kairer

Masonry was originally bossed and in almost every room there is evidence of stock being removed from the walls during the dressing process. The process of cutting back the stock is similar to the practice of using one block to span a corner of a room, though the two should not be confused.

An unusually shaped block (labelled 'A' in figure 3.21) is positioned on the inside thickness of the doorway recess within the east wall of Room 1 that leads to Room B (courtyard). The lower corner of the block is cut away to form half

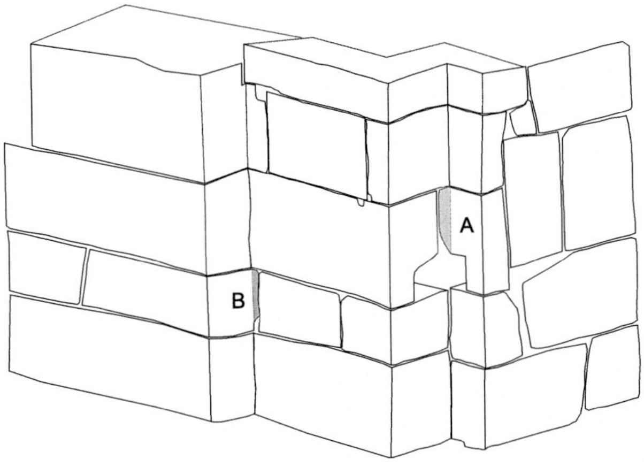

Figure 3.21. The tomb of Kairer: corner construction in the east wall of Room 1.

of a cavity that once accommodated a door fastening feature. The lock is housed within the doorframe signifying that this door was single-leaf and therefore opened outwards within Room 1 and opened against the south wall. The block was positioned above a block of the second course and was cut back 0.05 m. during the dressing process. The left side of the block extends into the wall and when it was cut back 0.05 m. of the front of the block remained to form part of the adjoining wall face. Because of the unusual use of this block it was simply positioned in a roughly dressed state and its final shape was decided once the wall was complete. The blocks in the above course have been skilfully cut to produce blocks that span round the corners to provide stability to the whole of the wall, perhaps even providing structural support for the blocks below. The block labelled 'B' is part of a stone block of the doorway leading to Room 2 slightly curves round to meet with the blocks of the second course of the east wall of Room 1. The distance is slight: 0.02 m., indicating that the whole length of the east wall (*i.e.*, the east wall proper of Room 1 and not the east wall of Room 1/2 doorway) was laid together and then dressed to form clean corners that are characteristic of these walls within the room.

The fourth course block on the left side of the south wall, of Room 1, curves round to span the southeast corner of this room (figure 3.22). Again the distance is slight (0.02 m.) suggesting that this is quite the typical amount of stock left on blocks – quite a small amount minimising the amount of dressing that was carried out. This would certainly suggest that the block was laid before the block which it meets on the east wall, giving a direction of work moving anticlockwise about this part of the room. The three courses below blocks labelled 'A' and 'B' in the figure are positioned at the corner of the room. They were therefore laid with a minimal bossed front as no stock is left at the corners. With a corner established it would make little sense to place a block 0.02 m. away from the established corner. Block 'B' was therefore laid after bossed block 'A' had been positioned. The work in this part of the room therefore moved from south to east in a clockwise direction.

Within the doorway between Rooms 2 and 3 (figure 3.23) a stone block labelled 'A' is on the north side and forms a complete part of the recess that defines the doorway. The block was laid as a whole and the recess was cut later when all the stone was laid, leaving stock 0.05 m. in thickness.

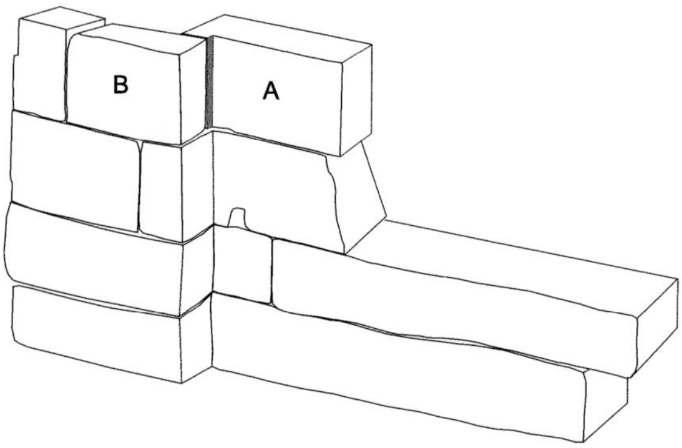

Figure 3.22. The tomb of Kairer: corner construction in southeast corner of Room 1.

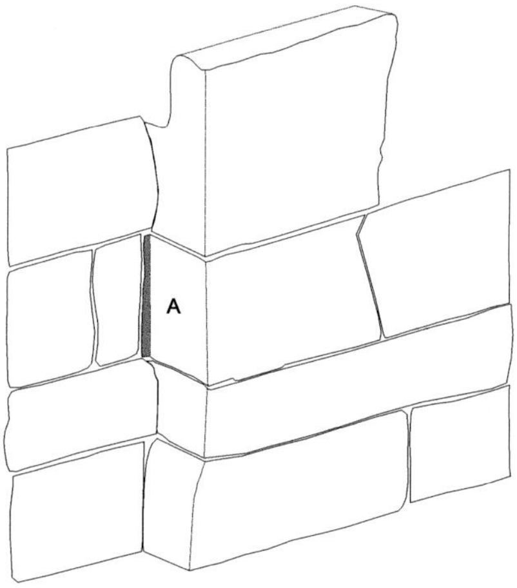

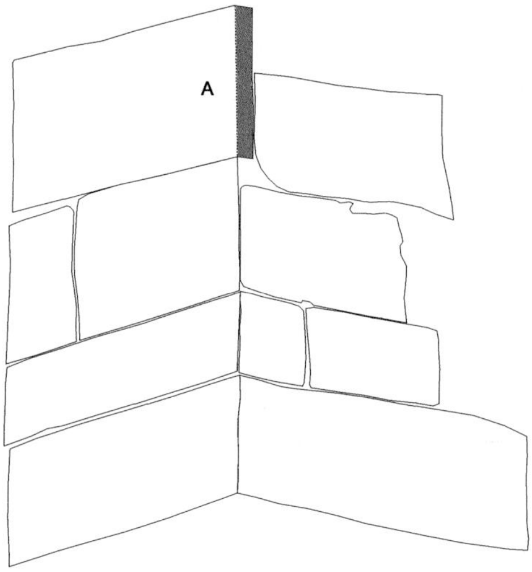

Left: Figure 3.23. The tomb of Kairer: north wall of Room 2.
Right: Figure 3.24. The tomb of Kairer: southwest corner of Room 2.

The fourth course block labelled 'A' is part of the south wall of Room 2 (figure 3.24). It is particularly large and is cut specifically to form part of the doorway recess between Rooms 1 and 2. On the west wall 0.07 m. of stock is visible on this block. Only the top levels of the first and second courses of the south and west walls are parallel with each other. The third and fourth courses of the west wall are unlike that of the south wall and are cut in much rougher way. The blocks below have rising joints meeting at the room corner, and more importantly, an L-shaped corner piece stone is used for the second course. This indicates that the corner of the room was established before this fourth course blocks were laid. It therefore must have been positioned before the block it meets with on the west wall. This would imply that work moved in a clockwise direction for this part of the construction.

Two blocks of the west wall of Room C span the northwest corner of this room (figure 3.25). A fourth course block, labelled 'A', spans 0.15 m. on the west wall and curves round to stretch for 0.10 m. of the north wall. The majority of the block lies on the west side suggesting this wall was laid first. This is

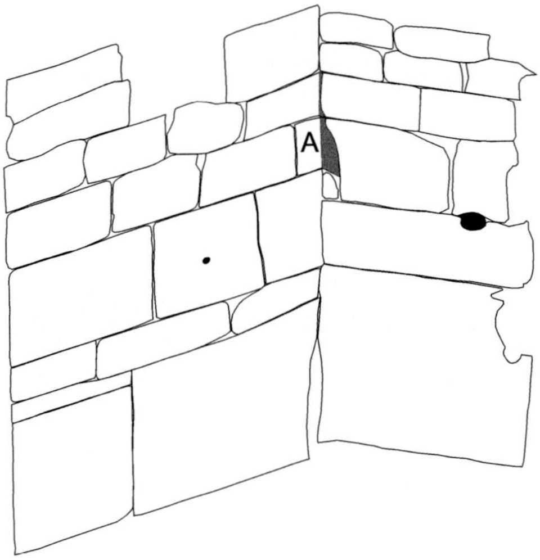

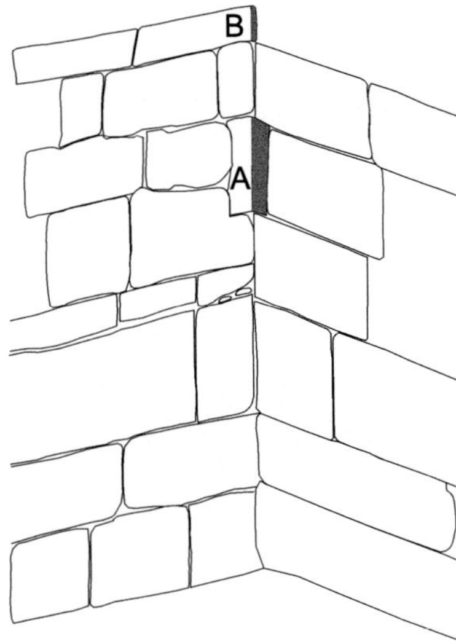

Left: Figure 3.25. The tomb of Kairer: northwest corner of Room C.
Right: Figure 3.26. The tomb of Kairer: southwest corner of Room 5.

confirmed by the adjacent block on the north wall being unusually cut to follow the shape of this corner stone. This gives a stock of 0.10 m. that is a considerable amount and may indicate the stone was decisively laid to form a corner, rather than merely being laid with a large amount of stock. The above block of the fifth course is larger (0.45 x 0.23 m.) and has a smaller amount of stock (0.05 m.) visible on the north wall. Again, the adjoining blocks on the north wall appear to have been cut to fit against this block.

Towards the top of the south wall of Room 5 there is a small block labelled 'A' with a height of 0.45 m. and width of 0.14 m. (figure 3.26) that stretches around the southwest corner of the room leaving visible 0.05 m. of stock on the west wall. It is placed within a stepped 'frame' of a block that has an uneven top joint: the joint is quite sloped with an irregular sided block being inserted above it. Despite the irregularity of the top, the corner cutting is neat and done purposefully to accommodate the block in question. This block must have been laid before the adjoining block of the west wall, giving a clockwise work direction moving from south to west. A top course block labelled 'B' stretches for 0.70 m. across the wall and has a narrow height of 0.16 m. It also goes round the corner leaving 0.05 m. of stock visible on the west wall. This again gives a clockwise work direction moving around the room, for this course. Between these two blocks there is a rising joint occurring at the corner of the room. This is formed by the side of the south wall block meeting against the length of the west wall block; suggesting that the west wall block was laid first, with the direction of work moving anti-clockwise.

The second course block labelled 'A' at the northwest corner of the north wall of Room 5 is cut rather irregularly (figure 3.27). The right side of the block is cut obliquely and has a height of 0.53 m. The lower part of the left side of the block (0.38 m.) continues into the west wall to form the corner of the room, leaving 0.05 m. of stock visible on the west wall. Above this stock there is a narrow tall

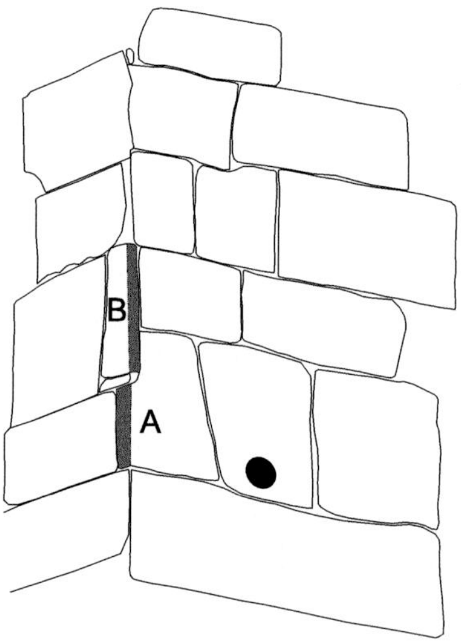

Figure 3.27. The tomb of Kairer: northwest corner of Room 5.

block labelled 'B' of the third course of the west wall that is 0.11 m. wide and 0.50 m. in height. This is another unusually cut stone that has been positioned to fill a small space left at the corner of the room. A strip of stock of this block is visible on the north wall; it is wider at the base (0.05 m.) and then gets narrower (0.02 m.) reflecting the uneven shape of the front of the stone before it was dressed. The corner of the room is established in the first course with a rising joint. It would therefore appear that the block on the north wall was laid before the west wall, giving an anti-clockwise work direction. The next block of the third course must have been laid before the block on the north wall, giving a clockwise work direction, opposite to the course below.

Corner Construction in the Tomb of Kairer

The top stone block of the east wall of Room 1 (labelled 'A' in figure 3.28) is cut in a shape that gives three exposed corners and spans a total length of 1.10 m. and width of 0.74 m. The block is positioned above four courses and forms the top course of the east wall and the recess before the doorway that leads to Room B. The height of the block is narrow (0.22 m.) but the maximum width and length is considerable. This block would have began as a roughly rectangular shape that was measured and hewn to a specific size so that it could form a top course that would stabilize this corner construction (minimum size 1.1 x 0.74 x 0.22 m.). The block below (labelled 'B') has also been hewn from one stone to form the recess of doorway. Presuming this block was originally rectangular, it has also been cut away considerably to form this L-shape. There has been a conscientious effort to construct a neat and stable corner in this part of the room. The corner shaped blocks are all positioned above a cavity within the third course that once housed a door fastening feature (discussed in Chapter 5). The door that once hung in this doorway closed Room B off from all other internal rooms. Room B was an open

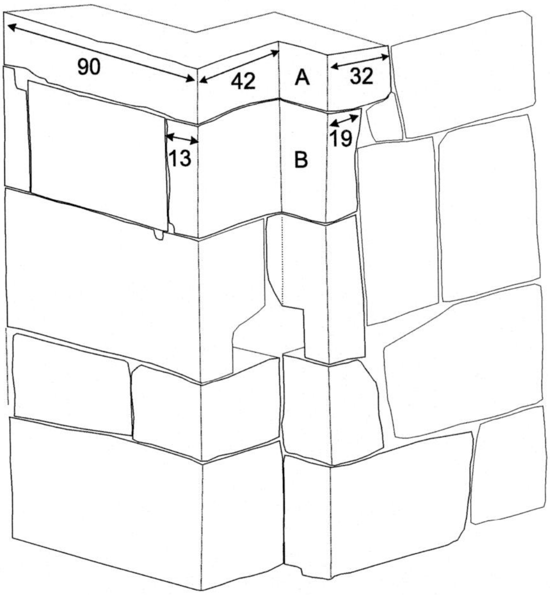

Figure 3.28. The tomb of Kairer: east wall of Room 1.

courtyard and thus a vulnerable part of the tomb in terms of security. The special emphasis on the bonding in this part of the tomb might be associated with the need to provide a secure doorway.

The shaded block in figure 3.29 effectively forms a corner in both Room 1 and Room 2; and forms the top block of the doorway between these two rooms. It is not possible to establish the total width of the block because there is not sufficient exposure of the sides, but with a total length of 1.41 m. and a maximum height of 0.70 m. it is of some considerable size (certainly over 0.30 m. in the central part as blocks in this wall with an exposed header are c. 0.25-0.30 m. in thickness). Looking at the top course blocks on the east wall of Room 2 there are two grooves, both being 0.09 m. deep, cut into two of the blocks at the south end of the wall. There is a parallel groove cut into the top right hand corner of a fourth course block that creates a space of 1.90 m. between the two blocks where a top course block could have been placed and subsequently secured into position.

The right side of block 'B' in Room 1/2 doorway (figure 3.30) forms a top corner piece with 0.11 m. curving round at 90 degrees to meet alongside a fourth course block of the east wall of Room 1. The bottom-bedding joint of the block is regularly horizontal but the top joint of this block is quite irregular. This is not just because of much smaller grooves that have been cut into this top right side of the block. One of the cuts, just in the interior of the corner, creates a space so that the large unusually shaped top course block (labelled 'A') of the east wall of Room 1 fits neatly into place. With this block being quite so individual it is understandable that greater attention was made for its proper fitting into position. The groves labelled 'a' and 'b', each 0.05 m. in width, were created when stock was removed from block 'B' when stonemasons dressed the wall. The groove labelled 'c' is harder to explain, as it does not appear to serve an obvious purpose. It is likely the result of an odd-shaped block being used, or inaccurate cutting.

Figure 3.29. The tomb of Kairer: doorway between Rooms 1 and 2.

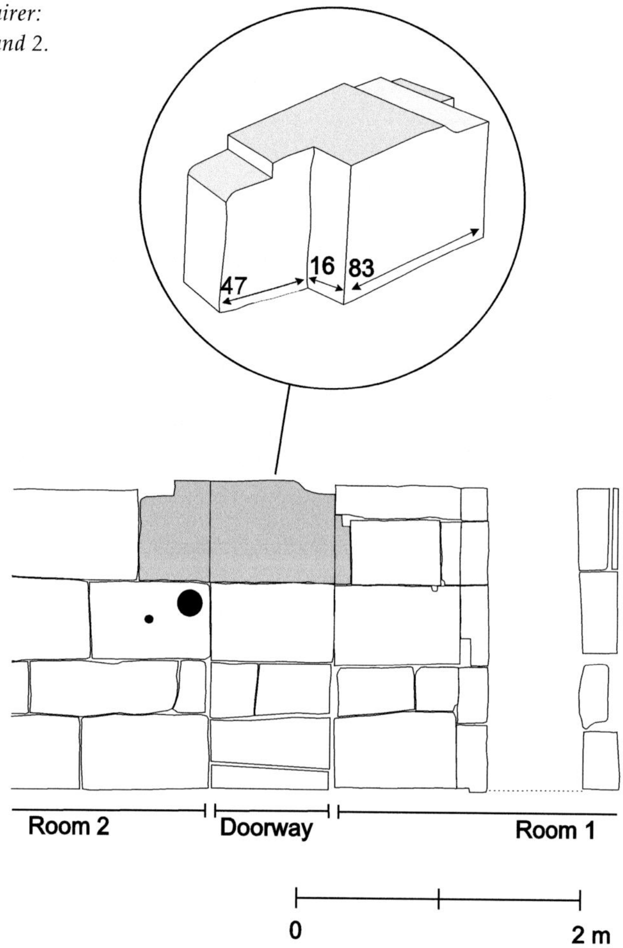

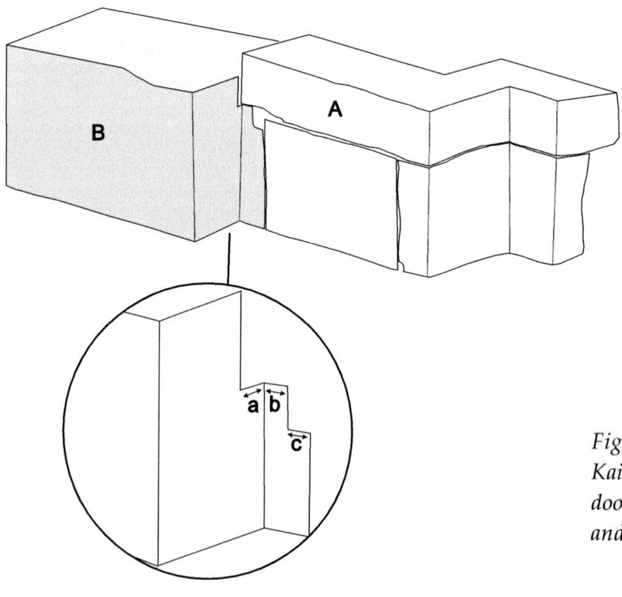

Figure 3.30. The tomb of Kairer: masonry in the doorway between Rooms 1 and 2.

Bossed Masonry and Corner Construction in the Tomb of Kagemni

The inside corners of the masonry within the tomb of Kagemni demonstrate that the blocks were laid with a thick amount of stock left on the face, as discussed in the publication of the mastaba (von Bissing, 1905: 2-3, pl. XXXI 1) and later noted by Petrie (1938: 49).

The north wall in Room 4 (figure 3.31) reveals how stock was left on the blocks at the two corners of the wall (von Bissing, 1905: pls. XXII, XXXII [W and G]). The wall consists of six courses of masonry laid using horizontal bedding joints and vertical rising joints (figure 3.32). Stock has been left on every corner of the wall and alternates between courses, indicating that the bossed masonry was laid in alternating layers of blocks that met against each other with each alternating between headers and stretchers. The amount of exposed stock seems to vary between 0.10 m. and 0.15 m. and often occurs in alternating courses at the corners of the rooms.

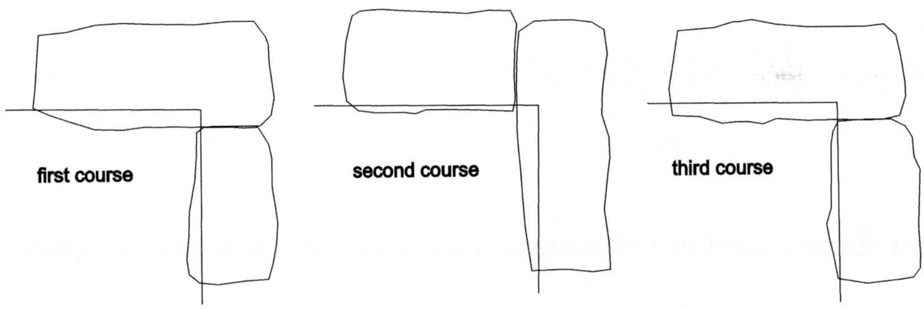

Figure 3.31. The formation of stock in alternating courses of masonry.

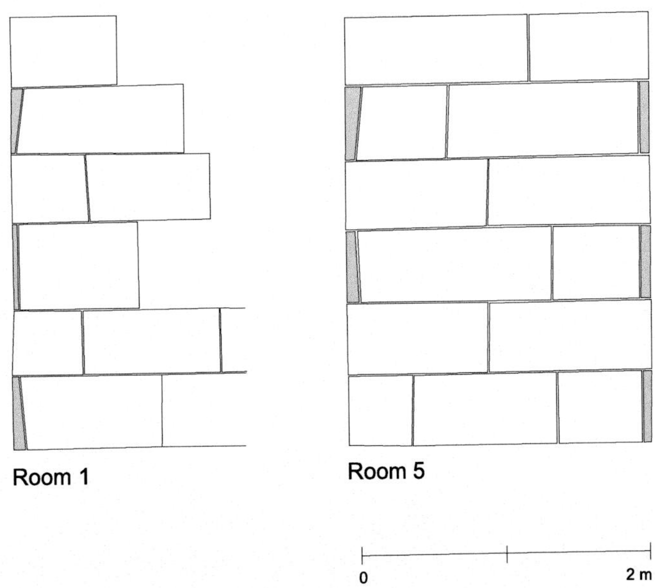

Figure 3.32. The tomb of of Kagemni: stock in alternating courses of masonry in Rooms 1 and 5. After: von Bissing (1905: pl. XXXII).

Figure 3.33. The tomb of Niankhba: south wall of Room E.

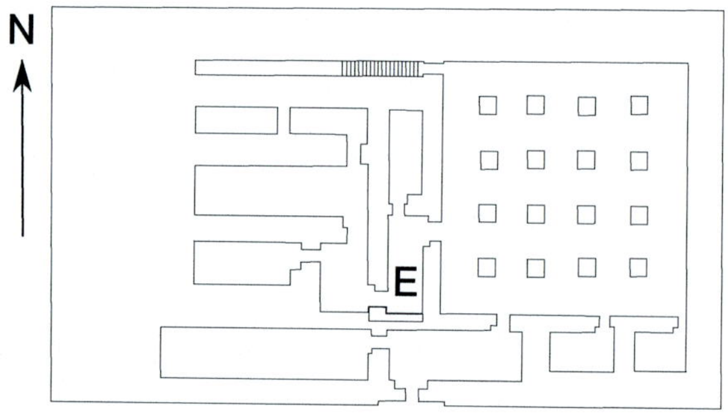

Bossed Masonry and Corner Construction in the Tomb of Niankhba

The corners of Room E (figure 3.33) both show evidence of stock being removed from blocks and the use of quoining. At the south wall of Room E is 1.80 m. in width, c. 2.00 m. in height and is composed of four courses of masonry. At the southeast corner the lowest block of the south wall reveals that it was dressed back by c. 0.05 m. The block is roughly dressed and is c. 0.15 m. in length on the south face and c. 0.05 m. on the east face, giving the thickness of stock that was left on this block before it was laid in place and dressed. The second course block above this also spans the corner of the room, with the south face being c. 0.85 m. in length and the east edge being c. 0.03 m. thick. The third course block above this also shows evidence of stock being removed. However, the corner of this block has been less well cut and the stock remains as more of a curved feature at the left side of the block, rather than a perfect right-angle cutting.

In the southwest corner of Room E the south wall meets with the doorframe of the doorway that leads to Room G. The south wall of the doorway is composed of four course of masonry and three of these blocks also form part of the masonry of the south wall of Room E. The first course block is a cornerstone that spans a length of c. 0.78 m. The block is cut in an L-shape that enables the block to form part of the south wall (c. 0.48 m.), the doorframe and part of the doorway wall (c. 0.30 m.). The rising joint of the second course block does not meet at the corner of the room. The east face of the second course block of the doorway wall forms the corner of the room and c. 0.02 m. of the block can be seen at the edge of the south wall. Hence the block was laid with c. 0.02 m. of stock that was removed when the wall was dressed. This block spans the whole length of the doorway (c. 0.85 m.). The third course block is a cornerstone that spans a length of c. 1.00 m., with c. 0.38 m. being part of the south wall masonry. The fourth course block is also a cornerstone, with c. 0.13 m. being part of the south wall masonry.

At the northeast corner of Room E (figure 3.34), the north wall meets with the doorframe of the doorway that connects Rooms E and D (pillared hall). The north wall is 1.10 m. in length, 1.90 m. in height and consists of four courses of masonry. The north wall of the doorway is 0.54 m. in length, 1.45 m. in height and consists of three courses of masonry. The first course block of the doorway spans the whole 0.54 m. length of the doorway and forms the northeast corner of the room, and c. 0.05 m. - 0.10 m. of the north wall. It is unclear whether this is the result of stock being removed from the block or deliberate quoining at this point. The second course block of the doorway is a cornerstone and spans the whole length of the doorway, forming 0.38 m. of the north wall. The third course block of the doorway spans the whole length of the doorway. It forms the corner of the room and c. 0.07 m. of the north wall. Like the first course block it is unclear if this is the result of stock being removed from the block or deliberate quoining at this point.

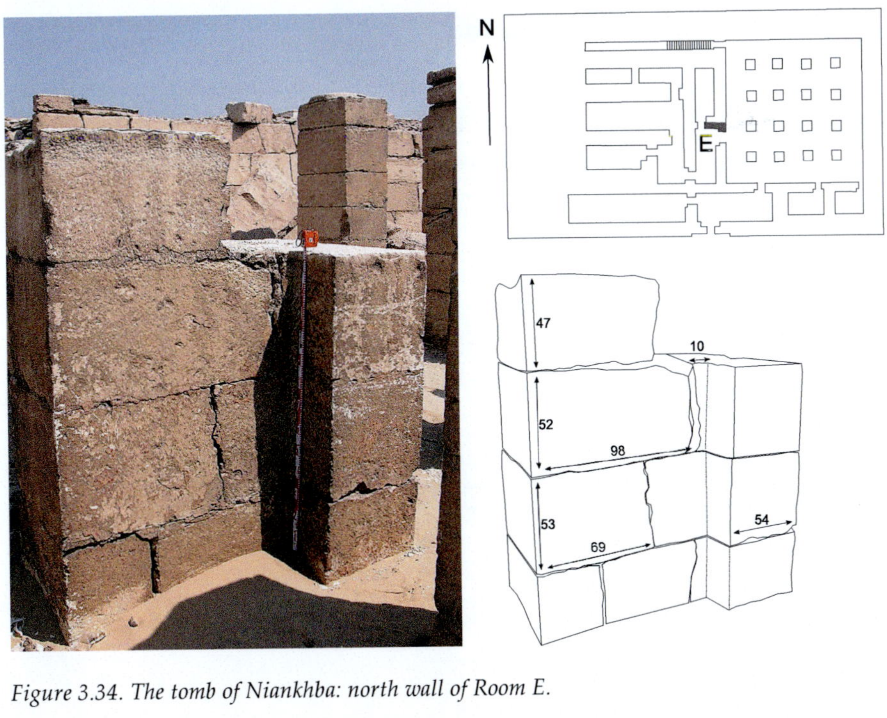

Figure 3.34. The tomb of Niankhba: north wall of Room E.

Summary of Bossed Masonry and Corner Construction

The evidence that masonry within mastabas was laid in a bossed state can be seen in the corners of rooms. The amount of stock left on a block seems to vary between a 0.02-0.15 m. and in some cases it would appear no stock was left on the face of the block, or that there was no stock at the edge of the block. The standard of bossed masonry must have depended on the source of the blocks. It is doubtful that there was a rigid policy of leaving a standard amount of stock on a block and it is more likely the result of the quarrying techniques used by individual groups of quarrymen. Some stone must have come to the mastabas from earlier structures and these reused stone blocks would either be dressed again or simply left and the other blocks were cut back to meet their face. The chippings taken from the front faces (and the sides) of the blocks were probably utilised within the gaps between skins of masonry. The evidence of stock is intricately connected with the construction of corners within the building and reveals bonding techniques. It gives an insight into the pattern of work if there is enough evidence to reveal in which direction the blocks were laid.

Scaffolding

Within Room C in the tomb of Kairer are curious holes along the north and south walls (figure 3.35). Three cylindrical holes appear at a height of 1.50 m. along the north wall; and on the facing south wall are three holes that correspond very

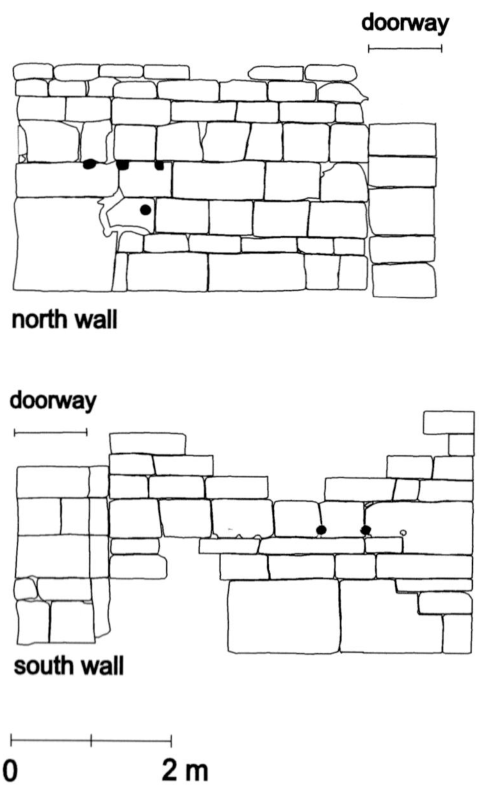

Figure 3.35. The tomb of Kairer: holes in the masonry of Room C.

closely. In Chapter 6 the most reasonable explanation for these masonry features is discussed: it is suggested that these holes once supported wooden shelving within this storeroom. However, there are other holes in this room that require explanation. Another, perfectly circular hole appears below the series of holes on the north wall at a height of 1.00 m. and a distance of 2.80 m. from the wall's eastern corner. This hole is unlike the others as it is perfectly round and in that it is actually carved within the body of a block rather than created at the block's edge. On the south wall a fourth course block has three grooves carved into the bottom, creating three slight holes. Other holes in the tomb include a hole in the west wall of Room 2 and two holes in Room 5, on the north and east walls. There are also quite wide spaces between some blocks elsewhere in the mastaba that could possibly be more than damaged sides. Similar holes have also been reported in publications of other Old Kingdom mastabas. For example, in the mastaba of Ankhmahor eleven evenly spaced small holes cut into the north wall of Room VII are reported, and further, less regular, holes cut into the walls of this same room (Kanawati & Hassan, 1997: 23). Within the Western Cemetery at Giza Roth (1995: 18) reports that the walls of shafts in a cluster of mastabas often show depressions cut into all four faces for footholds or possibly scaffolding.

Initial thoughts on the series of regular holes within Room C in the mastaba of Kairer were that they were false-work features and perhaps could reveal clues to the tomb's construction. With walls of Room C nearing a height of 3.00 m., some kind of scaffolding would have been required for the laying of higher courses (and possibly the roof – certainly the painting of the roof) and the final dressing of the masonry. In his study of historic masonry Bowyer (1973: 136) states that any building work over 1.20 m. in height requires scaffolding of some kind. Scaffolding would definitely have been required when building the mastaba of Ti which has exceptionally high ceilings; the height of corridor I and II is 4.50 m. and the walls are decorated to almost the ceiling height (Steindorff, 1913: 10-13, sheet 1, figs. 55-57). The ease of building the higher levels of masonry, and the roofing, must have been an easier task if there was an adjoining mastaba or wall, such as the enclosure wall of the Step Pyramid Complex, which Mehu built his mastaba against.

However, it is not just for construction that scaffolding would be required. It is evident that the faces of laid masonry were dressed after they had been laid, and the use of ladders for this purpose would have proved cumbersome (Clarke & Engelbach, 1990: 100). Instead wooden poles could be slotted into parallel holes carved into walls and stretched across the width of the room facilitating the final dressing of the wall and the decoration work by the artists. Similar false work features are found in medieval constructions in northwest Europe and are referred to as 'putlog' holes (Fitchen, 1961; 1986: 85-90). Workmen stood on the putlogs, which could support the weight of one or two men and a limited amount of equipment.

The shape and dimensions of the holes certainly accord with Arnold's (1991: 146) description of a putlog hole: "Putlog holes are mostly cut in the shape of round holes 20-30 cm deep and 20 cm wide." Similar devices have been found in other pharaonic masonry throughout Egyptian history and would have been utilised in most construction tasks (Arnold, 1991: 231-236; Clarke & Engelbach, 1990: 195). Scaffolding of light wooden poles tied together with a rope can be seen around a statue in the tomb of Rekhmira (Arnold, 1991: 231, fig. 5.19; Clarke & Engelbach, 1990, 105-106, fig. 232 Newberry, 1900: pl. XX). Once the wooden poles had been removed, the cavities were filled in and plastered to a smooth finish, homogenous to the clean surface of the rest of the wall, as was common practice with covering over joints and faults in the wall (discussed above). Work proceeded from the top downwards, with the putlogs being drawn out and reinserted at the next level down, if necessary in a tall room. The walls were painted in accordance with the surrounding decoration so that no visible trace of the holes remained. False-work features are thus often covered over and go unrecognised, except in undecorated rooms, such as storerooms.

3.3. Masonry Techniques at Saqqara

At Saqqara the technique to build the internal and external walls of mastaba superstructures is to use mixed masonry and construct the walls using two skins of limestone blocks and a core of limestone flakes and rubble. The rear of the blocks was left rough to reduce time cutting the blocks. Once the two blocks were laid the thickness of the wall was established and the builders would work upwards laying the blocks and dressing only the exposed surfaces and for some distance between the sides of each block. This practice can be seen in mastaba construction in both the Unas and the Teti Cemetery (figure 3.36) and in cemeteries outside of the Nile valley, such as at Balat (figure 3.37).

Figure 3.36. Cross-section of masonry within a mastaba in the Unas Cemetery (the tomb of Niankhba).

Figure 3.37. Cross-section of masonry within a mastaba in the Old Kingdom cemetery at Balat.

Figure 3.38. Cross-section of masonry within a magazine in the pyramid temple of Unas.

With this technique the width of a wall could be defined instantly and the space left between the two faces of the wall could be readily filled in with the chippings from the dressing of the masonry and from the readily available tafl. This process of building the wall reduces the need to dress all sides of the blocks and utilises local resources that would have reduced time and labour expenditure. In the masonry of the pyramid temple of Unas imported white limestone blocks are laid using this technique, but also with some alternating blocks forming the entire thickness of the wall (figure 3.38). The gap between the two skins is not a great as in private tombs and generally the blocks are cut with greater regularity on the rear and sides, reflecting more controlled procedure in building. In the private structures the masonry blocks of the lower course are consistently smaller in height and of a long length. This enabled the builders to swiftly mark out the positions of the walls and reserved the taller blocks for higher up in the wall, where the surfaces would be carved in relief decoration. Decoration below waist level is usually painted with a dado of varying detail. In undecorated rooms the masonry is often laid in a more random manner, unlike other rooms in the superstructure. The heights of courses within rooms are kept consistent, with only odd exceptions. This method could be achieved by using the same size blocks and checking heights of each course against the parallel wall, suggesting that for ease, the courses of each wall were laid at the same time. As the walls reached a metre in height wooden scaffolding would be required to complete the walls to the full height. This scaffolding would also be needed for the final dressing, relief carving and painting of the complete walls. The corners of rooms were constructed using a succession of alternating stretchers and headers. The reason for this is to create further stability at the corners of rooms with simple bonding.

4. Roofing

4.1. Introduction

The roofing of stone constructed mastabas in the Old Kingdom used a standard technique of stone slabs spanning the width of a room. The width of roofed rooms was therefore subject to the strengths of the stone slabs. Within the Unas Cemetery there are examples of roofing slabs *in situ*, and the common stone used is limestone, except for the roofing of the serdab in the mastaba of Mehu, which is constructed from sandstone. Norman de Garis Davies (1900: 3) found that the roofing slabs used in the mastaba of Akhethotep and Ptahhotep at Saqqara [D 64 complex], was a locally found "yellow stone" of a poor quality. For the roofing of large courtyards the slabs would be supported by rows of architraves supported upon columns. The stone used for architraves could also vary and Clark and Engelbach (1990: 12) discuss the various strengths of stone that was used: "limestone is not the medium for architraves; the most that can be spanned, for instance, by Tura or Ma'sara limestone is about [2.75 m.]. Even when such a space is spanned by an architrave it will not bear roof-blocks with any likelihood of lasting."

Although within mastabas in the Unas Cemetery limestone is used for architraves (discussed below), the only architraves found *in situ* was within the courtyard portico of the mastaba of Mehu. The columned halls within mastabas only contained architraves that had fallen to the ground.

In their discussion of roofing Clarke and Engelbach (1990: 9) quote George Reisner who was extremely familiar with the roofing techniques used in mastabas in the Western Cemetery at Giza: "slabs of limestone, on an extreme length of 250 to 285 cm., formed a practical roofing material; the longer slabs are from 50 to 80 cm. thick. The limestone in the walls lies in its natural position with the strata horizontal, as also do the roofing slabs and the architraves. The square pillars used in the 4th dynasty have the natural strata running vertically. The stone is so well selected and the architrave so carefully set that the splintering of a column is very rare indeed. The strain on the middle part of the architrave and the roofing-slab was not more than the stone could bear. The span over which the weight was borne was usually between 120 cm. and 150 cm."

Lighting in the tomb was often achieved by cutting slits at the joint between two adjoining roofing slabs (Petrie, 1938: 51), as can be seen in the restored roofing in the mastaba of Iynefert. In his description of the masonry within the offering-room of Ptahhotep in the mastaba of Akhethotep and Ptahhotep [D 64 complex] Davies (1900: 5) describes window slots within the tops of wall: "The east and south walls are pierced just below the ceiling by a shallow longitudinal opening, both wall and roof being cut away to form the shaft, which slants down into the chamber, presumably from the open air above. As the openings are at present blocked up and deeply buried, their further direction towards the outside of the mastaba could not be investigated. They were evidently designed to admit light or air, perhaps both. I do not know whether such apertures frequently occur in mastabas. Something similar exists in the pillared hall also, and I have observed the like in the hall of a mastaba in the necropolis of Gizeh." Within the Unas Cemetery different examples of roofing and lighting can be seen.

4.1.1. Roofing in the Tomb of Mehu

The roofing in the mastaba of Mehu (figure 4.1) was uncovered *in situ*, with just the roofing slabs in the offering-room of Meriankh (Room 5) being broken and disturbed (Hussein, 1942: 421). Hussein (1942, 421, pl. XXXIV) records that each roofing slab was composed of dressed limestone except for the seven roofing slabs above the serdab (Room 7) that were composed of sandstone. The lengths vary between 0.90 m. and 1.20 m., with a width of c. 0.45 m., and each slab overhangs the walls by 0.20-0.40 m. The more recent plans of the mastaba within Altenmüller's (1998) publication of the mastaba contain more specific dimensions for individual slabs. The roofing slabs used for rooms of the largest width (on average 2.00 m) use the same laying technique. The slabs span the width of the room and are all approximately 0.50-0.60 m. in width.

The corridor (Room 2) is 1.00 m. in width and because of the narrower width much wider roofing slabs can be used to roof this room: the largest has dimensions of 2.40 x 2.00 m. The same is true of the anteroom (Room 4) that uses one single roofing slab (3.00 m. x 2.25 m.). This places these roofing blocks at the extreme end of the scale in terms of dimensions. This is undoubtedly because of the narrow width of the corridor but the anteroom must be close to the maximum dimensions for a room that can be spanned with one single roofing slab. These internal rooms deep within the mastaba were illuminated by light-slots set between the height of the wall and the roofing. The main offering-room (for Mehu) was illuminated by a slot set within the top of the east wall, 0.86 m. wide and 0.06 m. in height (figure 4.2). There was possibly lighting in the anteroom, though the original masonry of the slot is not *in situ*. The location and size of the slot located within the top of the east wall of the secondary offering-room (for Ankhmeri) suggests this was a later addition made when this storeroom was converted to an offering-room for Ankhmeri (Altenmüller, 1998: 27, plans B and C). The same technique of lighting was also used in the nearby mastaba of Nebkauhor, where the columned hall was

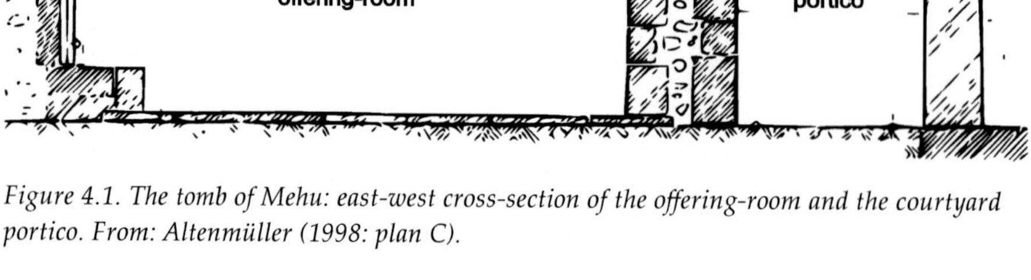

Figure 4.1. The tomb of Mehu: east-west cross-section of the offering-room and the courtyard portico. From: Altenmüller (1998: plan C).

Figure 4.2. The tomb of Mehu: arrangement of roofing slabs, with dotted lines representing walls. After: Altenmüller (1998: plan G).

lighted by sixteen slits cut in the roof, arranged in four rows of four slits, all equal distances apart (Hassan, 1938: 513).

The same technique for roofing the offering-rooms and the serdab is used for the roofing of the portico but here much longer slabs are used c. 3.70 m. in length (Hussein, 1942: pls. XXX, XXXV). The east side of the portico roofing is supported by three architraves that span the east-west width of the courtyard and are kept up by two square columns. Altenmüller (1998: 19) has attributed this portico to a third building in the use of the mastaba. The spacing between each column is approximately 1.75 m. which is wider than the usual dimensions (1.20-1.50 m.) of tomb architraves in the Western Cemetery at Giza (Clarke & Engelbach: 1990: 9).

4.1.2. Roofing in the Tomb of Seshseshet Idut

Four roofing slabs above the offering room (1.70 x 5.00 m.) survived *in situ* until they were broken into pieces during clearance of the mastaba (Macramallah, 1935: pl. IV A, B). Macramallah's publication does not include dimensions for the individual roofing slabs but each slab overhangs the walls by at least 0.20 m. and the masonry blocks of the walls are at least 0.30 m. in width. The blocks are therefore all at least over 2.70 m. in length and on average c. 1.45 m. in width. The scale bar in one photograph suggests that the nearest roofing slab is c. 0.30 m. in thickness and c. 2.85 m. in length (Macramallah, 1935: pl. IV B). The width appears to be much greater than the adjoining block. The two middle blocks overhang the west wall much more than the other two, but all slabs line up together rather closely on the east side. The tops of the slabs are smooth and the sides appear to be quite rough, though this could be from deterioration. The exposed backs of the masonry blocks are roughly cut flat but not smooth. There appears to be no sign of a second skin wall on the east and west sides suggesting that there was nothing but a rubble core between these internal walls and the backs of the exterior masonry. There is a gap of approximately 0.30 m. between the block above the lintel of the doorway entrance to the offering room and the south wall of the top course block of the offering room.

4.1.3. Roofing in the Tomb of Niankhba

Within the columned courtyard (figure 4.3) there are three fallen roofing slabs. The roofing slabs are roughly dressed limestone and are all at roughly 2.00 x 1.10 m. and 0.40 m. in thickness (figure 4.4). That only three remain is unsurprising considering the roof height (the tallest column is 3.48 m. in height). Only a few fallen roofing blocks remain in the comparable, but smaller (9.45 x 9.80 m.) columned hall within the mastaba of Nebkauhor (Hassan, 1975a: pl. IV C). The dimensions of the roofing slabs are comparable with the roofing slabs used to roof the courtyard in the multi-roomed mastaba chapel of Senedjemib Inti (G 2370) at Giza which are c. 1.40 m. in length and a thickness varying between 0.40-0.80 m. (Brovarski, 2001: 78, pl. 3). The courtyard is 12.00 m. square and the sixteen columns are arranged in four rows, with distances between them being fairly standard. There are no surviving architraves in this courtyard but Hassan (1975a: 14, pl. VI A) recorded two within the courtyard of the mastaba of Nebkauhor: "Two longitudinal, rectangular blocks of white limestone, forming the architrave of two pillars, were also found. The first part measures 2.60 m. long, 0.67 m. high, and 0.82 m. thick. One of its long sides is sculptured in low relief with a horizontal row of five figures facing [to the right], all of which represent the original owner of the Mastaba."

Unlike the courtyard of Nebkauhor the columns and walls are not decorated with inscriptions or scenes. The columned courtyard in the mastaba of Senedjemib Inti measures 5.57 x 10.7 m. and contains eight square columns which are arranged in two rows of four in an east-west line. Sixteen roofing slabs were found *in situ* that were carried on architraves that crossed the room in an east-west direction. In total there were originally thirty-three roofing slabs carried by ten architraves which were arranged into five rows that crossed the width of the room. Brovarski (2001: 78) provides the dimensions of the room: "The height of the hall of pillars from floor to ceiling is 3.25 m., the height of the base being 0.10 m., the height of the pillars 2.60 m. and the height of the architrave 0.55 m."

Assuming the columned hall in the mastaba of Niankhba was roofed in the same manner there would need to be four rows of architraves spanning the 12.00 m. of the courtyard. The north-south distance between the blocks and the wall is slightly less than in the other direction (between 0.10-0.30 m. less) so it might be reasonable to assume that the architraves spanned the room in a north-south direction. However, in any direction there would need to be twenty architraves, and using the dimensions of the three surviving roofing slabs, there would need to be forty-eight roofing slabs. The columned courtyard in the mastaba of Nebkauhor was probably lit by slits within the roof. Hassan (1938: 513) states that the hall was lit by sixteen slits cut in the roof and arranged in four rows of four slits, with each being an equal distance apart. He also comments that the underside of the roofing slabs were painted red to imitate granite, but gives no further details about the roofing and one can only presume he deduced the lighting arrangements with the courtyard from slits carved on the fallen roofing blocks, probably at the sides of meeting slabs. If this is an accurate observation then one would expect the courtyard in the mastaba of Niankhba to be designed in the same way.

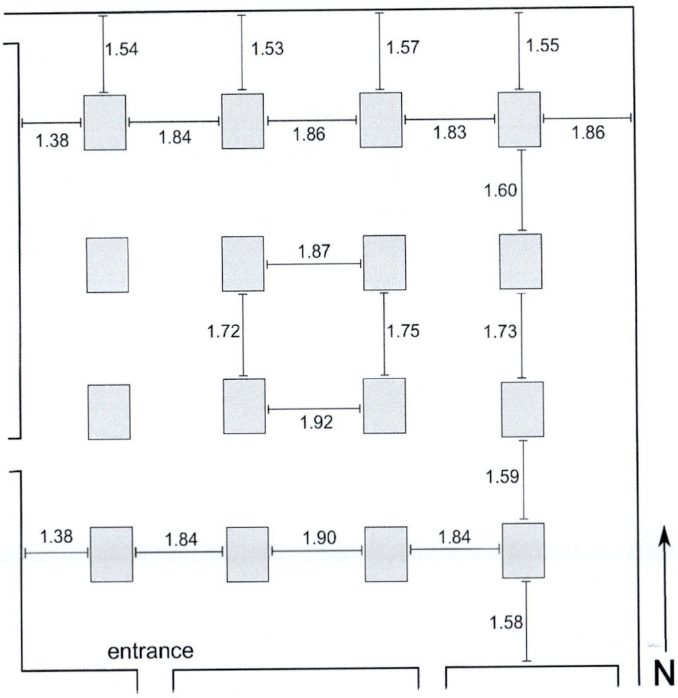

Figure 4.3, The tomb of Niankhba: columned hall (dimensions in metres).

Figure 4.4. The tomb of Niankhba: fallen roofing slab in the columned hall.

4.1.4. Roofing in the Tomb of Mitri

The western half of the serdab in the tomb of Mitri has three roofing slabs *in situ* (figures 4.6-4.7). The serdab contained several wooden statues that are now in the Egyptian Museum, Cairo (JE 51738, JE 52081, JE 93165, JE 93166) and the Metropolitan Museum of Art, New York (Rogers Fund 1926 nos. 26.2.2-26.2.2-6), but little has been recorded about the architecture of the tomb (Porter & Moss, 1981: 632). The sedab is 1.53 m. in width and the three roofing slabs span the width and rest on the top of the 0.40 m. thick walls (figures 4.8-4.9). Each slab

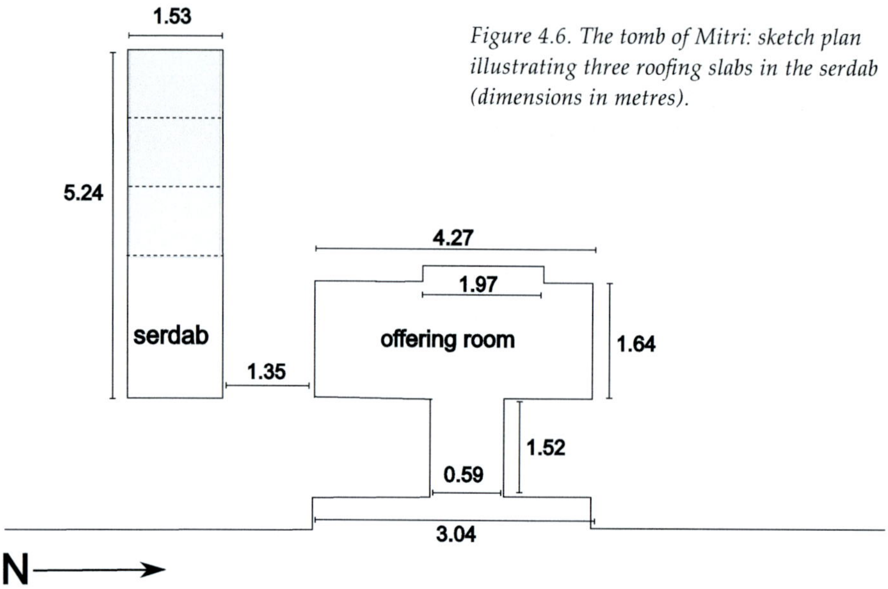

Figure 4.6. The tomb of Mitri: sketch plan illustrating three roofing slabs in the serdab (dimensions in metres).

Figure 4.7. The tomb of Mitri: entrance on the east face.

Figure 4.8. The tomb of Mitri: the serdab.

Figure 4.9. The tomb of Mitri: roof of the serdab.

is approximately 1.00 m. in width and 2.30 m. in length. This arrangement of roofing slabs is quite typical for a room of these dimensions and is how most rooms within mastabas would have been roofed.

4.1.5. Summary

The widths of corridors and rooms in mastabas were limited by the dimensions of limestone roofing slabs. Reisner's extensive clearance of mastaba superstructures at Giza revealed that roofing slabs had an uppermost length of 2.50-2.85 m. Both ends of roofing slabs would have to rest upon masonry walls and would therefore only allow a maximum width of 2.00 m. For rooms requiring greater dimensions columns and architraves would be used or the room would be unroofed. The roofing of a columned hall was quite a task and is indicative of the status of the tomb owner and the capability of the building team.

Roofing slabs positioned upon the top course of wall masonry were often engaged intricately in the masonry, rather than being just placed upon the top blocks. The roofing slabs would have to be lifted upon the mastabas and in some respect this would have imposed an upper limit on the height of a building structure. To reach these heights a form of ramp may have been used: one can expect that this was a similar method as used in the building of New Kingdom temples where ramps were made from mudbrick; or comparable to the mudbrick and rubble ramps in the Giza Cemetery that were used to access the burial shaft at the funeral ceremony. With the location of the mastaba of Mehu, one can see how the embankment next to the Step Pyramid Complex was useful for this; but also that it was not ideal to have such easy access next to an open courtyard. The architect may have made a compromise by building a parapet wall that improved the security of the superstructure. The need for lighting within a tomb was a consideration that must have been made during the planning of the roofing slabs. Light could be admitted to the mastaba through apertures in the roofing slabs or between the height of the masonry wall and the roofing slabs. Surviving evidence indicates that the false-door would be illuminated by a shaft of light. If lighting apertures do not exist in other extant roofed corridors or halls one must presume these rooms were illuminated by torchlight when needed.

5. Doorways

5.1. Introduction

In antiquity doors defined spaces within the internal plan of tombs. In tomb restoration schemes doors are very rarely reinstalled, even when pivot sockets in doorways remain in place. More often than not the only door to be replaced is that of the tomb entrance, and here the door is a modern thick iron bar gate. It is entirely possible to walk around a tomb and not consider what artistic representations and inscriptions are missing and this hinders our appreciation of the tombs style and decoration scheme. To illustrate this a selection of doors from the Old Kingdom that are of a style most likely to have been used within the Memphite multi-roomed mastabas of the late Old Kingdom is discussed. The chapter will then move on to consider the style of doorways within mastabas and what archaeological evidence can inform us of the doors that were once positioned within these doorways.

5.2. Doors from Old Kingdom Tombs

The rare find of a 5th Dynasty wooden door near the Teti Cemetery hints at the wealth of data absent from Old Kingdom tombs. The door of the royal master builder Kaemhesit is decorated in incised relief with a standing figure of the deceased and a smaller figure, called Hetepka (Egyptian Museum, Cairo, JE 47749). Around the figures incised hieroglyphs give the name and titles of the owner, names of family members, and standard offering formulae (McFarlane, 2003: 43-44). Kaemhesit was buried in a mastaba located about 20.00 m. west of the tomb of Mereruka, first excavated by James Quibell and Angelo Hayter in 1906-1907, and later investigated by Cecil Firth in one season between 1922 and 1923 (Quibell & Hayter, 1927; see also Porter and Moss, 1981: 542-543). Kaemhesit's door is constructed from a single piece of wood 2.22 m. in height (2.61 m. including the pivots), 0.68 m. in width and has a thickness of 0.08 m. (Capart, 1927: 11, pl. 13; Koenigsberger, 1936, 16; McFarlane, 2003: 42). Pivots at the top and bottom of one side allowed this single leaf door to be emplaced in socket holes. Both pivots have roughly the same shape, though the lower pivot is more pointed. This design is quite typical: the hinge was rarely used for mounting doors, and later many pivots (in particular for large doors) rested within a hard metal casing (Arnold, 2003: 76; for pivot casings see Koenigsberger, 1936: 20-23). The door was not found *in situ* but some distance away from the interior of the tomb. The names and titles inscribed on the door place little doubt that this door once hung within the tomb of Kaemhesit; and the width of the door accords with the size of doorways in Quibell and Hayter's plan of the tomb – these doorways being the tomb entrance and the entrance to the columned hall (Quibell & Hayter, 1927: pl. 1).

Kaemhesit's tomb and other mudbrick mastabas in this area were re-cleared and investigated by a Macquarie University team, under the direction of Ann McFarlane between 2000 and 2003 (McFarlane, 2003). Although no pivot holes were preserved in the floor paving this recent project has revealed that the entrance to the columned hall contains bolt holes within the internal recess (McFarlane, 2003: 42). Quibell and Hayter (1927: 19) also uncovered a wooden drum measuring 1.95 m. in length, with a diameter of 0.31 m. (Egyptian Museum, Cairo, JE 44175), which has been reassessed and published by MacFarlane (2003: 44, pls. 16b-c, 51b). Both ends of the drum had been carved flat to aid insertion within the wall above a door. The face of the drum (0.84 m. in length) was incised and painted with text that reads 'the royal master builder, the overseer of builders of the Residence, Kaemhesit'. This rare surviving tomb fitting is another example of an element of tomb design and decoration now absent from the archaeological record for many tombs.

Ahmed Moussa retrieved three wooden tomb elements from beneath the Unas causeway, just north-west of the tomb of Khnumhotep and Niankhkhnum (Moussa, 1972: 289-291, pl. 29). All three elements were decorated and inscribed with the name of the owner, Itisen, who held the titles 'overseer of the faience work' (*mr ṯḥnt*) and 'chief of king's adorners'. Two of these wooden objects are described as being lintels and the other was the lower part of a door leaf. One lintel is of a very large size, measuring 2.38 m. in length, 0.16 m. wide and 0.21 m. thick, and was accompanied by three adjoining uninscribed pieces of wood (average length of c. 1.60 m.). Moussa (1972: 289) believed that these pieces, and some "cylindrical pieces, which join them" may have formed part of the ceiling within a mudbrick tomb, and comments that this was a usual architectural feature in this type of tomb. The description of these objects certainly accords with the type of finds that was recovered from the excavation of the mudbrick tomb of Kaemhesit. The great size of this inscribed piece might also suggest that this is an architrave, perhaps part of a false-door. The other lintel was 0.77 m. in length, a size that corresponds with the width of the average tomb doorway. Moussa also found a highly decorated wooden door leaf measuring 1.40 m. high, 0.86 m. wide and 0.055 m. thick. The width of the door is typical for that of a doorway and it is probable that this is a single leaf door that sealed a doorway of the same width. The door leaf is decorated in sculptured high relief divided into scenes, with the standing figures of Itisen and his wife Neferet dominating the scene. Just as in the door of Kaemhesit all figures on the door are facing in the direction that the door opened – outwards with the figures moving into the room.

From Upper Egypt, the excavations at Elephantine discovered fragments of a wooden door that shares much of the same fine detail as the two doors described above (Junge, 1976: 98-107, fig. 7, pls. 30-32). The door is inscribed for a 6th Dynasty judge and overseer of scribes. The reconstruction of the door has a width of c. 1.00 m. and two registers. The upper register has a representation of the owner standing with a sceptre held in his left hand and a long staff in his right hand. Behind him stand his wife, with smaller male figures standing on either side of the couple. The lower register has traces of five figures, three of which are carrying scribal equipment.

The early 3rd Dynasty tomb of Hesira at Saqqara contained extraordinary wooden elements as part of its design; a long east–west corridor contained a row of six niches on the south wall, housing wooden panels carved in raised relief with representations of the owner (Quibell, 1913). The panels are regarded as some of the most sophisticated artworks produced in ancient Egypt and although not doors, the panels demonstrate the significance of wooden elements within tomb design (Egyptian Museum, Cairo, CG 1426-1430; see Porter & Moss, 1981: 437-439).

The doors discussed above are decorated and contain broadly similar content – representations of the owner with inscriptions giving the name of the owner, family members, and reference to his profession and status. These doors must have fitted in with the decoration scheme of the room. Doorways are often framed by a line border and the wall the door opened against was bare of decoration (*cf.* Duell, 1938: pls. 14, 162-165). It is worth considering what content went on the door depending on its location within the tomb. We know that the inside thicknesses of doorways vary in content – *e.g.*, representations of the owner, subsidiary figures, and scenes of offering bearers and vessels (Harpur, 1987: 43-57). The latter content is found within the doorways to offering-rooms and attached storerooms (the type of storeroom typically found within the multi-roomed mastaba) and one would expect the decoration to be more suited to the scene content of the doorway thicknesses, rather than featuring the more biographical aspect found on the doors described above.

5.3. Representations of Doors in the Old Kingdom

The rock-cut tomb of Sekhentiu and Neferseshemptah at the south of the causeway of Unas has an exceptionally well preserved painted bedroom scene (Moussa & Junge, 1975: 19, frontispiece, pls. 1-2). The north wall of the tomb has three registers and the middle register represents a bedroom with a door at the very left. The double leaf door is fastened shut with two blade bolts. Both door leafs are decorated with alternate longitudinal stripes of red and brown pigment and mounted with conical shaped pivots. The outside edge of the door leafs and the pivots are painted black. This is a fine Old Kingdom example of the representation of doors within tomb decoration. Within this corpus we often see double leaf doors within domestic and religious contexts, such as the doors of statue niches (Fischer, 1996: 91-102). These doors regularly have a blade bolt as a method of fastening the door. Doors decorated with images of the deceased with his family and workers appear to be restricted to the burial place. They contain images and inscriptions that fit into the repertoire of decoration found in the tomb; they therefore not only compliment the tombs decoration scheme but are integral to it and contain biographical data about the owner that is important. They are, however, missing from nearly all tombs. Their obliteration from the archaeological record is more likely because of the materials relative value in ancient Egypt, its susceptibility to decay (rotting, insect activity) and the easily reusable nature of the object within a cemetery that was in use through to the Roman Period.

There are types of false-door that realistically capture the image of a working door, described by Arnold (2003: 89) as "a door with every technical detail translated into stone." The false-doors from the tomb of Seshemnefer at Giza display an image of a double leaved door including the battens, a blade bolt, the upper and lower pivots and the well defined lower pivot sockets (figure 5.1) (Junker, 1938: figs. 34 and 36). The outside of the door from the tomb of Kamhesit was reinforced with seven horizontal battens, held in place by mortise and tenon joint. False-doors are decorated with battens (*i.e.*, the back of the door is on show) and Fischer (1996: 91-102) believes this supports the commonly understood concept that the deceased enters the offering room from the burial chamber, and goes further to propose the false-door is the door of a naos. Doors reinforced with battens can also be seen in some tomb decoration and the  hieroglyph representing a door leaf with pivots (Fischer, 1996: 93-94, fig. 5, pl. 12; Gardiner, 1957: 496). The inside of some Old Kingdom tomb passages have horizontal channels carved within the wall; presumably to accommodate the battens of the door when open (Fischer, 1996: 92, fig. 3).

Doors were not only used to close the entrances to rooms and there are a few examples of doors being used to close a naos (or shrine) within a tomb. The columned hall in the mastaba of Mereruka contains a niche with a statue of the owner set into the north wall. Two socket holes are cut into the limestone threshold

Figure 5.1. Artist's impression of false-doors in the tomb of Seshemnefer, Giza. From: Junker (1938: fig. 34).

of the naos to support wooden doors (Duell, 1938: 8; Firth & Gunn, 1926a: 15; Kanawati *et al.*, 2010: 39). Fischer (1996: 92-93) also comments on the interior decoration of painted horizontal bands that imitate the batons of the doors. The doors are now gone and although this design feature is not entirely lost, a full appreciation of the spectacular tomb architecture is. A further false-door within this tomb (on the west wall of A11) repeats the concept of a naos door; being a combination of the palace-façade style with a central niche imitating in great detail the outside of a double leaf door, closed with a blade-bolt and completed by fifteen batons and upper and lower pivots (Duell, 1938: pl. 107). The earlier 5th Dynasty mastaba of Ptahhotep (D 62), west of the Step Pyramid Complex of Djoser, contains a comparable shrine that perhaps influenced the architecture in the mastaba of Mereruka (Porter & Moss, 1981: 596-598). The shrine is positioned at the south end of the west wall of the large columned hall, placing it to the left side of those that crossed the courtyard to make offerings in the chapel (Hassan, 1975c: fig. 12; Porter & Moss, 1981: fig. LX). The outer section of the niche has a width of 1.24 m. and a height of 2.20 m. and is framed by torus moulding and a lintel. On the underside of the lintel two sockets have been carved at each end that would both have held the upper pivot of a door leaf. The statue would have been placed within the shrine and a double leaf door would have hidden it from view. The sockets are 0.06 m. in diameter and 0.14 m. deep; both door leafs would have been at least 2.20 m. in height with a width of about 0.62 m. By comparison the upper pivot on the single leaf door of Kaemhesit is 0.20 m. in height with a diameter of 0.05 m. (McFarlane, 2000: 42).

Excavations at the 5th Dynasty cemetery at Abusir South have uncovered another example of doors being used to close an offering area (Bárta & Vachla, 2001: 34-35). The paved floor within the offering chapel preserves the lower pivot socket for the door that opens into the room but also two lower pivot sockets that once were positioned in front of an offering area. According to Bárta and Vachla (2001: 34-35): "The square inner chamber of the chapel, with finely dressed limestone walls, measures only one square mete in surface area. It has no western wall; instead, there are two *in situ* sockets hollowed-out in the stone, indicating that the area behind was screened off from the chapel by a two-leaf door. Instead of a false-door in the west wall there was a niche."

5.4. Doors Within Tombs

There is a characteristic style used in the building of doorways in Old Kingdom tombs. The door is hung within a doorway defined by a single recess, but for greater decorative effect, even two recesses (figure 5.2). Doors were mounted using turning pivots that sat within two sockets (figure 5.3). The lower pivot rested within a circular hole that was carved into a paving stone or the threshold (Goedicke, 1965: 200). In some cases the socket was carved in a harder stone than the surrounding paving, for greater durability (Hölscher, 1951: figs. 42 e-f, 44). Grooves could be cut in the paving stone in front of the socket to allow the pivot to be lowered into position. The upper socket could be positioned in the lintel or

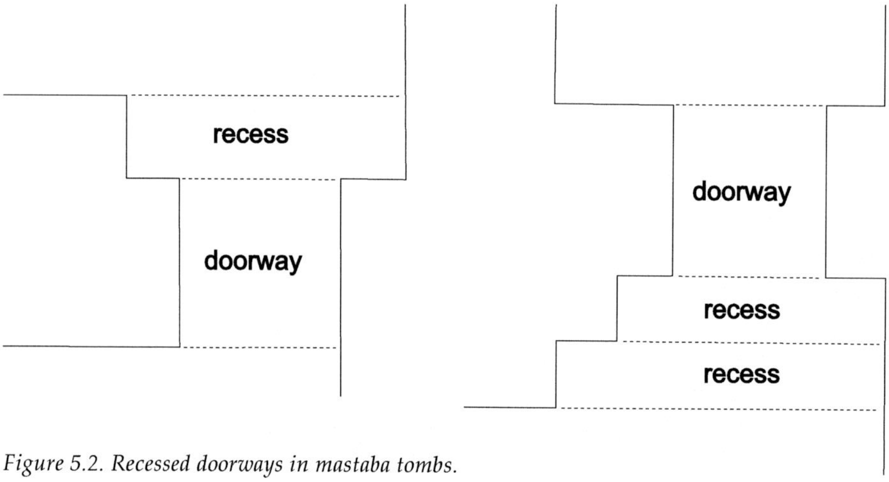

Figure 5.2. Recessed doorways in mastaba tombs.

1. lintel
2. doorjamb
3. pivot sockets
4. slot for inserting door

Figure 5.3. Method of hanging a door. From: Arnold (2003: 75).

an adjacent block that formed part of the ceiling of the doorway, if the door does not hang directly underneath the lintel; as in the case of doors positioned within long doorway passages. Once more, for reasons of insertion, the pivot socket was often positioned within a separate wooden block that was inserted within a cavity cut within the lintel/stone block. This upper socket consisted of different wooden parts that allowed the height of the socket to be repositioned to a lower height once both pivots of the door were in their respective sockets (figure 5.4) (Arnold, 2003: 75; Koenigsberger, 1936: 31-34, figs. 34-38).

Lintels above doors in Old Kingdom tombs are often damaged, which may suggest that the masonry was broken up to allow the door to be successfully removed. This implies that once the upper pivot socket fitting was in place it was hard for it to be dismantled. Likewise, the paving stone that often forms the threshold, where the stone lower pivot would be, is also more than often missing. Certainly once the door was hung it would be hard to quickly remove it and smashing away the paving of the threshold or breaking apart the lintel was quicker than sawing the pivots off the door itself. Indeed, presumably if the door is intended to be reused elsewhere, as a door, then this would be destructive. It is likely that doors were removed for reuse within other tombs, or the wood was recycled for the manufacture of other goods.

5.5. Fastening Doors

As stated above, false-doors can reveal the appearance of doors in the Old Kingdom. These are always double leaf doors and are sealed with a 'blade-bolt'. This is the most commonly recognised form of sealing a door and appears as the —•—

Figure 5.4. In situ *wooden upper pivot socket in the tomb of Kagemni. From: von Bissing (1905: pl. III.2).*

hieroglyph: a wooden or metal bar that rests within two U-shaped loops on one leaf and which could be slid into a locked position within the loop on the other leaf (Gardiner 1957: 496). Architect and Egyptologist, Otto Koenenigsberger, made a comprehensive survey of door fastening features (Koenigsberger, 1936: 47-52). However, most doors within mastabas are single leaf and the methods of fastening these doors are not as well known. A close inspection of doorways within mastabas can reveal where doors were hung and how they were fastened. A range of carved features within the doorframes show the variety of ways that a door could be fastened. In his study of the architecture of the 20th dynasty mortuary temple of Ramesses III at Medinet Habu, Uvo Hölscher (1951: 34-37, fig. 46) studied the doorways and found at least six different methods of fastening doors within the temple. The present author has found parallels with nearly all of these methods within Memphite tombs and shall use a similar system to Hölscher's fastening types to illustrate specific examples found within late Old Kingdom mastabas. In this method there are six typologies, with types A, B and C using a pin-bolt; and D, E and F using cord to tie a door shut (figure 5.5). Throughout this survey of door fastening methods of Old Kingdom tombs references will be made to Types A-F listed below.

In Types A and B the bolt is fastened to the door, on the outside and the inside respectively. A sliding bar would have sat within loops and could be secured within a hole carved into the doorframe: similar to the blade bolt hieroglyph. In Type C the bolt sits within the doorframe, and can be pulled out in to a locked position. In Types D and F rope is used to fasten the door. The rope is passed through a carved hole within the doorframe or tied to a projecting knob. Once secured the cord could be sealed.

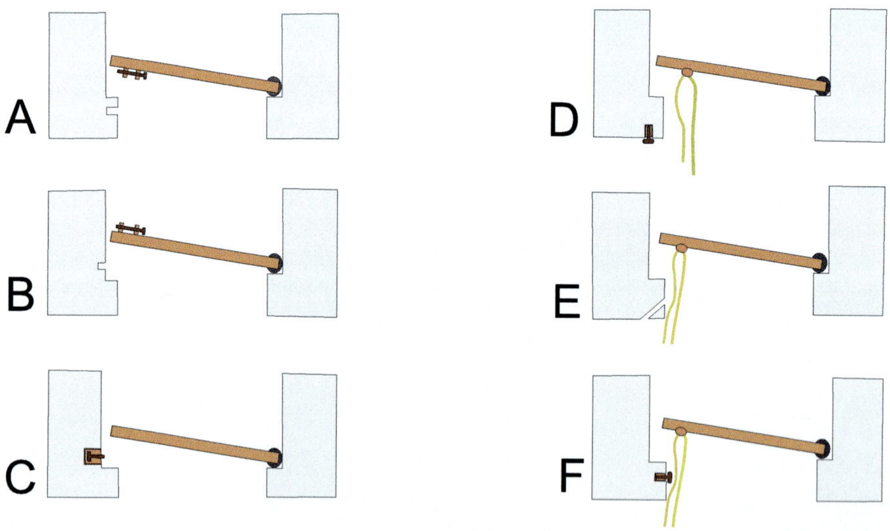

Figure 5.5. Classification of different door fastening methods.

Types A, B and C are known as pin-bolt locks and have either circular or rectangular sockets carved into the doorframe. In the later case it is more likely that the socket housed the bolt, as in Type C. Often these square sockets contain another smaller socket that goes deeper into the doorframe (Koenenigsberger, 1936: 47-52). This mortise would hold the bolt, probably encased in some form of wooden structure that was held tight within the shape of the mortise and secured with mortar. Ludwig Borchardt (1910: 22, 60, fig. 75) found evidence of door fastening features within the northern group of storerooms in the mortuary temple of Sahure at Abusir. Holes were positioned within the wall of the doorways revealing that the door was held closed by a rope or chain to a knob that sat within the cavity of the wall (figure 5.6). Bolts in the form of a lion have been recovered from temple doors of later periods (Borchardt, 1907, fig. 17; Koenigsberger, 1936: 53-58, taf. VIII-IX). The rope and seal type of door fastening is often used in combination with Types A, B and C; the security advantages of this combination are logical, though some types might be later replacements. Hölscher (1951: 37) found three different types of fastening used on one door within the palace complex of Ramesses III at Medinet Habu.

5.6. A Survey of Doorways Within the Unas Cemetery

Between 2000 and 2005 the author recorded examples of tomb door fastening features in the Unas Cemetery. The survey results are included here alongside data gathered from publications.

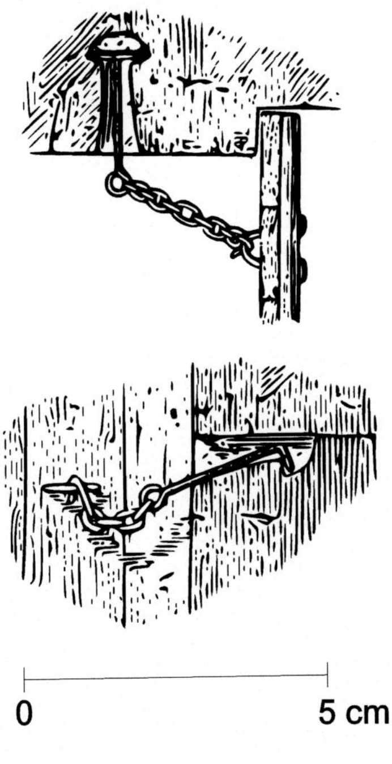

Figure 5.6. Chain fastened door from the pyramid temple of Sahure. From: Borchardt (1910: fig. 75).

5.6.1. The Tomb of Kairer

The ceiling of the tomb entrance has not survived but further inside the tomb there are walls surviving at greater heights, with two doorways containing evidence of door fastening methods. Within Room 1 surviving cavity features reveal that this room could be sealed off from all other rooms. The doorway leading to Room B, the largest surviving room in the mastaba (an open courtyard), was once sealed with a door that was positioned within a recess at the east end of Room 1 (figure 5.7). The paving stones in this area are missing, but door-fastening features reveal that the door was hung on the south side of the doorway and would have opened inwards against the south wall of Room 1.

The doorway in the east wall of Room 1 gives direct access to Room B, an open courtyard. Cut into the north side of the recess that defines the doorway is a square shaped cavity containing a deep drill hole, set within the corner, 0.85 m. above the floor (figure 5.7 labelled 'a'). The cavity is considerably large and its depth (0.20 m.) suggests it held a substantial locking mechanism, according with the Type C method of fastening a door when the bolt sits within the doorframe. A pierced flat slab of wood was probably set within the square cavity to provide the bolt socket greater protection (*cf.* Arnold 1992: 17, fig. 2, pl. 6). Directly opposite the cavity, on the south wall, there is a smaller cavity (0.10 x 0.12 x 0.20 m.) positioned 0.90 m. above the floor (figure 5.7 labelled 'b'). This cavity is positioned 0.10 m. from the east side of the wall. This represents the thickness of the door; it is likely that this was an extra method employed to fasten the door. A bar could be placed across the inner face of the door once it was closed.

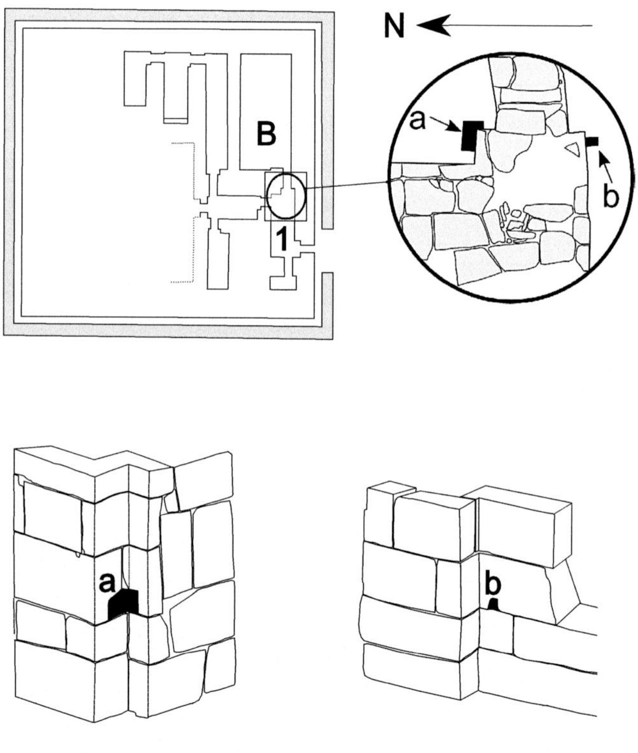

Figure 5.7. The tomb of Kairer: doorway between Rooms 1 and B.

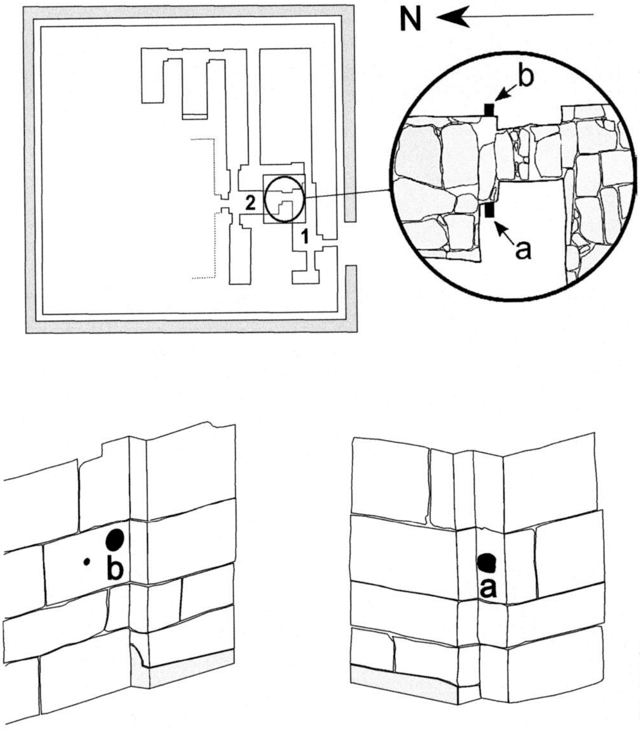

Figure 5.8. The tomb of Kairer: doorway between Rooms 1 and 2.

The doorway from Room 1 to Room 2 was closed by a door hung within Room 2 (figure 5.8). The paving within this room is intact, apart from the northeast corner, where it would seem a pivot stone piece is now missing, as is so often the case in tomb paving. That the door was hung on the east side of the doorway is not only suggested by the design of the door, but also by the surviving cavity feature on the west side of the doorway. Set within the west side of the door recess is a distinctive cavity feature, positioned 1.00 m above the floor (labelled 'a' in figure 5.8). A cylindrical hole 0.13 m. in diameter and 0.15 m. deep is carved within a rectangular recess 0.17 x 0.25 m. and 0.02 m. deep. The cavity conforms to Type C door fastening method, where the bolt sits within the doorframe.

5.6.2. The Tomb of Khenut

The entrance to the tomb of Khenut is defined by a single recess, with a doorway built with three recesses which widen out as one enters the tomb. The doorframes are composed of several courses of stone that are cut to a shape. These form the first inside recess. The lintel is one stone block (c. 0.30 m. thick) that rests upon the edges of both doorframe blocks. The stones that would have been adjacent to the lintel, forming the ceiling of the doorway, are now missing and consequently there is no evidence of an upper pivot. The paving stone on the east side of the doorway is also absent and no lower pivot has been preserved. Immediately within the entrance of the tomb there are two cavities that provide evidence for how the entrance door was fastened (labelled 'a' in figure 5.9). Rectangular cavity features on the west doorframe are carved into the lower part of the third course block next to the entrance doorframe. Both are similar in size (the largest is 0.30 x 0.17 x 0.05 m.) and contain a deeper circular hole 0.05 m. deep. A pierced flat slab of wood was probably set within each cavity to provide the bolt socket greater protection (*cf.* Arnold 1992: 17, fig. 2, pl. 6).This would accord with the Type C door fastening method, where the bolt sits within the doorframe. Munro (1993a: 42) reports that Bieger uncovered a wooden block in the eastern corner of the outside door of the tomb of Khenut, underneath 0.22 m. of plaster. The block was described as being very weathered with traces of red colour. The shape and the dimensions of the block are very similar to the cavities within the walls (0.30 x 0.185 x 0.07 m.), with a projecting tenon joint with a diameter of 0.075 m. It seems likely that this wooden block is part of the door fastening mechanism and fitted into one of the mortise cavities in the doorway of the tomb of Khenut (*cf.* Type C). The two mortises differ in that the interior hole is positioned on opposite sides of the rectangle: this difference could perhaps add to the strength of a double locked door and be part of the door fastening design. Alternatively, one of the mortises is earlier and the other is a replacement. The wooden door would have been held in the 0.10 m. space between the bolt and the wall of the recess. Further within the doorway

c

b

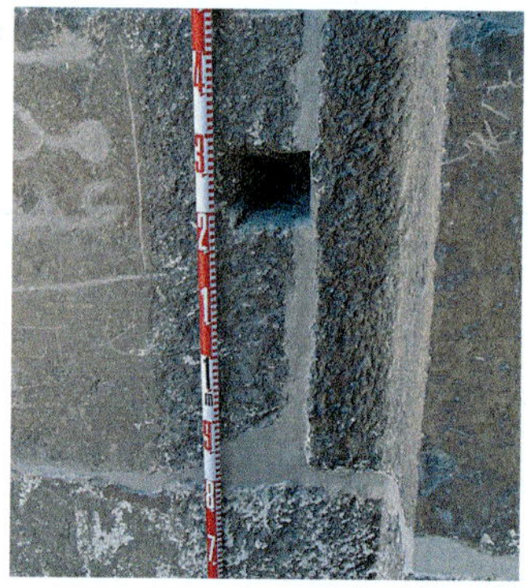

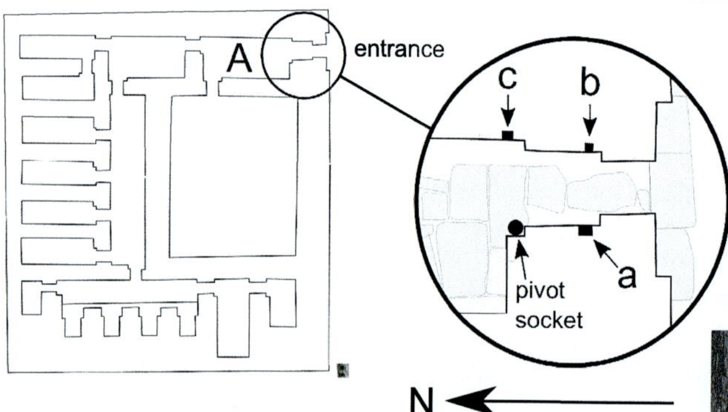

a

Figure 5.9. The tomb of Khenut: entrance doorway.

on the east wall, just within the second recess, there is a square shaped hole carved into the second course stone block of the wall. With sides of 0.10 m. and a depth of 0.07 m., positioned 1.18 m. above floor level (labelled 'b' in figure 5.9). This hole is 1.00 m. within the doorway and may represent evidence that another door was once positioned at this point.

At the end of the recessed doorway, on the west side, a pivot socket is cut into the paved floor. Corresponding with this pivot socket is a bolt hole carved into the opposite east wall (labelled 'c' in figure 5.9). The hole is 0.07 m. in diameter and 0.95 m. above floor level and would once have held the bolt when the door was fastened shut. The gap of 0.06 m. between the edge of the socket hole and the recess thickness suggests that the bolt was fastened to the inside of the door and that the door was positioned between the socket hole and the recess thickness when it was fastened shut (Type C). The wooden door must have been quite substantial as the doorway is much wider than any other within the tomb (1.50 m. compared to the typical width of around 1.00 m.). The presence of only one lower pivot socket is not secure evidence that this was a single leaf door, as the paving stones at the opposite side of the doorway (east) are missing. However, the presence of only one fastening feature on the east doorframe would seem to confer that there was a single leaf door pivoted at the west side of the doorway. The door would not have opened against a wall, as seems to be the usual arrangement in tombs. This part of the east wall in this room is decorated and might suggest the door was a later addition (Munro, 1993a: 52-53, pl. 33).

The south side of the doorway between Rooms A and H contains evidence on how the door was fastened (figure 5.10). Room A is the first room within the mastaba and Room H is the largest room, an open courtyard. The cavity on the south doorframe is positioned about 1.00 m. above floor level. The roughly square shaped hole (0.20 x 0.18 m.) is carved into the south side of the doorframe, but also cuts into the inside thickness of the recess. The west side of the frame, which forms the corner of the west wall of Room A has been filled in with cement during restoration work. It would seem that the cavity passed through the north side of the block and pierced the south side. The edge of the block has a part missing that is roughly the same height as the hole on the north side and is 0.10 m. deep. With this hole now being filled in it is hard to be definite that this part of the door-fastening system or merely a break in the edge of the block. However, its position and size makes this element more characteristic of a door-fastening feature. It seems most likely that the door here was fastened in method similar to Type E: a door fastened with a rope that passed through the corner of the doorframe. Though the size of this cavity is somewhat puzzling; it is much larger than what one would expect for a hole for just rope to be passed through. The size of the cavity is more similar to the Type C method, where the bolt sits within the doorframe. Indeed this cavity feature is very similar to the door fastening mechanism in Room 1 in the tomb of Kairer, discussed above. Both holes cut into the very inner corner of the doorframe. It may be possible that the door was sealed with two methods: a door bolt that sat within the doorframe, and a rope that passed through the outer corner of the doorframe.

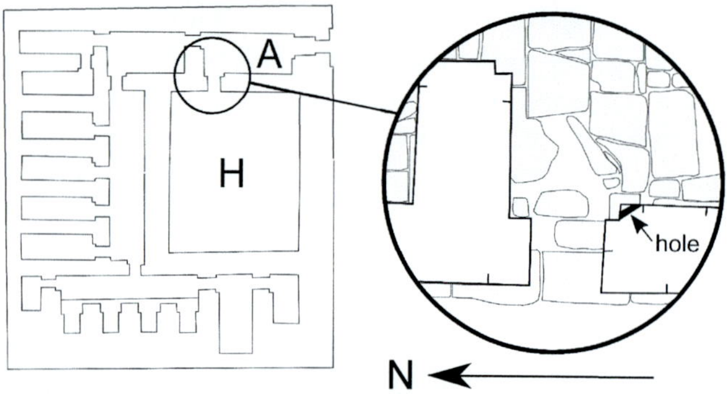

Figure 5.10. The tomb of Khenut: doorway between Rooms A and H.

The doorway between Rooms B and M1 was sealed at the north end, within Room M1 (figure 5.11). It gives access to two storerooms (Rooms M1 and M2) of the same size (4.60 x 1.10 m.).The west doorframe survives to four courses in height. The top block is cut in an L-shape and contains two holes positioned about 1.25 m. above the floor. A diagonal hole has been carved through the top corner of the block of the doorframe leaving two rectangular holes, separated by 0.03 m., both measuring 0.05 x 0.03 m. (labelled 'a' in figure 5.11). This is typical of a door fastening method whereby a rope passed through the corner of the doorframe that held the door locked (Type E). This demonstrates that the door pivoted in the south-east corner of the room and would have opened outwards against the east wall.

On the north side of the doorway between Rooms M1 and M2 is a carved hole (labelled 'a' in figure 5.12). A pivot socket is cut into the floor in the south-east corner of Room M2 indicating that a single leaf door opened outwards into Room M2. The location of the hole in the doorway is on the opposite of the pivot socket, suggesting it was used to keep the door fastened shut. A similar hole is positioned

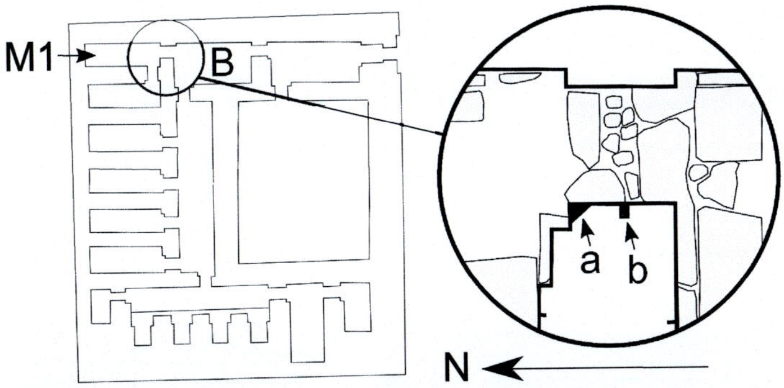

b

a

Figure 5.11. The tomb of Khenut: doorway between Rooms B and M1.

in the west wall of the doorway between Rooms B and M1 (labelled 'b' in figure 5.11 and 5.13). These roughly carved holes are not like the neat cylindrical holes that were made to receive a bolt when a door was fastened shut using a pin bolt mechanism (Types A-C). It is more plausible to conceive that these cavities once contained a projecting wooden knob, similar to Type F, which would have been used to anchor a rope that was attached to the door (figure 5.13). In combination with the Type E method, the door would have been fastened at two different points 0.30 m. apart. Or alternatively one type of fastening method could be an older redundant feature.

5.6.3. The Tomb of Nebet

The ground plans of the adjoining tombs of two queens of Unas, Khenut and Nebet, correspond with each other and one may assume both shared similar architectural characteristics. Indeed, the ground plans seem to only differ for the recessed doorways that form the entrances on the south side – one is the reverse of the other. The tomb of Nebet could not be accessed for detailed examination so the observations discussed here are gathered from Munro's (1993a) publication. Just as in the entrance to the tomb of Khenut, there is a pivot socket located within the third and final recess, 2.00 m. deep inside the tomb (figure 5.14). The door would

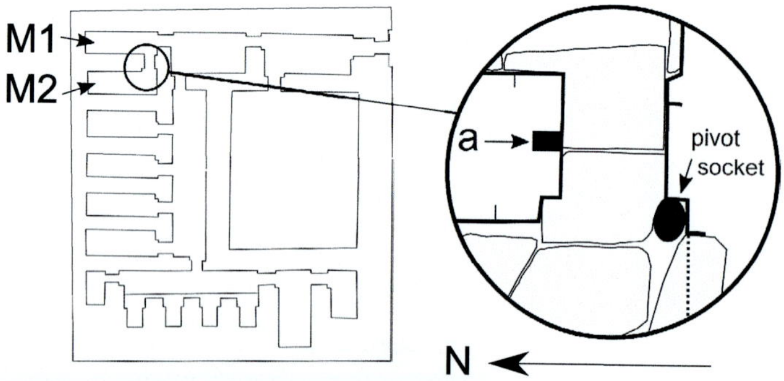

a

Figure 5.12. The tomb of Khenut: doorway between Rooms M1 and M2.

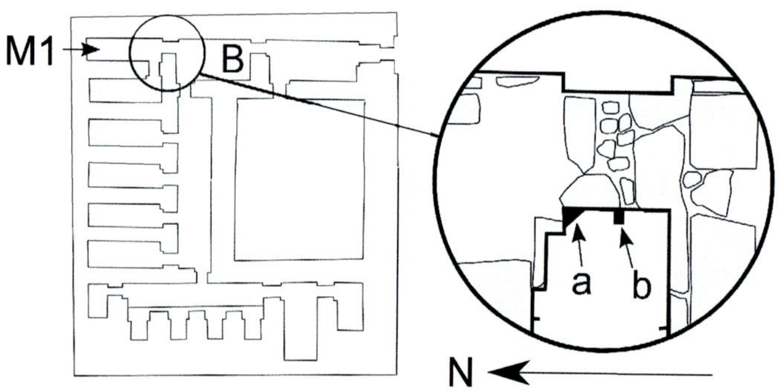

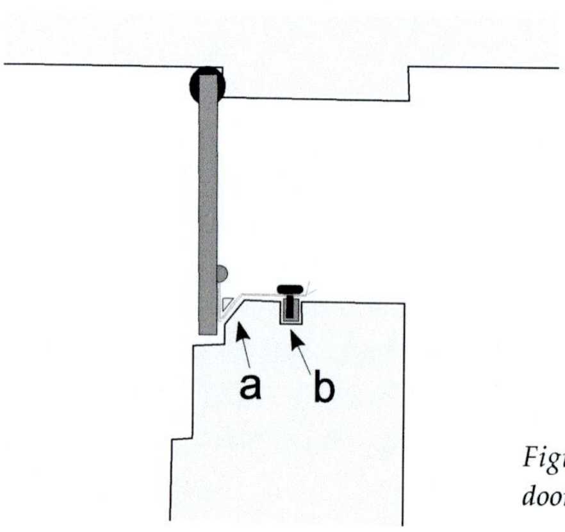

Figure 5.13. The tomb of Khenut: doorway between Rooms B and M1.

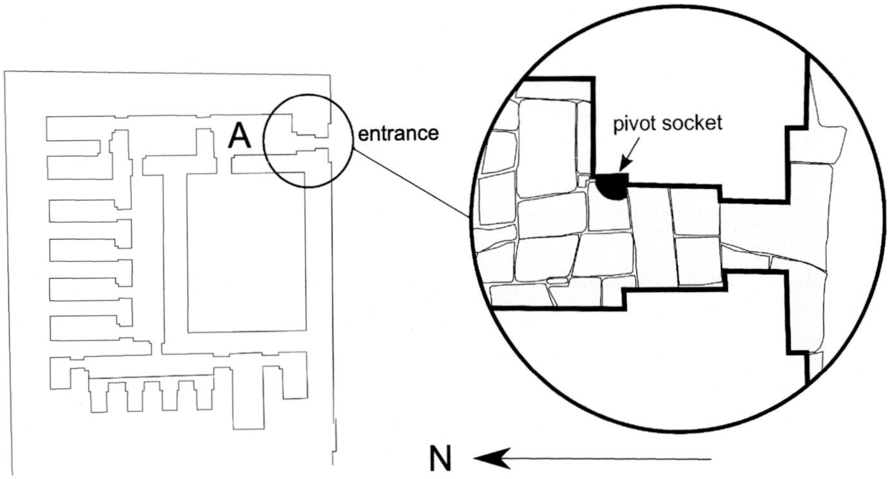

Figure 5.14. The tomb of Nebet: entrance doorway.

have opened outwards towards the east; and just as in the tomb of Khenut, it opens out into the middle of the room, rather than against the wall. The paving stones in the entrance and within Room 1 are completely intact, unlike in the tomb of Khenut. This demonstrates at this part of the doorway only a single leaf door was used; something that could not be entirely proven in Khenut's tomb as the paving stones were missing on the opposite side of the surviving lower pivot stone. In the subsection entitled 'Architectural and Technical Details' (Munro, 1993a: 42-49), Munro states that there are distinctive recesses ('aussparungen') in the corners of the second doorway recess in both tombs and within the stone framework above in the tomb of Nebet (commenting that the entrance to the tomb of Khenut is too damaged for this to be observed). These features must be the rectangular internal cavities observed in the entrance of the tomb of Khenut (see figure 5.9, labelled 'a'). Though, curiously, in this tomb no lower pivot socket is recorded on the plan (Munro, 1993a: insert 2). Munro believes that the front door to the tomb was a double door, and does make comment that this is a remarkably narrow doorway to be sealed with a double-leaf door (1.10 m.). This does not seem to correspond with the presence of the cavities at mid-door height on the insides of the doorways. The entrance passage to the tomb of Nebet would also appear to have further small cavity features along the wall at mid-door height. Munro considers that they do not appear, at first, to have a meaningful purpose to hold the bars of a door bolts, but rather thinks that they may have served some purpose in a locking device allowing the doors to be locked from the outside; making reference to the complicated mechanism outlined by Koenigsberger (1936: 58-63, fig. 74). This may be the case, but their function is better elucidated when considered in conjunction with the nearby pivot socket on the east side of the doorway. These holes are most likely to be the same as those in the tomb of Khenut, and are quite likely to be associated with a door being fastened with a rope (Type D or F).

At the north end of the west wall of Room A is a doorway which gives access to Room H, a large open courtyard (figure 5.15). A pivot socket is carved into the floor of Room A in the north-west corner. As in Khenut's tomb the courtyard door would have opened inwards against the north wall of Room A. The doorway in the north wall of Room A is defined internally by a recess 0.20 m. deep and provides access to all other chambers in the tomb. A pivot socket is cut into the floor at the north-east corner of the room. In the ceiling directly above is a rectangular cavity cut into the lintel (Munro, 1993a: pl. 12; Saad, 1940: pl. LVIII). This would once have held a block of wood carved with a hole that formed the upper pivot socket. Again, this corresponds to the design in the tomb of Khenut where a lower pivot socket is cut into the northeast corner of the room. In both tombs the door would have opened inwards and against the east wall of Room A.

A preserved pivot socket in one of the storerooms, Room M4, indicates that doors in the storerooms were pivoted on the west side and opened outwards against the west wall of the room (figure 5.16). An elevation drawing for a north-south section of the tomb of Nebet illustrates how the doors within the store rooms were kept fastened. A cylindrical hole is carved in the middle of the doorway at height of 1.00 m. above the floor (labelled 'a' in figure 5.16). The hole is 0.10 m. in diameter and is located towards the top of a second course block. If all doors were pivoted on the west side of the doorway then it is consistent that the fastening feature should be on the doorframe opposite. When the door was closed against the recess thickness of the doorway (0.20 m.) this would have placed the door about 0.30 m. away from the hole. Possibly, this hole accommodated some sort of wooden knob used to secure a rope between the door and this point. This would be similar to the Type F method of fastening a door that involved using a rope and a projecting knob, held within the doorframe before the door.

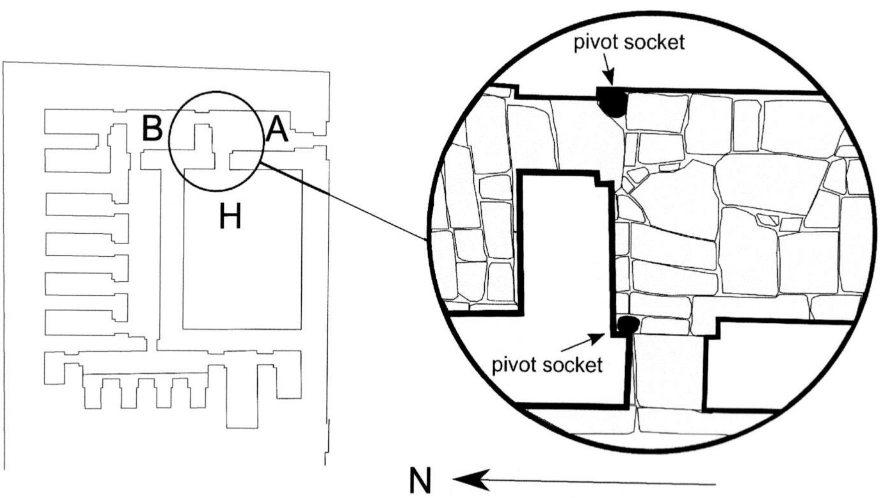

Figure 5.15. The tomb of Nebet: doorways in Room A.

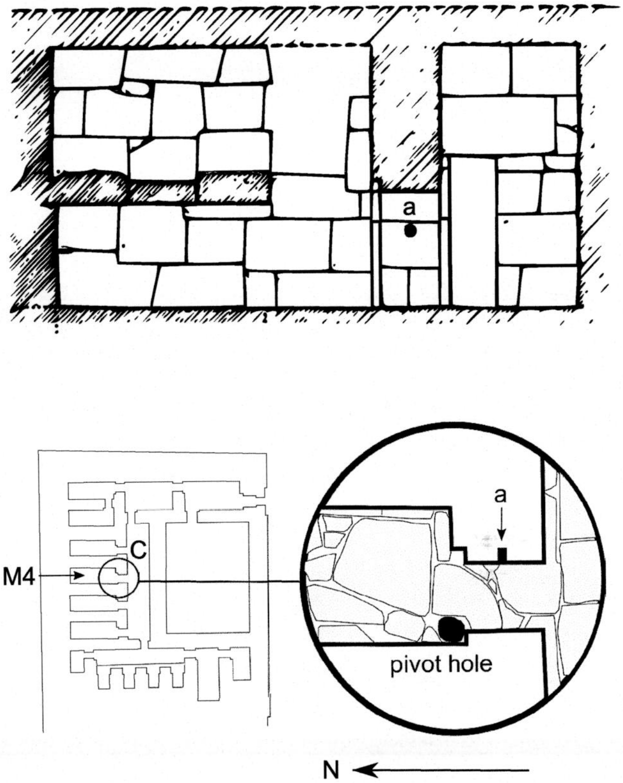

Figure 5.16. The tomb of Nebet: doorway in Room M4. From: Munro (1993a: insert 3).

5.6.4. The Tomb of Seshseshet Idut

Lauer (1976: 80, pl. IX) states that the doorway between Room 4 and Room 5 (the offering-room) contains an upper pivot socket on the east side. A rectangular shaped cavity contains a wooden block carved with a socket hole that would have accommodated the wooden upper pivot of the door, just as described by Arnold in his reconstruction of doorway fittings in the 12th Dynasty pyramid of Queen Weret II at Dahshur (Arnold, 2002: 79, fig. 24). In their publication of the tomb Kanawati and Abder Raziq (2003: 38-39) give dimensions of all doorways within the mastaba and include descriptions of door fittings in two other doorways. In the recess of the doorway between Rooms 1 and 2 there is a square hole carved into the east wall of the recess at a height of 1.02 m. above floor level (labelled 'a' in figure 5.17). This bolt socket is 0.22 m. wide, 0.18 m. in height and 0.18 m. deep. Another bolt hole is located in the north wall of the recess of the doorway between Rooms 2 and 4 (labelled 'b' in figure 5.17). This square hole is carved at a height of 0.56 m. above the floor and is 0.09 m. in width, 0.15 m. in height and 0.13 m. deep. The difference in height between the two bolt holes might suggest that they were not constructed at the same time, and that the security of the tomb was improved on more than one occasion. The staircase within this tomb (in Room 3) makes the superstructure more vulnerable to intruders. An additional locked door between Rooms 2 and 4 would have increased the security of Room 5, the offering-room.

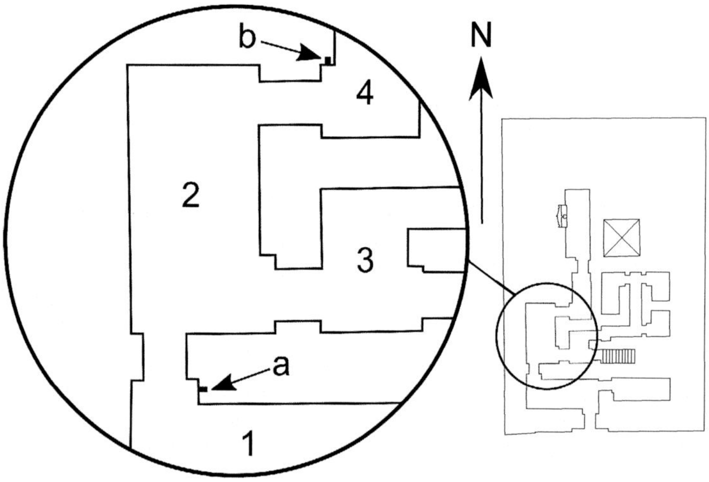

Figure 5.17. The tomb of Seshseshet Idut: doorways in Rooms 1 and 4.

5.6.5. The Tomb of Iynefert

Further in from the doorway entrance, on the east doorway wall, are two shallow holes carved into one stone block. One has recently been filled in with cement and utilised to hold a metal gate that now seals the entrance. These holes may have been bolt sockets, implying that the doorway was sealed with a single leaf door pivoted on the west side which opened outwards into the tomb (Kanawati & Abder Raziq, 2003: 14).

The east side of the doorway between Rooms 1 and 2 is pierced with a hole that cuts through the corner of the doorframe (labelled 'a' in figure 5.18). The hole is 1.08 m. above floor level, with each opening 0.06 m. wide. If a door was pivoted on the opposite side of the doorway a rope could be passed through the hole and fastened to the door to keep it closed – as like fastening method Type E. The upper pivot socket of the door is on the opposite side but it is not exactly opposite the door fastening feature (labelled 'b' in figure 5.18). The upper pivot socket is 0.46 m. away from the inside hole in the doorway, and is a rectangular shaped recess that would have once accommodated a wooden feature (like the one *in situ* in the tomb of Seshseshet Idut), which contained the actual socket that the pivot sat within. The external dimensions of the pivot socket are 0.35 x 0.17 m. with internal dimensions being 0.33 x 0.13 m. with the hole at one side of the rectangle being 0.12 m. in diameter; the depth of the socket is 0.18 m. (Kanawati & Abder Raziq, 2003: 15). If the door was closed it would have been pressed against the frame of the doorway. A rope could be attached to the doorway and secured at the slot that is carved into the corner of the doorframe at the opposite end of the doorway, as suggested in figure 5.19.

The doorway from Room 2 to 3 is 0.89 m. long and was once closed by a door that hung within Room 3 (figure 5.20). The door was pivoted on the east side and would have opened outwards against the east wall of Room 3. The doorway is 0.71 m. wide and is defined by a recess 1.00 m. wide and 0.14 m. deep. The limestone block that forms the lintel and ceiling of the doorway is very

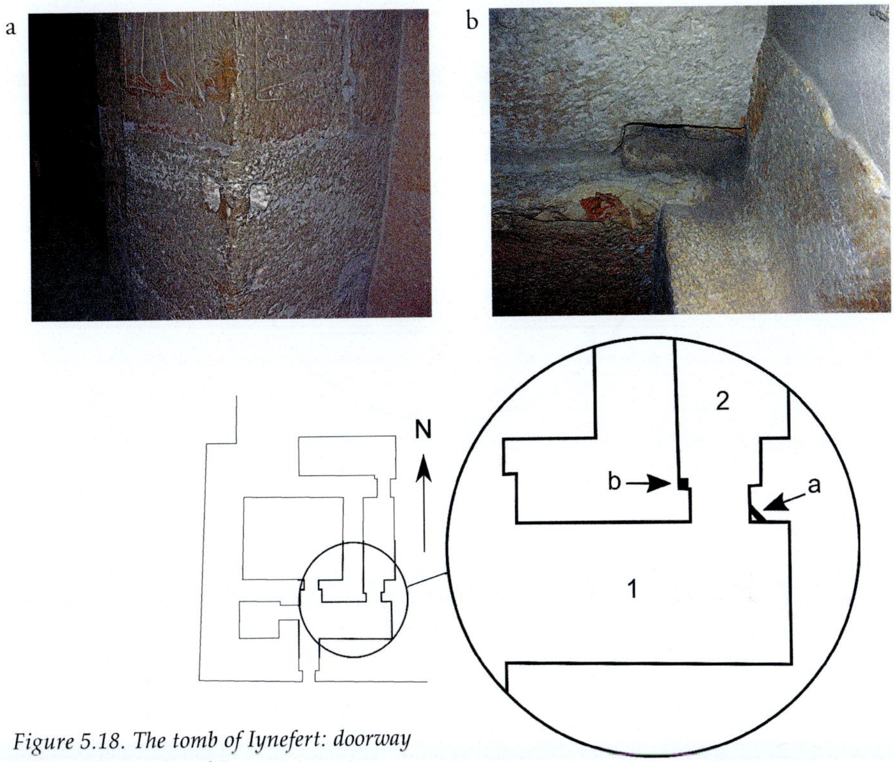

Figure 5.18. The tomb of Iynefert: doorway between Rooms 1 and 2.

large and has been carved to create a 0.14 m. deep rectangular void above where the door would have hung. The east side is damaged, exposing a rectangular cavity containing a circular socket. There is trace of plaster within the cavity that may have been used to hold the wooden upper socket piece in place. It is quite possible that the void within the ceiling of the doorway was once filled with a composite lintel, perhaps of a different material, such as wood.

5.6.6. The Tomb of Nebkauhor

The tomb of Nebkauhor could not be accessed for detailed examination but the publication by Selim Hassan (1975a) includes descriptions of how doors were fastened at different points within the tomb. Similar to the entrance passages in the tombs of Niankhba, and Khenut and Nebet, the doorway widens through a set of three recesses (Hassan, 1975a: pl. IV [A]). Hassan describes a rectangular hole located in the left-hand doorframe of the entrance that he believes to be a bolt-hole (Hassan, 1975a: 7). However, the dimensions of the cavity (0.17 x 0.13 m.) and Hassan's (1975a: 7) assertion that the passage was "originally closed by means of a double-leaved wooden door which could be bolted from the inside", do not correspond. If this was a double door a bolt-hole in the left doorframe would not seem necessary. It could be plausible that a double leaved door might have the extra security of a bar placed behind it, but Hassan does not record that there was any similar cavity on the right side of the doorway. It is more logical to deduce that this

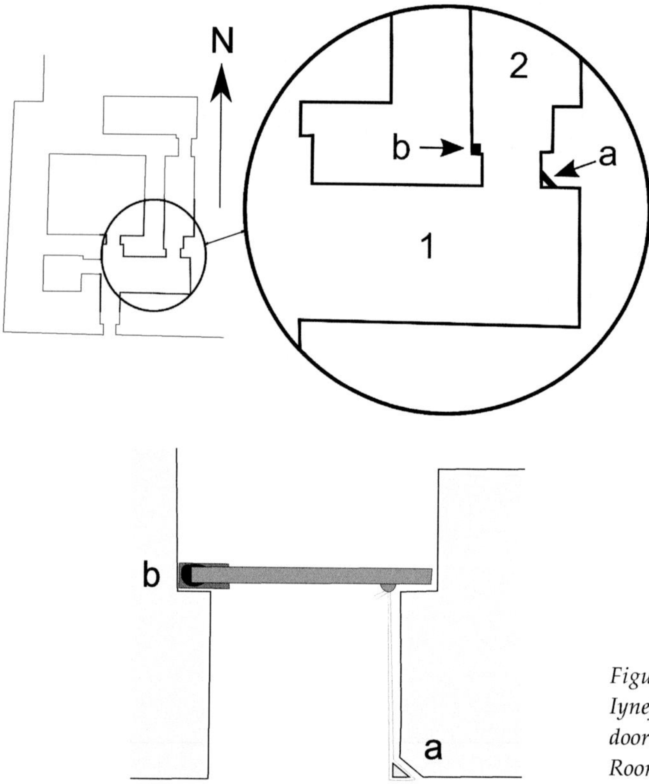

Figure 5.19.The tomb of Iynefert: reconstruction of a door in the doorway between Rooms 1 and 2.

Figure 5.20. The tomb of Iynefert: doorway between Rooms 2 and 3.

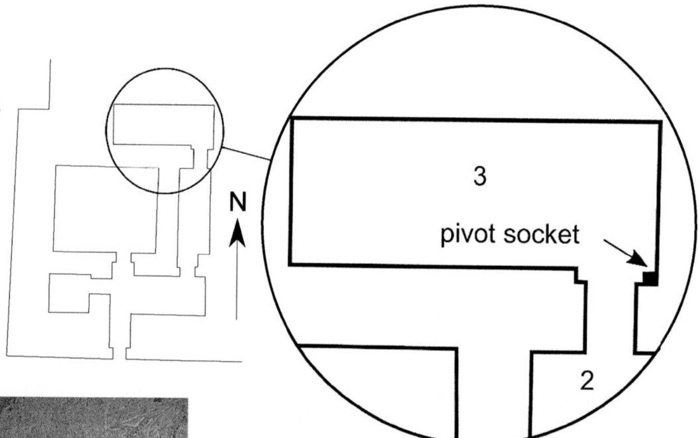

doorway was once sealed with a single leaf door that was pivoted on the east side and fastened shut in a method involving the rectangular hole on the west side of the doorway. Only the lowest two courses of the doorway survive *in situ* and both sides are described as being of white limestone. The west side survives to a height of 1.33 m. and is decorated with two registers of painted carved relief decoration (Hassan, 1975a: 6-7, pl. IV [B]). The east side survives to a height of 1.26 m. and is uninscribed. If the door was pivoted on the east side it would have been opened against this wall, and it is consistent that this wall is undecorated, unlike the facing west wall that would have been seen when one was admitted to the tomb. The size and shape of the cavity suggest that this was not merely a hole for a bolt to rest in. It is more likely that his cavity was constructed as a mortise to contain a rectangular wooden unit that housed the bolt, or a smaller hole to receive the bolt if the bolt was fixed to the door. The hole is positioned 0.65 m. above the floor, but it is not specifically stated how far within the doorway it is located.

Further within the tomb Hassan (1975a: 58-60, pl. XLVII) describes the door fastening features within a series of five storerooms. The doorways in Rooms 8, 9, 10 and 11 have holes bored across the corners of the doorways (labelled 'a' in figure 5.21). This type of hole indicates that the door was fastened with rope, which was attached to the door and passed through the hole (Type E), just as Hassan (1975a: 59) considered: "Probably a length of rope was passed through this hole and attached to the bolt, either for the purpose of sliding it in or out of its socket, or for the purpose of sealing it after the door was finally closed." This indicates that all doors within the northern row of storerooms were pivoted

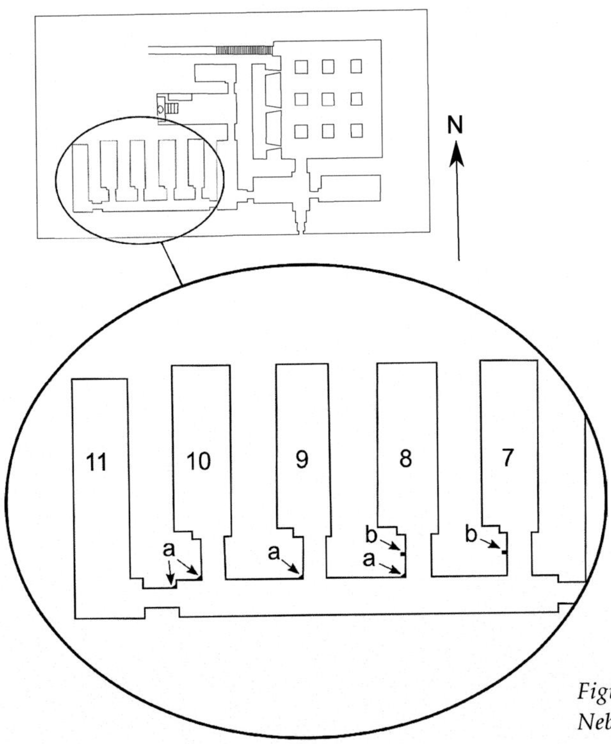

Figure 5.21. The tomb of Nebkauhor: storeroom doorways.

at the corner of the room, on the east side of the doorway and opened outwards against the east wall, rather than opening in the middle of the room. The door in Room 11 was pivoted in the corner of the room, on the south side of the doorway and also opened against the south wall. Further door fastening features are recorded within the west sides of the doorways of Rooms 7 and 8: there are cylindrical holes carved into the stone, described by Hassan as 'bolt-holes' (labelled 'b' in figure 5.21). Each hole has similar dimensions: the hole in Room 7 is 0.10 m. in diameter and 1.06 m. above floor level; the hole in Room 8 is 0.09 m. in diameter and 1.01 m. above floor level.

Although not described in the text a plate within Hassan's publication (1975a: pl. XLI B) shows a cylindrical hole carved into the left wall of the doorway between the offering-room (Room 4) and the attached side-room (Room 5). This indicates that this doorway was once fitted with a wooden door that opened outwards against the east wall of Room 5. With a hole in the middle of the doorway wall, below the height of the registers, it would seem that the door was fastened with a rope that was attached to a knob fixed in the hole within the west doorway wall.

5.6.7. The Tomb of Mehu

The descriptions of the doorways by Altenmüller (1998: 25-27) provide ample evidence for door fastening methods, indicating all five doorways within the tomb were fitted with wooden doors (figure 5.22). The floor of the entrance has a pivot socket (0.12 m. in diameter and 0.08 m. deep) carved on the south side indicating that the door opened outwards and against the south wall of the entrance chamber (Room 1). The entrance was extended when a thickness of surrounded walls was added to the east side of the exterior (Altenmüller, 1998: 17-19). A rectangular niche is located in the north side of the recess and

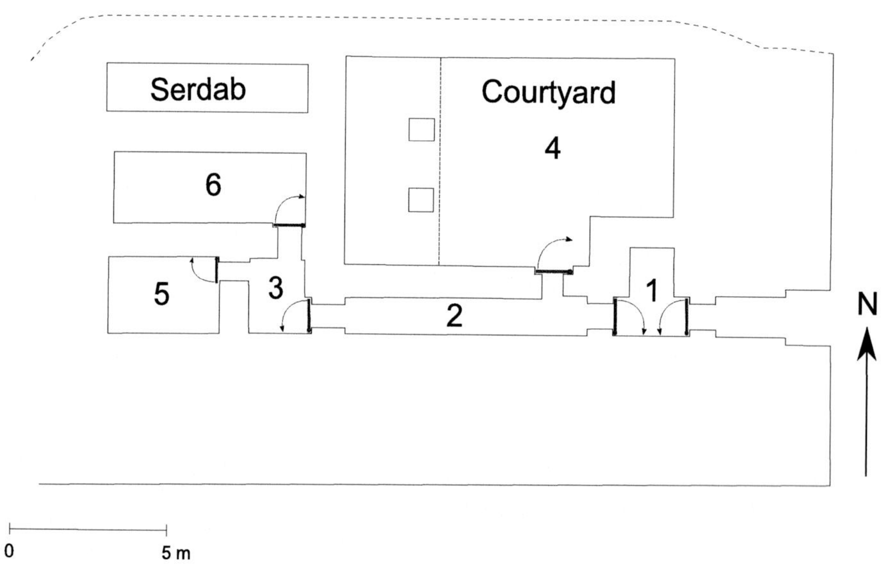

Figure 5.22. The tomb of Mehu: directions that doors open.

measures 0.18 m. in height, 0.10 m. in width and 0.61 m. in depth. The depth of this recess might suggest that a bar rested within it and was pulled out some distance behind the door when in closed position, suggesting that this door fastening system is similar to Type C, where the bolt is kept within the doorway. There was a door which fitted in the other doorway of this entrance chamber that would seal off the room completely. The doorway leading to the long east-west corridor (Room 2) has a lower pivot socket on the south side, indicating that the door opened inwards against the south wall of Room 1. The north side of the doorway contains a niche, measuring 0.18 m. in height, 0.11 m. in width and has a depth of 0.25 m. This niche would have functioned in the same way as the recess on the doorway described above. The external dimensions of the niche are the same and the difference in depths might indicate that the bolt in the first niche did not pass through the whole length, and did not function as simply a long bar that could be pulled out and pushed back when required. Indeed, the bolt may have been fixed to the door and only fitted into the niche when the door was closed, like in Types A and B door fastening methods.

The doorway between Room 2 and the open courtyard (Room 4) contains a lower pivot socket on the east side; and within the lintel of the doorway an upper pivot socket was also preserved. The socket is a square shaped niche 0.12 m. wide and 0.12 m. deep that would have contained a wooden fitting with a socket to accommodate the door pivot (Altenmüller, 1998: 26). Similar upper pivot socket features are also found in the doorways between Rooms 2 and 3 (dimensions: 0.27 x 0.17 x 0.12 m.), Rooms 3 and 5 (0.16 x 0.16 x 0.16 m.) and Rooms 3 and 6 (0.16 x 0.16 x 0.16 m.). With three upper pivot socket features sharing the same dimensions this would appear to be a standard size and all doors were pivoted in the same manner using a fitted wooden block containing a cavity to fit around the upper pivot of the door. In all these doorways the door opened outwards into the other room and against a flat wall.

5.6.8. The Tomb of Ptahshepses Impy

Although not a multi-roomed mastaba, the tomb of Ptahshepses Impy has been included in the survey as it contains excellent preserved examples of different door fastening mechanisms. Only one side of the entrance has survived (figure 5.23). A single-leaf door would have been hung on the south side of the doorway – the side now missing. There are two cavities carved into the north side doorjamb. The top cavity is a cylindrical hole, positioned 1.10 m. above the threshold. This would have received a bolt that was fixed to the outside of the door like Types A and B methods of fastening a door. The cavity 0.10 m. below is a carved square with a circular hole set within the centre, just like a door fastening feature in the tomb of Kairer (figure 5.8) and similar to those in the tomb of Khenut (figure 5.9). A pierced flat slab of wood was probably set within the square cavity to provide the bolt socket greater protection (*cf.*, Arnold 1992: 17, fig. 2, pl. 6). This type of cavity would have held a lock that could have been secured behind a closed door: like Type C.

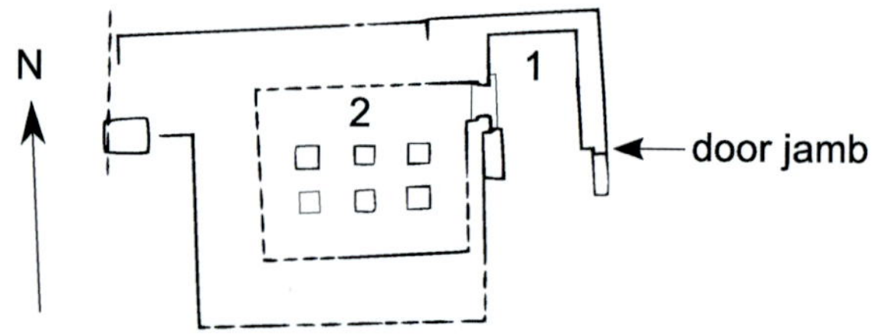

Figure 5.23. The tomb of Ptahshepses Impy: doorway in Room 1.

The distance between the edge of the cylindrical holes and the edge of the doorframe represent the thickness of the wooden door. It is likely that the tomb initially only had one door lock and that later another form of fastening the door was added for additional security, or because the other door fastening method had fallen out of use. The columned inner chamber of the tomb contains the shaft to the burial chamber of Ptahshepses Impy. The north side of the threshold contains a curious hole (figure 5.24). The door to the tomb was fitted behind the doorjamb a good distance away from the outside edge of the threshold. The purpose of this hole is confusing and it seems unlikely that it could have served any purpose. What seems more likely is that the threshold is a recycled doorjamb. The cavity is carved through the corner of the rectangular block. At one end the hole is circular and on the other (shorter width) side the hole is a slim rectangle. The carving is purposeful and appears like a cavity carved to fasten a door using a rope. These types of locks (like Type E) are often associated with doors in storerooms/magazines. The thickness of the block is rather thin and quite similar to the blocks used in small mastabas behind Ptahshepses Impy, to the immediate east of the mastaba of Khenut. It might be that this is a doorjamb taken from a tomb in this area. Archaeological and textual evidence specify that doorway elements (*i.e.*, lintels, thresholds and doorjambs) were ideally constructed from finer imported stone and consequently these elements are prime materials to be removed and reused at later periods, if possible.

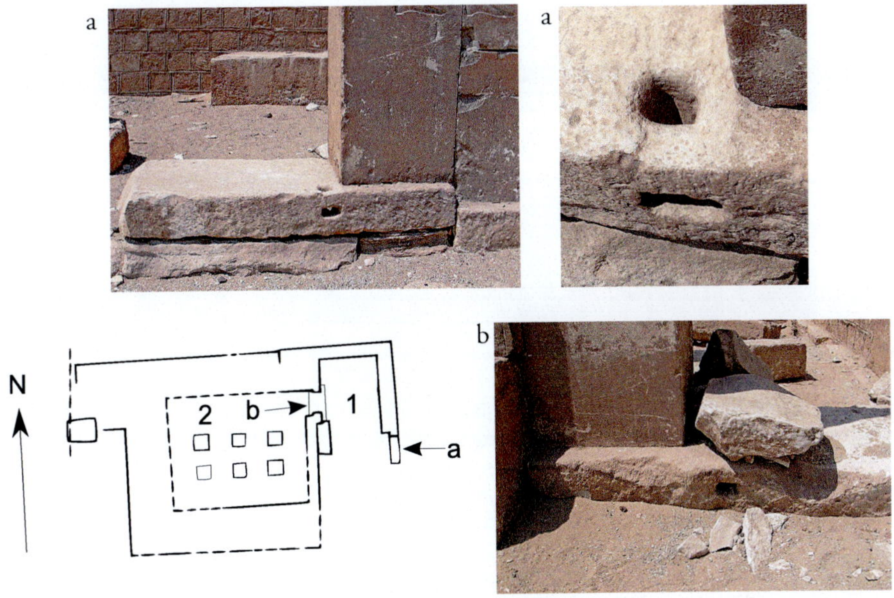

Figure 5.24. The tomb of Ptahshepses Impy: doorway between Rooms 1 and 2.

The threshold to the inner columned hall has a similar hole carved through the side. The stone is of imported limestone. The doorjambs are reconstructions. In both cases the holes are carved at the opposite end of where the door was pivoted; though it seems unlikely that the holes could have served some function associated with the door.

5.7. Other Memphite Tombs

The corpus of data collected in the Unas Cemetery is supplemented with evidence of door fastening features in other parts of the Memphite necropolis, in particular the Teti Cemetery.

5.7.1. The Tomb of Mereruka

With a superstructure that is formed of three separate chapels, containing a total of thirty-two rooms, this tomb preserves ample evidence for the fitting of doors. Improving on Duell's 1938 publication a Macquarie University expedition recorded architectural features in the tomb completed from 2004 to 2009 and published in three volumes which include good coverage of doorways, pivot sockets and door fastening features. (Kanawati & Abder Raziq, 2004; 2008; Kanawati *et al.*, 2010; Kanawati *et al.*, 2011).

Located in the northwest corner of the tomb complex is a group of five storerooms, each designated to an individual phyle ('gang') by labels incised on the door lintels (Duel, 1938: pl. 199[B]). Four of the storerooms (A17, A18, A19 and A20) have holes carved through the corner of the doorframe, at heights above floor level varying between 0.60 m. and 0.77 m. (labelled by arrows in figure 5.25;

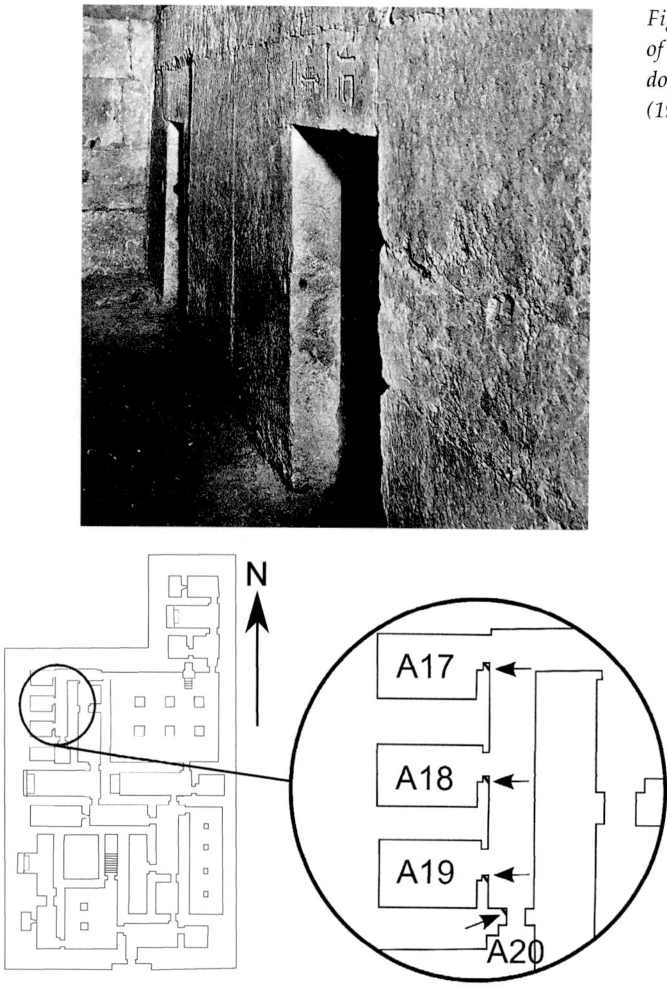

Figure 5.25. The tomb of Mereruka: storeroom doorways. From: Duell, (1938: pl. 199 A).

Duell, 1938: pl.199[A]; Kanawati *et al.*, 2010: 40-41). Doors were pivoted on the opposite side to the holes and a rope could be passed through the hole to fasten the door shut, as fastening method Type E, a method which is also used in other tomb storerooms (*e.g.*, the tomb of Nebkauhor).

At the southern end of Room All is a doorway to A12, one of the smallest decorated chambers in the tomb. This is a side-room adjoining the offering-room (A11), and was probably used as a storeroom for supplies of products and utensils required to perform ceremonies for the afterlife of the tomb owner (Harpur & Scremin, 2006: 341). Preserved pivot sockets in the floor and ceiling of the south-west corner of the A12 show that the door opened outwards against the south wall of A12. On the north side of the entrance to A12 a corner of the doorframe is broken away which appears consistent with door fastening method Type E, a type typically associated with storerooms/magazines (figure 5.26).

Figure 5.26. The tomb of Kagemni: doorways between Rooms A11 and A12. From: Duell (1938: pl. 105 B).

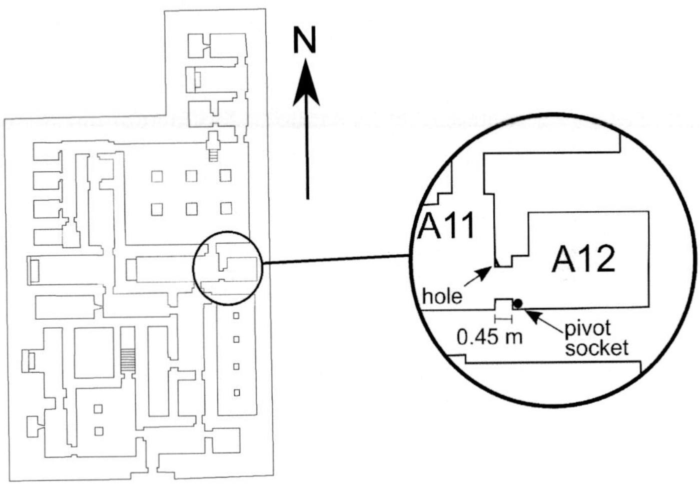

5.7.2. The Tomb of Kagemni

Friedrich von Bissing (1905: 1-5) provides an excellent account of door construction within the first chapter of his publication of the tomb. Understandably, the work is somewhat lacking in photographs and diagrams one now expects in a contemporary archaeological report but the clear descriptions make up for this loss. The chapter 'Allgemeine beschreibung der mastaba des Kagemni' reveals the unusual archaeological preciseness not ordinarily encountered in tomb publications of this time.

A wooden upper pivot socket was preserved in a doorway between Room 7 (offering-room) and Room 8 (storeroom) (figure 5.4) (von Bissing, 1905: pl. III. 2). Directly beneath is a lower pivot socket carved into the stone paving slab. A single leaf door would have been pivoted on the west side of the doorway and opened outwards, against the west wall Room 8. This type of room (a side-room of the offering-room) is mainly decorated with registers of men bringing vessels and chests, part from the space against which the door would have opened against, which is left blank. Von Bissing (1905: 3) interprets this to mean that the door was rarely left unopened. There is no description of a method in which the door may have been fastened shut. The wooden upper pivot socket has been placed inside a recess which was cut into the west side of the lintel. The pivot socket is 0.37 m. in length, 0.20 m. in width and has a depth of 0.08 m. The socket is carved at one side and has a diameter of 0.12 m. It is within this socket that the upper pivot would have rested when the door was in position. Von Bissing does not describe the unexposed parts of the wooden pivot socket or how it is held in place. The feature corresponds with the upper pivot sockets in the tombs of Seshseshet Idut and Mehu (described above) and with Arnold's (2003: 75) reconstruction of an upper pivot socket; and one can expect that this exposed part is one part of the device that is likely to be composed of two or three elements.

In both of the doorways between Rooms 4 and 5 and Rooms 2 and 3 there are similar shaped slots carved into the walls. The slots are 0.08 m. in height, 0.05 m. in width with a depth that varies between 0.07 m. and 0.14 m. In each case the hole is located on the opposite side of the remaining pivot sockets: on the east wall of the doorway between Rooms 4 and 5; on the south wall of the doorway between Rooms 2 and 3. This certainly suggests that these slots have some purpose with the functioning of a door. However, both slots are not directly opposite the door pivots, each is c. 0.22 m away from the doorframe. They are therefore not slots to receive a bolt. On these slots von Bissing (1905: 2) suggested that they held a device (made of wood and copper), to which a rope could be fastened, which in turn was connected with the door latch, and, when the door was locked, could be sealed. This seems the most logical reasoning for these slots and is similar to Type D method of fastening a door that uses a rope, rather than a bolt (*cf.* Koenigsberger, 1936: fig. 55). The door would be larger than the doorframe and when closed the sides would be pressed against the stone of the doorframe. If a knob was inserted into the slot then a rope connected to the door could be bound around the knob and this would keep the door tight in place.

Another type of door fastening device in the doorway between Rooms 2 and 4 is a hole drilled at the corner of the doorframe that von Bissing describes as a hole to allow a strong rope to be passed through that could be tied to the door to fasten it shut (von Bissing 1905: 2). This hole would have been used to fasten a door and is typical of Type E fastening method that uses a rope. A slot is described at the doorway between Rooms 1 and 2, which has unusual dimensions: 0.35 x 0.02 x 0.04 m. The long rectangular slot is directly opposite the door pivot, which does suggest that it has some function associated with the door. Von Bissing (1905: 2) suggests that this long slot may have once held a bolt that could be slid out in front of a closed door. This seems plausible, yet also quite unusual. Room 2 provides the only access to the rest of the tomb and the sealing of the doorway would have prevented access to all of rooms beyond Room 1; von Bissing (1905: 2) believes that this door would have been fastened shut during ceremonies held within the tomb.

5.7.3. The Tomb of Khentika

The doorway between Rooms 1 and 4 is an unusual style for tomb architecture. The doorway is not built from the normal masonry of large blocks that meet against one another with little or no gap. In this standard method the inside thickness of the doorway recess is cut into the corners of the blocks. In Khentika's tomb, however, the doorway between Rooms 1 and 4 has been reduced in width on either side using columns of small blocks. These additions remove the recess that once defined the doorway. Originally the door opened into Room 1 against the south wall (labelled 'a' in figure 5.27). Major architectural changes were made from the original plan and the tomb entrance was moved from the north side of the superstructure to the east, with a new entrance being made through the east wall of Room 1 (James, 1953: 17-18, fig. 8-9). The door between Rooms 1 and 4 needed to open in the other direction, so it could be pushed open in the direction of a person entering the tomb (labelled 'b' in figure 5.27).

Located on the south wall of Room 9, a large columned hall, are three doors to Rooms 10, 11 and 12 (storerooms). At the entrance to Room 10 two holes are carved within the second course block that forms part of the east doorframe (figure 5.28). A small rectangular hole has been made on the right side of the block, near the edge, positioned c. 0.70 m. above the floor. The other hole is larger, and located on the top corner of the block, c. 1.10 m above the floor. The lowest hole corresponds with fastening method Type E, a door fastening method frequently associated with storerooms/magazines. A closer examination of the

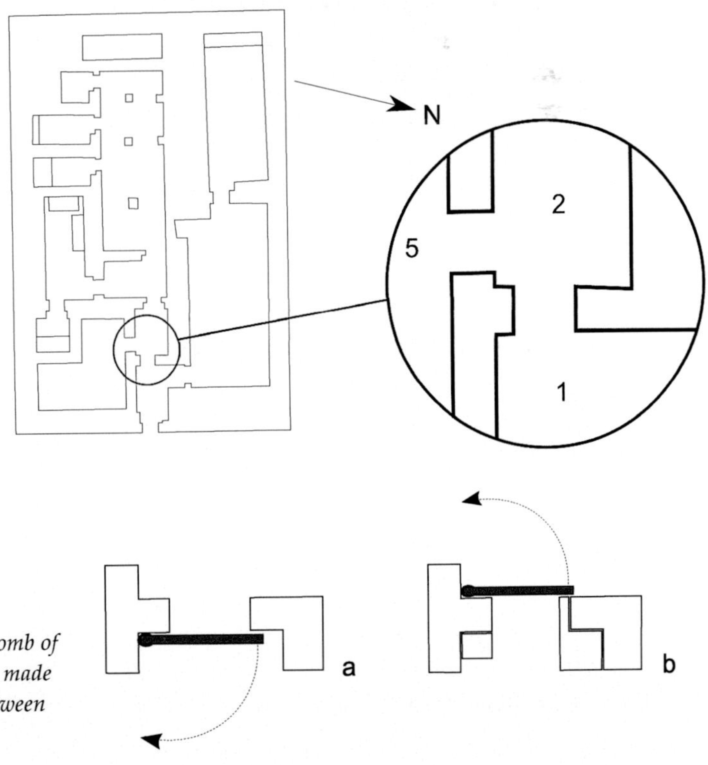

Figure 5.27. The tomb of Khentika: changes made to the doorway between Rooms 1 and 2.

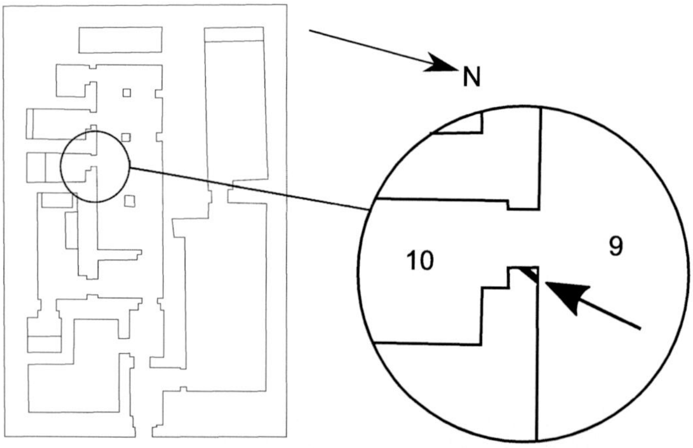

Figure 5.28. The tomb of Khentika: doorway between Rooms 9 and 10. Photograph courtesy of The Egypt Exploration Society.

other hole also suggests that this was of the same type. In this case it would seem the corner piece, which held the fastening rope within the block, has broken away. This is understandable considering the vulnerability of this element of the stone block, at a corner, when a hole has been bored diagonally through it; and also perhaps constant wear. Could it be that there were two fastening methods of the same type? It is perhaps more than likely that the upper hole was the original door fastening feature. After some wear and tear the hole became useless and another hole was cut into the corner of the block.

5.7.4. The Tomb of Ankhmahor

The doorway between Rooms 3 and 5 contains two holes on the southern thickness. One is positioned 0.15 m. within the doorway just below the decoration level, measuring 0.08 × 0.05 m. with a depth of 0.09 m. (Kanawati & Hassan, 1997: 21). It was likely used as a door fastening method, perhaps to accommodate a door bolt (*cf.* Types A-B). Although Alexander Badawy (1978: pls. 48 and 57) included photographs of the doorway he does not refer to the holes. Within this publication plate 48 clearly shows that there is a second hole cut through the corner of the doorway thickness and the west wall of Room 3. Kanawati and Hassan (1997: 23) provide dimensions for the hole but do not regard it as being part of a door fitting. Rather they (1997: 23) include the hole as one of a number of 'curious' holes within the tomb: "Curiously, a number of small holes were cut through the angles of several walls, possibly in order to attach or secure something in place. While their purpose remains uncertain, it is possible that these provided a hitch for tethering animals." The hole measures 0.03 x 0.06 m. and is 0.63 m. above the doorway threshold. This hole is very much like that used in Types E and F for fastening doors, rather than tethering animals.

5.7.5. The Tomb of Debehen

The rock-cut tomb of Debehen at Giza uses imported white limestone to case the walls and to create rooms within the hewn chamber; the very stone Debehen refers to his monumental inscription within the entrance chamber (Hassan, 1943: fig. 118, pl. XLVIII). One wall passes between the tomb at the north and divides the tomb into two rooms. A lower pivot was found within the threshold that was carved from one piece of limestone, and indicates that the door opened inwards against the east wall of the tomb. Hassan (1943: 174-175) records a door fastening feature of this doorway: "In the left-hand side of the doorway, at a height of 1.15 m. from the threshold, are two bolt-holes, one circular and one rectangular. The presence of these two holes seems to indicate that two types of bolts were contemplated for use on this door. The rectangular hole was probably made to receive a sliding bar, as there are indications on the opposite jamb of the hole in which it would have entered; but the scheme was abandoned before the cutting of this second hole was completed." The description given by Hassan seems familiar with the methods used within mastabas, indicating security measures of the same kind were used in different types of tomb. However, the internal structure of the tomb of Debenhen is rather like a mastaba, with the limestone masonry within the tomb being used to section off areas of the hewn tomb. The use of two methods to fasten the door is seen in some of the tombs discussed above, with the features described being very familiar to the fittings found within the doorjamb in the mastaba of Ptahshepses Impy.

5.8. Doorkeepers

The design of doorways within tombs follows a conventional style, with a doorway defined by one or more recesses and doors opening outwards against a wall which are sometimes left clear of decoration. Wood was a prestige material and would have been used carefully within the tomb, just as imported stone was used for key elements and in certain places within the structure. The surviving wooden door of Kaemhesit has an upper pivot length of 0.20 m. which correspond with the depth of upper pivot sockets recorded in tomb doorways. The upper pivots of doors would have been secured in place within the door sockets. Several doorway lintels included in this survey show signs of damage, seemingly inflicted in the removal of the valuable wooden doors. Wooden doors were used in tombs to close off entrances to rooms and to close off certain areas within the tomb. Used in combination with fastening methods doors could be locked and doorways sealed shut. Before the invention of the 'tumbler' lock (c. 1000 BC) the method of locking a door was easy to break.

Security depended upon mud sealings applied over rope fastenings were stamped with an individual design. The sealing would have to be broken to open the door and by this method the security of storerooms could be monitored. For improved security the door could also be guarded. Of all the tombs included in this survey that have entrances with masonry surviving to a sufficient height (c. 1.00 m.) there is evidence of door fitting features and door fastening features. The entrance to the tomb could be considered the most important doorway that required sealing shut. Indeed, in some examples there was evidence of more than one method of fastening a door (such as the tombs of Ptahshepses Impy and Khenut). In some examples there was evidence of more than one door being used within the length of a doorway (*e.g.*, the tombs of Nebet and Khenut). Substantial holes carved through the corner of both the doorframe and the recess thickness, have been found in doorways that leads to an open courtyard (*e.g.*, the tombs Kairer, Nebet and Khenut). The holes once contained the bolt mechanism that fastened the door shut (Type C). There is also a similar substantial bolt hole described in the doorway leading to the open courtyard in the tomb of Ankhmahor, within the Teti Cemetery (Badaway, 1978: 11-12; Kanawati & Hassan, 1997: 20). The stairways in the tombs of Neferseshemre, Kagemni and Mereruka all have doorjambs that would enable the staircase to be closed and the tomb secured (Kanawati & Hassan, 1997: 22). The door in all examples would have opened inwards so it could be locked from the inside – *i.e.*, sealing off the open courtyards. The need for a locked door here appears necessary as the open courtyard was a room within the tomb without a roof. However, an intruder could gain easy access to the tomb by climbing the wall and dropping down into the courtyard. Munro considers this a possibility in the tombs of Khenu and Nebet (Munro, 1993a: 42), as does Deborah Vischak (2003: 150) in the tomb of Ankhmahor. Some scholars interpret that this seemingly practical arrangement is also an architectural response to the concept of the afterlife. Inspired by James Allen's contextual analysis of the Pyramid Texts inscribed on the walls of the burial chambers of king Unas (Allen, 1994: 5-28), Vischak relates the architecture of the tomb of Ankhmahor with the decoration scheme, which together helps to fulfil the needs of the deceased in the next world (Vischak, 2003: 133-157). Vischak (2003: 150) considers the door bolt to be used in both the realm of the living and the dead: "it is possible that Ankhmahor was perceived to draw back the bolt of the door, located on the room 1-side, the direction from which he would be coming, to open his way to the sunlit sky of the porticoed hall, room 6, in a manner similar to that of the king as expressed metaphorically, in the Pyramid Texts". Vischak continues to consider any parallels with the open courtyard and the king's journey as described in the Pyramid Texts.

Other common types – the rope fastening method – is found frequently in storerooms and in some cases used along with another method. This method could be viewed as less effective than a metal or wooden bolt being secured within the doorframe. However, this method of fastening a door is useful to ensure that a room is not entered without breaking some form of seal. When the door was closed the rope would be secured in a knot, covered with clay and impressed with a seal design. The only way to then gain access to the room would be by breaking the seal or cutting the rope. In all examples it is apparent that the measures to keep a door secured shut could not keep out the determined intruder and it seems logical that the security of tombs also required guards.

A common component of the multi-roomed mastaba is an entrance side-room. The walls of these rooms are not decorated and the location beside the tomb entrance suggests that this room functioned to accommodate tomb personal, perhaps a doorkeeper. This proposed function seems plausible when looking at the layout of rooms in the tomb of Kairer (figure 5.29). Room A is an unpaved room with roughly smooth walls that measure 2.20 m. north-south and 1.00 m. east-west. The room is entered through a doorway on the west wall of Room 1, immediately beside the tomb entrance. From this position no one could enter without going past the room, which is also opposite the doorway of an open courtyard, a vulnerable part of the tomb where intruders

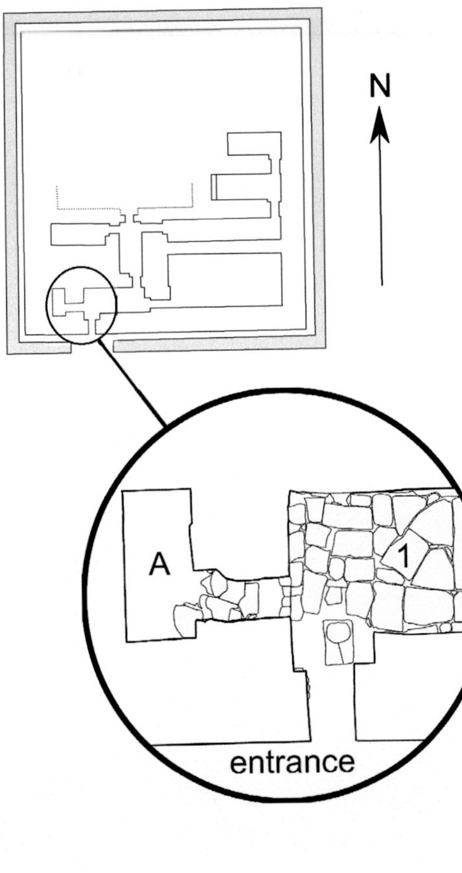

Figure 5.29. The tomb of Kairer: entrance side-room (Room A).

could possibly scale over the walls. Similar side-rooms can be seen in the layout of six other Memphite tombs: Iynefert, Idut, Nebkauhor, Niankhba, Mereruka and Neferseshemre (figures 5.30-5.31).

The provision of a room within the tomb for a doorkeeper was a security measure to safeguard the tomb space and its contents. As discussed above doors within tombs could only provide relative protection and could be forced open with reasonable force. Locked doors ensured certain areas of the tomb could be

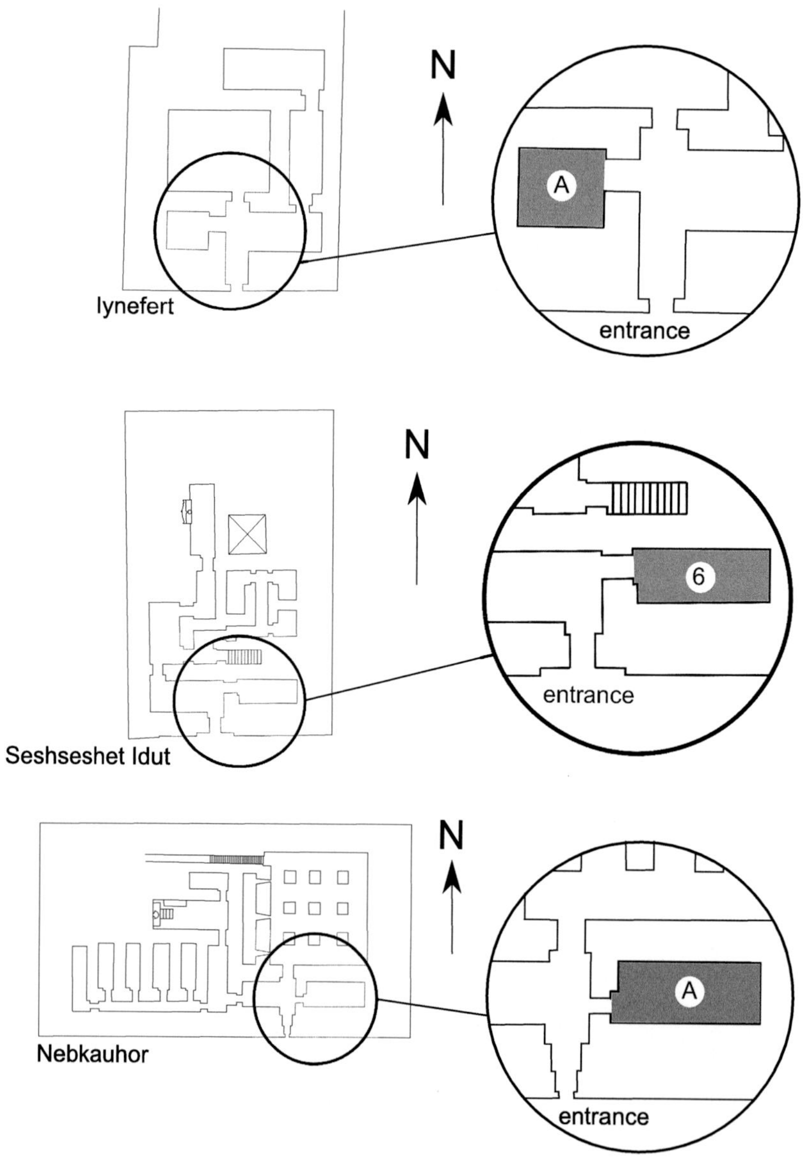

Figure 5.30 . Entrance side-rooms (shaded) in the tombs of Iynefert, Seshseshet Idut and Nebkauhor.

off-limits, with broken seals indicating trespass. An on-site doorkeeper could act as a guard for the tomb providing all-day protection. The room may also have functioned as a sleeping area for one guard or potentially a shift of guards on duty.

In the tomb of Mereruka (figure 5.31) Room A2 is located at the east side of Room A1, the entrance chamber to the tomb. In his commentary on the tomb Prentice Duell makes several references to the relationship between the mastaba ground plan and that of the Egyptian house, which is reflected in his comment on

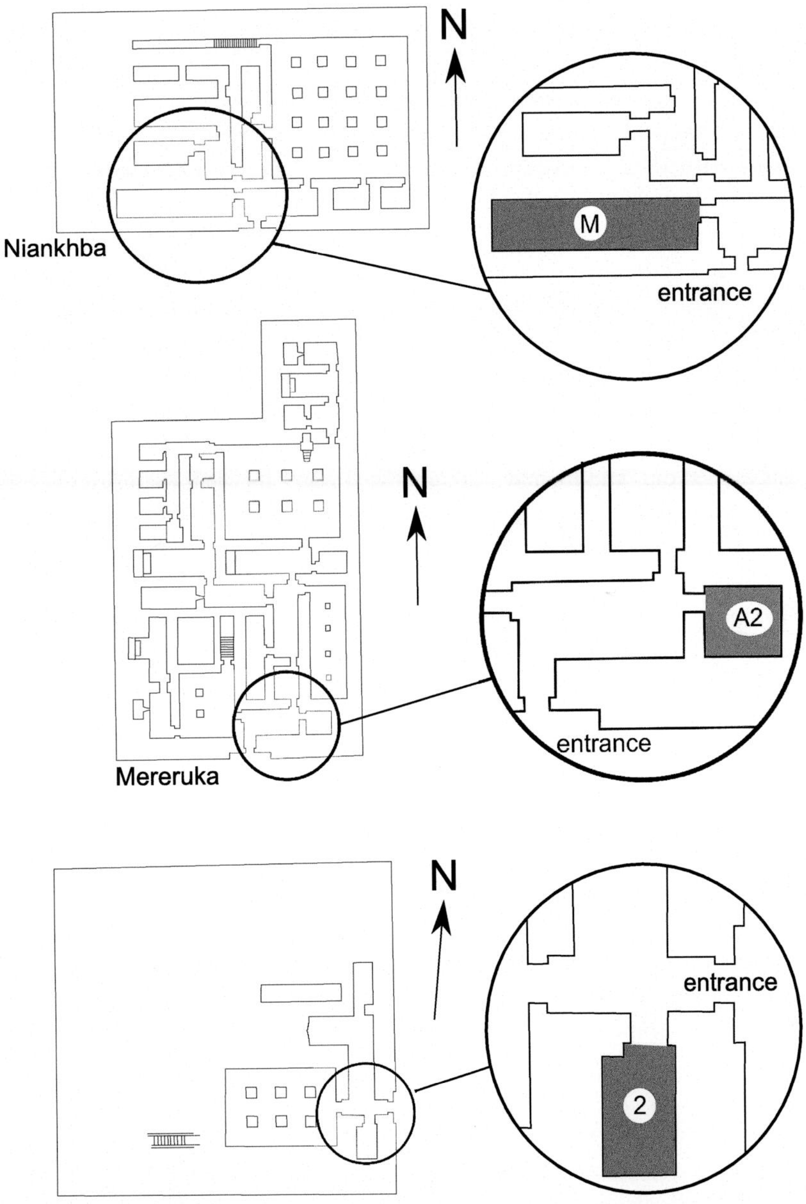

Figure 5.31. Entrance side-rooms (shaded) in the tombs of Niankhba, Mereruka and Neferseshemre.

this room (Duell, 1938: 9): "There seems to be no reason for this room unless one regards the plan of the mastaba as representing that of a house, where this would be the anteroom for the doorkeeper, adjoining the vestibule." Room A2 was probably the doorkeepers' room within the Mereruka's tomb and was a later addition to the tomb layout. The doorway to the room was cut through the decorated east wall of Room A1 which Duell (1938: 9) believed was "hollowed out as an afterthought from what had been a corner of solid masonry." This addition was made because the tomb entrance was not originally planned to be located on the south side. This considerable effort indicates the great importance of this room and does not entirely fit with Duell's deduction that the room is merely replicating the plan of a typical house, a concept shared by Badawy (1978: 11-48).

The doorkeeper's role was not just to provide security for the tomb but to also assist with the functioning of the mortuary cult, as Bolshakov (1997: 25) observes: "As far as we can judge by the appeals appearing in the late Old Kingdom and calling passers-by to offer or to read out an offering-formula, everybody was allowed to enter cult chambers, no matter who these visitors might be – relatives of the buried person or strangers. Cult chambers were protected by morals; however, in order to prevent them from penetration by undesirable visitors, bolted doors were used and, probably, doorkeepers might have been engaged." Texts inscribed on the exterior walls of 6th Dynasty tombs insist that those entering the tomb be pure and it is plausible that that it was one of the doorkeeper's functions to ensure this was carried out, and he may have provided water for visitors to ritually cleanse themselves with before entering the tomb. Such as inscribed on the entrance façade of the tomb of Ankhmahor (Kanawati & Hassan, 1997: 28, pls. 2, 35) which reads: "[With regard to] any persons who shall enter this tomb in an impure state, having consumed the abomination which is abhorrent to an excellent *ꜥkh*, and not having purified themselves according to the manner in which they should be pure for an excellent spirit one who regularly did what his lord favoured – [I shall seize his neck] like a bird's and put fear in him so that the spirits and those on earth see and are fearful of an excellent *ꜥkh*." (Strudwick, 2005: 264).

Ewer and basin sets were essential equipment for ritual purification, represented in offering scenes in tomb decoration and appearing as burial goods, such as a pair of bronze ewer and basin sets from the tomb of Tjetji in the Teti Cemetery (Metropolitan Museum of Art, New York, Rogers Fund 1926 nos. 26.2.12-15; Firth & Gunn, 1926a: 30, fig. 31; *cf.* Radwan, 1983: 22-23). They were used for washing hands and feet before presenting offerings, something one can imagine taking place as a ritual performance before entry within the tomb. As much as the small rooms found off the entrance chamber may be seen as repeating the plan of a house, they should also be considered as a practicality in death as much as in life. As a doorkeeper would work in the house of the elite it should be expected that the same would continue to be done so in death. By the use of a range of door-fastening features, that fulfilled different purposes, the tomb could only ultimately be secured if there were trustworthy guards within the tomb or the cemetery in the least.

6. Courtyards, Columned Halls and Storerooms

Buried within the Unas Cemetery were some of the highest ranking people who lived between the reigns of Unas and Pepy II. Of particular interest are the tombs of Nebet and Khenut, Unasankh, Iynefert, Seshseshet Idut, Nebkauhor, Niankhba, Kairer, Neferseshemptah and Mehu. These tombs emulate details of pyramid temples on a smaller scale in their design. It was a style of tomb architecture prevalent with the elite of the time. Known as multi-roomed mastabas because of the complex arrangement of rooms within the superstructure, they are a type of non-royal tomb that emerged during the reign of Nyuserra (Bárta, 2005: 105-128; Brovarski, 2001: 11-35; Harpur, 1987: 106-110; Jánosi, 1999: 27-37; Spencer, 1975: cols. 400-409; Strudwick, 1985: 30-35, figs 2-5). These tombs are elaborate structures consisting of an internal plan that is never repeated. A shared characteristic of the design is a long offering-room oriented east-west with a false-door occupying the west wall. This design is the norm for most tombs with only a few exceptions (such as the tombs of Unasankh and Seshseshet Idut). Other common architectural elements of the multi-roomed mastaba are open courtyards, columned halls and storerooms. The function, significance and meaning of these features will be considered below, but with a particular emphasis on the variety of storerooms provided for the mortuary cult as this has received less study.

6.1. Courtyards and Columned Halls

The cultic and symbolic function of courtyards in multi-roomed mastabas is comparable with those found in the mortuary temples of the 5th and 6th Dynasty. Besides the offering-room, the courtyards and columned halls inside tombs also served as a place of ceremonies for the afterlife of the tomb owner. They were a location for rituals of the funerary cult, enabling the dead to participate in such ceremonies through several means:

- statues could be located within the courtyard
- statues within an adjoining serdab
- false-door or stela
- burial shafts and descending corridors are frequently located within the courtyard
- the image of the deceased within the relief decoration.

They are another architectural innovation derived from pyramid temples, first included within a mastaba by the vizier Ptahshepses at Abusir, during the reign of Nyuserra (Bárta, 2005: 105-128). Starting off as open courtyards they developed into grand columned halls such as the magnificent example in the tomb of Mereruka in the Teti Cemetery. In discussing the evidence for the facilities for slaughter within Old Kingdom pyramid temples Christopher Eyre (2002: 186;

but see also Malek, 1988: 23-34) also considers the function of courtyards within mastabas as a place of ritual sacrifice: "Architecturally and functionally [the columned hall] of Mereruka served some of the purposes of the open court of large 5th Dynasty tombs: a place of access, offering and the performance of ritual, and so possibly sacrifice." The open courtyards in the mastabas of queen Khenut and Nebet contained false-doors that would have allowed the deceased to partake in the rituals performed in this area (Munro, 1993a: 118-123). The same potential could be achieved with statues placed in the area, often behind a wall in a serdab *e.g.*, the tombs of Nebkauhor, Ti and Ptahhotep I [D 62]). Burial shafts are regularly located in the courtyard or hall (*e.g.*, the tomb of Kairer). Bárta (2005: 113) interprets these shafts as "channels through which the deceased left the burial chamber to go and take part in offerings in the courts".

The largest room in Mereruka's tomb is a columned hall, measuring 9.20 m. north-south and 11.80 m. east-west (Duell, 1938: pls. 124 A, 126 A-B). Set within the floor in the centre of the room is a large tethering stone 0.36 m. high with a hole 0.15 m in diameter (Kanawati *et al.*, 2010: 39, pl. 61). The shape of the block and its location at the centre of the hall suggest it is more than a reused construction piece set into the ground by tomb robbers who entered a shaft (Duell, 1938: 8 no. 54). The engaged statue of Mereruka set within a niche in the north wall indicates that this was a room that was used for cult ceremonies which may have included the sacrifice of an ox. Part of a similar pierced stone was found in the entrance chamber within the mastaba of Ptahhotep (Davies, 1901: 4, pl. II). The broken piece is 0.30 m. thick, has a maximum width of 0.64 m. and is pierced with a hole 0.24 m. in diameter. Mortar was attached to the stone and it would seem that this pierced block was once fixed within a part of the tomb as a tethering stone; adjoining the room where this pierced stone was found is a large columned hall (Davies, 1901: pl. I).

Yvonne Harpur (1987: 57) suggests that scenes of men leading oxen on the walls of entrance doorways and interior scenes of men overthrowing an ox imply animals were taken into the tomb to be sacrificed. Salima Ikram (1995: 84), however, sees potential problems with bringing an animal within the mastaba: "The tethering-stone in the tomb of Mereruka would imply that a sacrificial beast was tethered and offered in the chapel. This would be difficult from a practical point of view as the room is pillared, and wrestling a fully grown ox to the ground and slaughtering it would require more space for manoeuvring. If it were a calf the operation might be performed more easily in the constrained space. It seems most likely that the animal was brought into the chapel, presented as an offering, and then removed outside and killed or perhaps turned over to the funerary priests to dispose of as a sacrifice at a later date." Mereruka's tomb has an exceptionally complex design and one should consider how less difficult it would be to lead an animal into the open courts or columned halls inside the mastabas within the Unas Cemetery. In all cases these ceremonial rooms adjoin the entrance chamber or are connected by a straight corridor. It would be quite possible to bring a young animal within a few rooms before restraining for slaughter in the courtyard or columned hall.

Harpur (1987: 57) comments that butchery scenes are also shown on several entrance walls in association with statue-dragging and might represent part of another ceremony that took place outside the tomb: "The combination of these activities suggests a sacrifice made before the statue of the deceased, prior to its passage through the chapel and enclosure within the serdab." Eyre (2002: 187-188) makes reference to a tethering stone found in a forecourt outside of the tomb complex of Seshemnefer and Tjeti at Giza and suggests that sacrifice took place outside of the tomb. Indeed, it could be that animals were sacrificed in different parts of the tomb complex depending on the ceremony. Eyre (2002: 187-188) concludes: "...it seems characteristic that a place of slaughter is situated very close to the place of offerings, and forms a part of the ritual complex. In a private funeral, a sacrifice seems to have taken place at the entrance to the tomb or in front of the false-door/stela, and cult at the tomb envisages sacrifice at the point of offering."

Staircases within multi-roomed mastabas are often located within or near an open courtyard or columned hall, but the function is not clear (Jánosi, 1999: 34).

Tomb owner	Staircase location
Ptahhotep I [D 62]	off columned hall
Nebet	separate corridor
Khenut	separate corridor
Niankhba	columned hall
Nebkauhor	columned hall
Seshseshet Idut	separate corridor
Ankhmahor	open courtyard with a portico
Neferseshemre Sheshi	columned hall
Kagemni	separate corridor
Mereruka (within Wa'tetkhethor section)	open courtyard with a portico

The function of stairs within mastabas might be associated with slaughtering activities taking place within or outside the tomb proper. Like within the pyramid temple of Raneferef the stairs could provide access to the roof for meat to be dried in the sun, as discussed by Verner (1994: 151-153) and Eyre (2002: 182). If prepared meats were to be presented as offerings it is reasonable to suppose that some of the preparations could take place within the tomb (just like in the temple) and that the meat was then distributed to the staff of the mortuary cult.

A funeral scene within the mastaba of Niankhkhnum and Khnumhotep contains a representation of the final part of the ceremony that Bolshakov (1997: 101) calls, "standing on the tomb". He (Bolshakov, 1997: 101) noted the high frequency of funeral scenes located near stairs, an open courtyard or a columned hall. John Wilson refers to a similar scene within the Giza tomb of Debehen that depicts offering bearers ascending the roof of a tomb, which he (Wilson, 1944: 213, pl. XVIII) translates as "standing on the roof for invocation-offerings". Wilson asserts that the ceremony would be repeated as part of the mortuary cult of the deceased. This implies that courtyards and columned halls are not only places for periodic ceremonies (especially festivals) but also associated with gatherings of family members ascending the roof to watch the coffin be lowered into the burial chamber through a shaft. This does pose the question of how a coffin was lowered within a roofed hall (were the roofing slabs left off until after the burial?). Roth (2002: 107) discusses another ceremony that took place on the roof of the tomb, associated with the lowering of statues within the serdab, suggesting another function for a staircase.

6.2. Storerooms for the Mortuary Cult

Within some multi-roomed mastabas the mortuary cult of the owner was maintained by staff organised using a phyle system, described by Roth (1991: 91-118) as a 'passing phenomenon' in her review of non-royal phyles in the Old Kingdom. Based on the criteria listed below Roth identified thirty individuals who established a mortuary cult that was run by using this system:

- Monumental copies of mortuary cult legal documents that make reference to phyles.
- References to phyles by name and titles of cult functionaries found within tomb scenes.
- A complex of five storerooms within a tomb.

The arrangement of storerooms for the mortuary cult is clearly visible in the architecture of multi-roomed mastaba tombs, an innovation that appeared during the second half of the 5th Dynasty (figures 6.1-6.3) (Bárta, 2005: 113). Within the Unas Cemetery the tombs of the queens Nebet and Khenut, and the vizier Nebkauhor, contained a set of five storerooms indicating the use of a phyle system. This was an extravagance which imitated the architecture of pyramid temples and trespassed on the mortuary cult prerogatives of the king. Storerooms in sets of five and ten can be seen in royal mortuary temples from the reign of Khafre (Brinks, 1979: pl. 7). Each storeroom belonged to individual phyles of *kꜣ*-priests that worked on a five month cycle of rotation. However, in some cases each phyle was divided into two groups, creating ten groups of *kꜣ*-priests working in a ten month cycle, like the system used in royal cults (Roth, 1991: 116). The cult personnel worked in rotation and included: inspectors of the *kꜣ*-priests (*sḥḏw ḥmw-kꜣ*), *kꜣ*-priests (*ḥm-kꜣ*) and scribes of the phyle (*sš n zꜣ*) - a title sometimes shared with that of *ḥm-Kꜣ*, suggesting one priest held two roles (Roth, 1991: 113). We only have a narrow understanding of how private mortuary cults functioned when cult personnel were subdivided in a phyle system. Roth (1991: 111) surmises that the system was adopted by non-royal individuals as an expression of wealth and status. The copying of a royal system can be considered alongside tomb designs being inspired by nearby architectural styles and artists repeating detailed decoration schemes, It was a costly practice and unsurprisingly all of the known Memphite tombs with an arrangement of five storerooms belong to members of the royal family and highest officials (two queens and five viziers): queens Nebet and Khenut (Munro, 1993a:

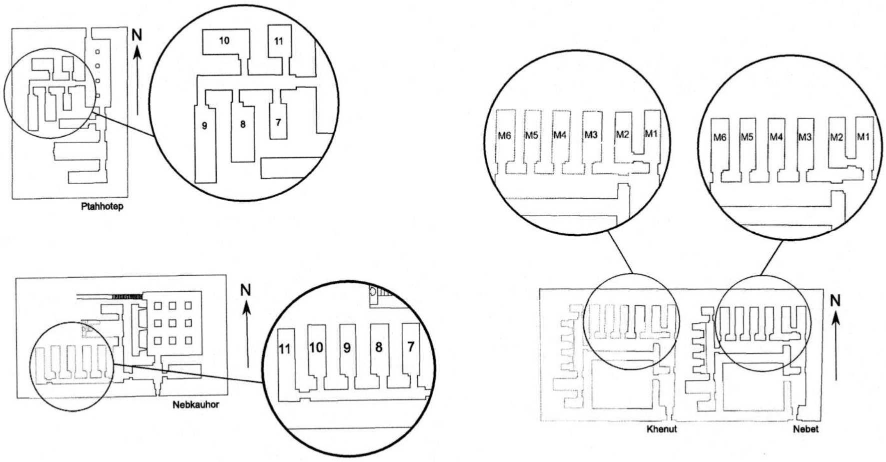

Figure 6.1. Storerooms in the tombs of Khenut, Nebet and Nebkauhor.

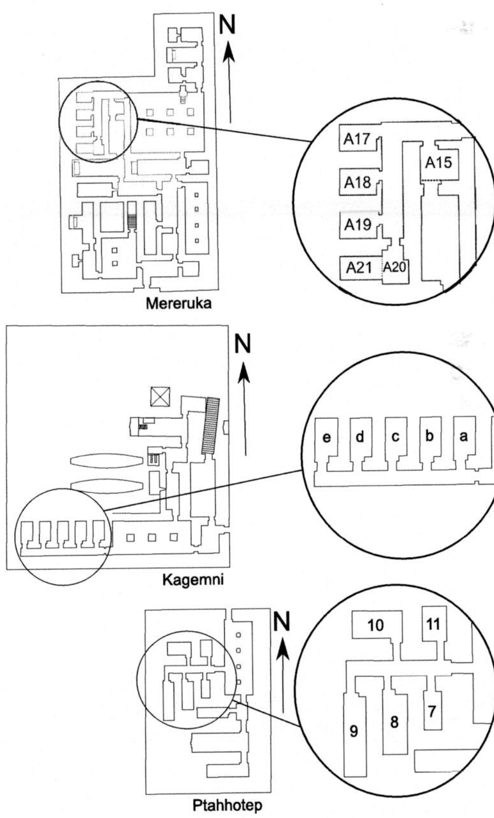

Figure 6.2. Storerooms in the tombs of Mereruka, Kagemni and Ptahhotep (LS 31).

Figure 6.3. Storerooms in the tombs of Ptahshepses at Abusir.

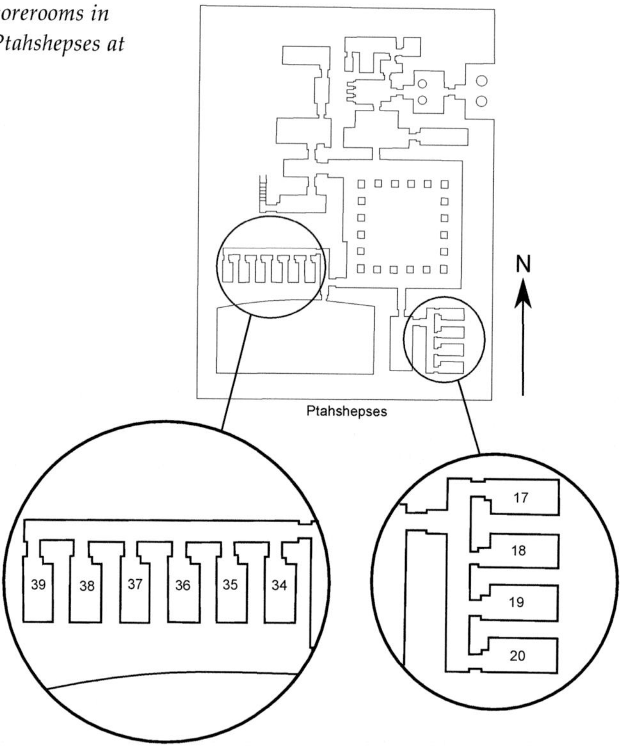

insert 2); Ptahshepses (Verner, 1994: 175); Ptahhotep (LS 31) (Lepsius, 1849: 42); Nebkauhor (usurped from Akhethotep/Hemi; Hassan, 1975a: fig. 1); Kagemni (Firth & Gunn, 1926a: pl. 51); and Mereruka (Duell, 1938: pl. 2).

During the clearance of the tomb of Nebkauhor, a broken limestone lintel was found on the corridor floor outside a storeroom (Hassan, 1938: 514; 1975a: 59, pl. XLVIII[D]). The lower part of the block was inscribed with two rows of text:

"Storeroom of the *nḏs* phyle, under the direction of the dignitary, the elder of the hall, the inspector of the *kꜣ*-priests, Bebi.

The assistant inspector of the *kꜣ*-priests, Imi."

The lintels above the five storerooms in the tomb of Mereruka are labelled with the name of each separate phyle (Duell, 1938: pl. 199 B). As in the label from the tomb of Nebkauhor each room is called *šnꜥ*, which has variously been translated as 'storehouse' (Faulkner, 1962: 269) or 'magazine' (Gardiner, 1957: 517). The purpose of the rooms was to provide a separate storeroom for a particular phyle of priests. But what else do we know about the function of each individual room? In his review of the components of the Old Kingdom tomb Bolshakov (1997: 25) clearly explains the difference between storage rooms of the earliest examples and magazines within tombs: "Storerooms of the classical Old Kingdom were intended for keeping equipment and victuals priests made use of for officiating their services; thus, they were functionally quite different from earlier magazines filled with items supposed to be used by the deceased himself, mainly food." He

(Bolshakov, 1997: 91) continues to consider the designation of the storerooms in the tombs of Mereruka and Nebkauhor as '*šnʿ* houses' and compares them to the '*šnʿ* houses' found within households of the Old Kingdom elite: "Such a designation is quite reasonable because storerooms were intended for keeping and perhaps for preparing food offerings, and so they had the same functions in the tomb as the '*šnʿ* houses' in the nobleman's household." In this consideration Bolshakov also includes the singular storerooms attached as a side-room to offering rooms in tombs dating between Unas and Pepi I (Harpur, 1987: 108). It is these storerooms that are sometimes decorated with processions of offering-bearers and registers of vessels and carrying chests that will be considered below. In all known storeroom complexes intended for the use of phyles there is no wall decoration and we should regard the functions of these two different types of storerooms separately. The design of the phyle storerooms in mastabas imitates those of the pyramid temples. Deep stone shelves in the storerooms in the pyramid temple of Pepy II divided the rooms horizontally into two levels (Leclant, 1977: pl. 11; 1979: pls. 6-7; 1982: pl. 50; 1983: pl. 22). The design can be traced to the 5th Dynasty pyramid temples of Sahura, Raneferef and Nyuserra at Abusir where the storerooms were built with an upper storey.

6.3. Storerooms in Pyramid Temples

In the pyramid temple of the 5th Dynasty king Sahura, the northern storerooms are arranged on both sides of a long north-south orientated corridor accessed by a lockable door off a single columned hall (labelled 'A' in figure 6.4). There are five doorways, which are built from granite and positioned equally on opposite sides of the corridor. Above each doorway is an inscription labelling the room, and on the thickness of each doorway were remains of door fastening features (Borchardt, 1910: fig. 75). A hole within the wall indicates that the doors were fastened in place by a rope wrapped around the door and a knob that sat within the hole positioned in the doorway wall. Each storeroom has a floor area of 4-6 m^2 and is split into two floors with stairs leading to an upper storey. Each floor is c. 2.50 m in height, this being half the height of the outside corridor (figure 6.5). The second unit of storerooms (labelled 'B' in figure 6.4) were interpreted by Borchardt (1910: 22-24) as a facility for storing less valuable commodities as the doorways contain no door fastening features, with just one lockable door at the entrance to the corridor. In these storerooms the staircase is located at the front and is accessed from the corridor (figure 6.6). Borchardt (1910: 22-24) notes that the stairs are very steep and that there was no evidence of a wall between the top floor rooms and the corridor and proposes that the space was filled by a low stone wall or railings. However, it seems more plausible that these upper-storeys were not roofed and that they served a function as a space for drying meat from the slaughterhouse.

The storerooms within the pyramid temple of Raneferef are arranged in two units: one at the north and another at the south-east. The temple complex was built in mudbrick and some of the storerooms contained preserved lower parts of staircases, which are arranged in the same manner as within the northern storerooms

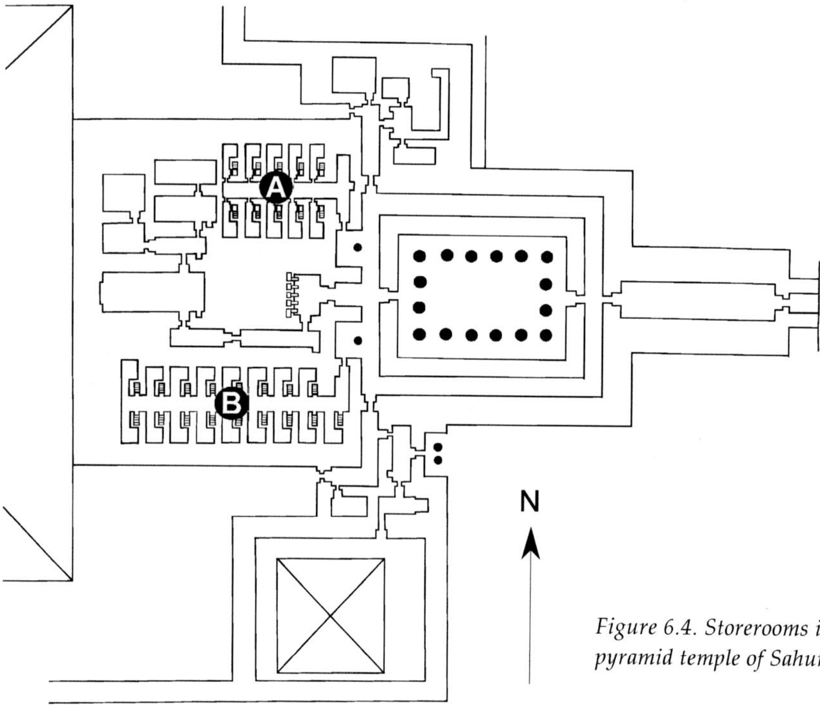

Figure 6.4. Storerooms in the pyramid temple of Sahura.

in the mortuary temple of Sahura. The second storey of these mudbrick storerooms was presumably a wooden platform. Eyre (2002: 183) considers the rooms' use for food preparation: "To the south of the vestibule a central corridor is flanked by six pairs of long, narrow rooms, probably all roofed with mud-brick vaults. In some of these rooms the preservation of staircases suggests the existence of light wooden platforms at half the height of the room, comparable to the arrangements for hanging meat seen in both the model of Meketre and in tomb scenes. Remains of mud-brick benches in some rooms are more likely to represent storage than working fixtures, although deposits of ashes and some traces of hearths in these storerooms might imply some cooking (or drying or even smoking of meat)" A staircase is located on the corridor of the south-east group of storerooms and Verner (1994: 150-154) connects the function of this staircase with the associated 'Sanctuary of the Knife' area and proposes that this gave access to the roof where the meat would be dried out. It is not entirely impossible that the upper-storeys of these storerooms were a walled small open area for the drying out of meat in the sun or other methods of meat preparation (*cf.* Eyre, 2002: 181-190). This type of storeroom design continues into the Middle Kingdom mortuary temples of Senusret I: "The western part of a mortuary temple ordinarily contains four groups of two to five elongated chambers each with two floors and therefore having rather low ceilings. These rooms are considered to be magazines." (Arnold, 1988: 49). Arnold (1988: 49-50) considers that because of the height of the second shelf a wooden ladder would have been needed to reach this upper level of the room. With each phyle being divided into two divisions in royal mortuary cults it is sensible

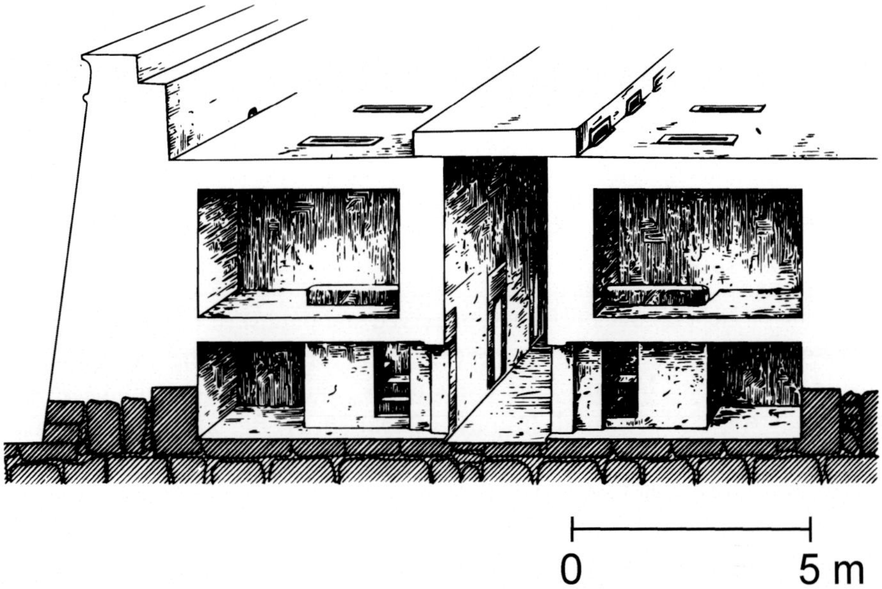

Figure 6.5. Borchart's reconstruction the north group of storerooms (A) in the pyramid temple of Sahura. From: Borchardt (1910: fig. 17).

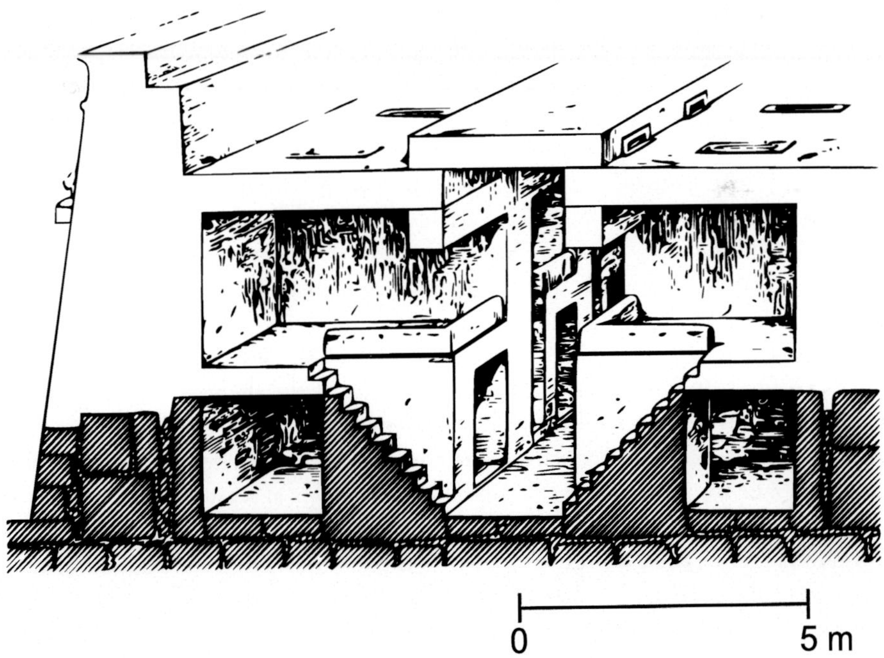

Figure 6.6. Borchart's reconstruction the north group of storerooms (B) in the pyramid temple of Sahura. From: Borchardt (1910: fig. 19).

to assume that the shelf divided the room allowing for two divisions to share the room in an organised manner. The design was also adopted in the storerooms of some private tombs in the Old Kingdom and it is a feature Roth (1991: 101) regards as typical for phyle storerooms of this time.

6.4. Tombs with Five Storerooms

6.4.1. The Tomb of Nebet

The tomb of Nebet is one of the best preserved and published tombs in the Unas Cemetery, providing excellent evidence for the use of shelving in storerooms (figure 6.1). Rooms M1-M6 form a row of six storerooms all of similar size at the northern end of the tomb (Munro, 1993a: 33-34, fig. 2, 4, insert 2). The rooms have to be passed to reach the stairs, statue niches and offering-room with attached side-room. M1 and M2 are accessed via a doorway 0.75 m. in width at the northern end of Room B. M2 is connected to M1 by a doorway of the same width, at the south end of the west wall. The doorways for M3-M6 are all evenly positioned along the north room of a long east-west corridor 11.25 m. in length and 2.15 m. in width. The doorways are of a similar size with a maximum width of 0.75 m., and all 0.80 m. deep. The fastening methods of the doors are discussed in Chapter 5. All doors in M2-M6 were pivoted in the south-west corner of the room and opened outwards against the west wall. The recess of each doorway is c. 1.10 m. in width and c. 0.10 m. deep. The height of each doorways is c. 1.58 m., with the rooms being c. 3.70 m. in height. In rooms M2-M6 blocks of stone have been used to span across the width of the room providing a shelf. Each shelf is positioned between 1.40-1.50 m. above floor level, with the depth varying between 3.05-3.20 m. The stone block shelves are between 0.30-0.50 m. in thickness and set between the second and third courses of masonry of the east and west walls. In a section drawing of M3 it can be seen that the shelf is not a level surface and that the central block is shallower than the other two (see figure 6.7) (Munro, 1993a: fig. 4 section D-D). Whether this is the same for the other storerooms and a functional feature of the shelving is not stated.

The shelves occupy an area which spans over about two thirds of the room, leaving a space of c. 0.70 m. from the edge of the door when in the full open position. The top edge of the shelf in all storerooms is at least 2.00 m. above the floor. If the function of the shelves was to be a surface to support objects then some form of ladder or stool would be needed to access objects that were stored further back from the edge of the shelf; indeed, it would be perverse to construct such a deep shelf if all of the surface area was not needed. The minimum distance between the top of the shelves and the ceilings in all the rooms is between 1.80-1.90 m., a height that would be sufficient to allow a person to stand upright. It can be seen that the shelving essentially creates a mezzanine level within the storeroom. This may or may not be related to the phyle being divided into two groups; it might just be better use of space within the storeroom or a method to zone off areas for very separate purposes or activities. The lack of shelving in M1 suggests a different

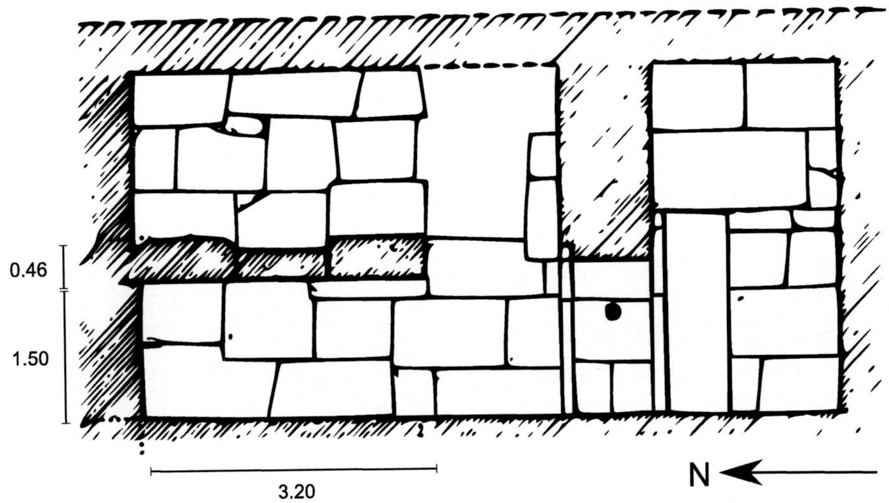

Figure 6.7. Cross-section of a storeroom in the tomb of Nebet. Dimensions in metres. From: Munro (1993a: pl. 4).

purpose for this room, and may imply a different status of M2, that is joined with M1 by a doorway and is separate from the other four storerooms. Being the largest and at the end of the corridor this could be the principle storeroom used by the first phyle (*imi-wrt*), as is often the case (Roth, 1991: 18, 37-40). The dimensions of M1 and M2 in the adjoining tomb of Khenut are comparable with that of the analogous rooms in the tomb of Nebet; and the surviving trace of the floor plan also suggests the same for the other four storerooms (Munro, 1993a: insert 2).

6.4.2. The Tomb of Nebkauhor

The storerooms in Nebkauhor's tomb similarly arranged in a linear design as in the tombs of Nebet and Khenut (figure 6.1), but follow more closely the layout of storerooms in the pyramid temple of Niuserra in Abusir (Brinks, 1979: pl. 15). All five storerooms are located at the south side of the tomb, accessed from a narrow east-west corridor, 9.80 m. in length and 1.00 m. wide (figure 6.8). The storeroom doorways are all of a similar size with a maximum width of 0.67 m. The masonry in Rooms 10 and 11 is better preserved, with the height of each doorway being c. 1.50 m. Lintels above each doorway may have been inscribed with a phyle name, as one example was found during the clearance of the tomb (discussed above). Room 10 is the better preserved of the northern row of storerooms and Hassan (1975a: 60) describes it as being built from masonry courses of both local and 'white' limestone and surviving to a height of 1.50 m. Interestingly Hassan (1975a: 39-40). describes 'roofing slabs' that were left *in situ* in this storeroom and storeroom 9 at the east: "[Storeroom 9] was originally roofed with large slabs of white limestone, two of the northernmost of these remain *in situ*. Above this chamber, there was originally another one of the same dimensions, which was also used as a store. The walls of this chamber are now very dilapidated...

[storeroom 10] was also roofed with large limestone slabs, two of which, measuring 1.50 m. long and 0.38 m. thick, remain *in situ* at its northern end." With only 'roofing slabs' being positioned *in situ* at the northern end of the storeroom, at the same distance from the south wall, it is incorrect to consider these narrow blocks as roofing. Like in the tomb of Nebet (and Khenut) these are stone shelves that only spanned the northernmost end of the storerooms and this is why no further 'slabs' were found *in situ* in the storerooms. It seems Hassan considered the whole of the storeroom to be roofed and a second storey above provided another storeroom of the same dimensions. It is unclear if he considered the entrance to this second storey being from the corridor, or from a second storey corridor directly above. One plate in the publication of Hassan's clearance of the storerooms shows Rooms 8-10 and the doorway and rear of the east wall of Room 11 (Hassan, 1975a: pl. XLVII). The walls of Rooms 7-8 have not survived to the same height as the other three storerooms but there are no shelving blocks *in situ*. This is likely because the walls only survive to the height that the shelving blocks would have been placed upon. The published photograph illustrates how the shelves were positioned in place and gives an indication of their size: the two blocks laid next to each other give a shelf with a depth of at least 1.70 m. that covers just under half of the room length. The walls between each storeroom are constructed from two outer casings of limestone blocks with a central filling of rubble (figure 6.8). The shelving blocks are positioned upon the tops of the third course of masonry. The top of the shelving meets with the height of the doorways (c. 1.50 m.) and with a thickness of c. 0.40 m. this would have allowed for space of c. 1.10 m. beneath the shelving (*cf.* the storerooms in the tomb of Nebet which are c. 1.50 m. above floor level). The maximum height in the corridor is c. 2.84 m.; it would be reasonable to

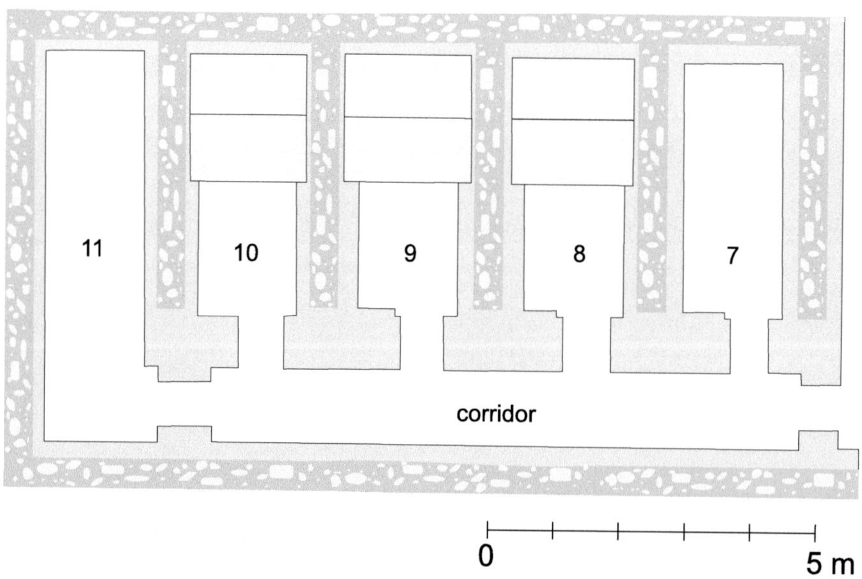

Figure 6.8. Rooms 7-11 in the tomb of Nebkauhor.

assume that the ceiling height of this corridor was the same as that of the ceilings within the storerooms and provides a minimum height of at least 1.34 m. above the shelving (*cf.* the tomb of Nebet, c. 1.80 m.).

However, it would seem unusual if not all storerooms contained a stone shelf like those *in situ* in Rooms 9-10. There was shelving in all five storerooms within the tombs of Kagemni and Nebet, which are all of a similar linear design. A photograph in Hassan's publication of Nebkauhor's tomb (1975a: pl. XLVII) shows that there could have been stone shelving in Room 8 and the east wall of Room 7 does not survive to a height sufficient to support a shelf. Hassan does not mention any shelving in Room 11, though there is also less information provided about this room, suggesting that it was less well recorded (Hasan, 1975a: 59). Indeed, no mention is made of the north wall, so this is possibly missing and consequently it is likely that the shelving would have been removed too. The walls between each storeroom are constructed of two facings of limestone blocks and a rubble core filling, like Type 3 in Arnold's classification of masonry in freestanding walls (see figure 3.1) (Arnold, 1991: fig. 4.72). The blocks are dressed on the exposed front and the sides, but the rear of the block is left rough. The wall between the storerooms and the corridor is constructed in a different method using thicker blocks that span the width of the wall, like Arnold's Type 2 in his classification of freestanding walls (Arnold, 1991: fig. 4.72). The doorframes are constructed from whole blocks that have been cut at the corners to create the recess style of the doorways.

6.4.3. The Tomb of Kagemni

The tomb of Kagemni began to be cleared by a team directed by Jacques de Morgan in 1893, followed by work under the direction of Victor Loret between 1897 and 1899. However, the full extent of the tomb was not realised until after the clearance of the entrance and the substantial western extent of the tomb by a team working for Cecil Firth between 1920 and 1926 (von Bissing, 1905; 1911; Firth & Gunn, 1926a: 20-23). Firth's work uncovered a linear series of five storerooms all located on the north side of a long east-west corridor. The storerooms are described as being originally in two storeys but there is no further detail or illustration of this feature. Each storeroom is about 2.20 m. in length and 1.50 m. in width, although this is only an approximation taken from Firth and Gunn's published plan (Firth & Gunn, 1926b: pl. 51). The upper courses of the storerooms are not preserved and it is not known if the lintels of the doorway were inscribed like in the neighbouring tomb of Mereruka. However, considering the similar design of the storerooms and the proximity of Mereruka it would be surprising if the same system of labelling the storerooms was not employed (Roth, 1991: 103). Details about door pivots or fastening features are absent from the report.

6.4.4. The Tomb of Mereruka

Five storerooms are arranged in a group in the north-west corner of this tomb complex (figure 6.2; Kanawati *et al.*, 2010: 33-41). The rooms are all of a similar proportion and are accessed from an L-shaped corridor 1.15 m. in width that has an entrance at the north-west corner of the columned hall. Some time after this part of the tomb was built and decorated a doorway was made between storeroom A15 and Room A9. The storeroom remains undecorated and it is unclear if this doorway altered the function of the room turning it into more of a thoroughfare. Indeed, Duell (1938: 9) considers that the reason has more to do with the symbolic functionality of the tomb: "a doorway was cut through the north wall into Storeroom A15, possibly to give the ka of Mereruka access to Chapel A13 and its altar through the doorway in its west wall." There are remains of a stone shelf 1.60 m. above floor level in A15, which once spanned the east side of the room (Duell, 1938: 8; Kanawati *et al.*, 2010: 40). The west wall of Room A20 was cut away to extend the room/ This area was labelled separately as Room A21 by Duell (1938: pl. 1). This alteration to the plan might be connected with the changes that were made by connecting Room A9 and Room A15. If the function of Room A15 was altered to that of a corridor it was no longer a secure room and thus not suitable for a phyle storeroom. To create more storage space Room A20 would have been the sensible choice to extend as there were no rooms occupying space to the west of it.

6.4.5. The Tomb of Ptahhotep (LS 31)

The tomb of Ptahhotep (figures 6.2, 6.9-6.10) was recorded by Lepsius, who numbered it LS 31, but since his work in the 1840s the tomb has once again been buried beneath sand and the exact position is unknown (Lepsius, 1849: 42; Porter & Moss, 1981: 653-654). According to Lepsisus's map the tomb is located approximately 320 m. south of the enclosure wall of the Step Pyramid Complex, and a short distance north of New Kingdom tombs of Ra'ia (LS 28) and Harmin (LS 29) (Lepsius, 1849: 33). Inscribed texts within the columned entrance hall provide information on the career of Ptahhotep who held the office of vizier. Porter and Moss (1981: 653) date this tomb to the middle 5th Dynasty or later. The east-west offering room (Room 4) has an attached side-room (Room 5), an architectural arrangement quite typical of the late 5th to early 6th Dynasty.

To the west of a large columned hall (Room 1) is a narrow east-west corridor (Room 6) that gives access to five irregular shaped rooms. Room 9 being the largest (5.00 m N-S x 1.94 m E-W) and Room 11 the smallest (2.09 m. N-S x 1.35 m. E-W). Although not of uniform shape the number, and the presence of shelving within all five rooms, suggests that they were used as storerooms for phyles of priests (Roth, 1991: 95). Roth (1991: 95) notes that the rooms are of an irregular size and shape but considers that they are storerooms: "Though the rooms are quite large, they seem to have been undecorated, or at least no decoration was recorded. The arrangement of the rooms is reminiscent of the storerooms in the mastaba of *mrrw-k3*. It seems likely that they were storerooms, and their number indicates the presence of a phyle system."

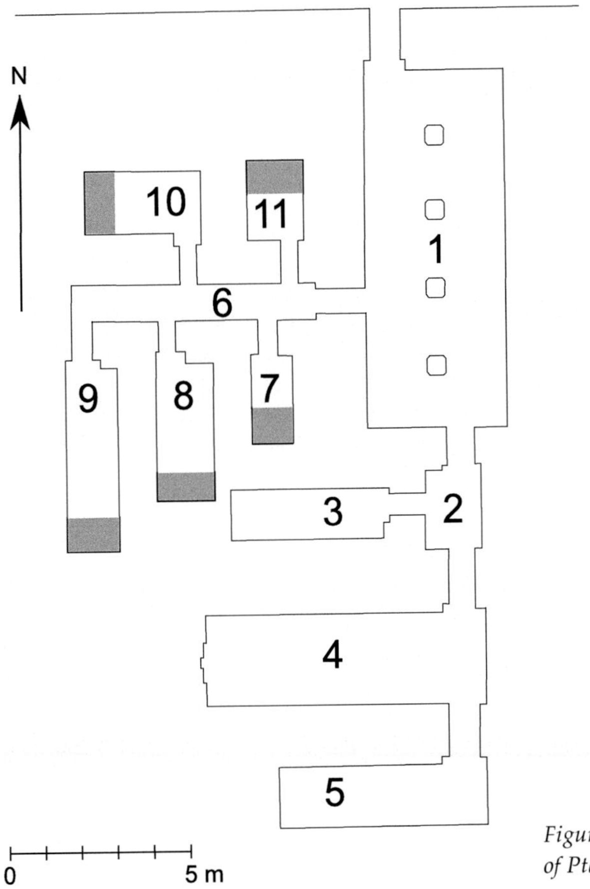

Figure 6.9. Rooms 7-11 in the tomb of Ptahhotep (LS 31).

A cross-section of the tomb reveals the height of the shelving, which is positioned just below the height of the doorways (figure 6.10). The shelving in Room 10 is 0.17 m. thick with a space of 1.30 m. between the shelf and the ceiling. In Room 11 there is a space of 1.29 m. between the top of the shelf and the ceiling. Lepsius's (1849: 42) drawing suggests the shelving is constructed from stone and incorporated into the masonry of the walls.

Having one room much larger than the others is not unusual in the design of phyle storerooms. Indeed, Roth (1991: 18, 37-40) states that the larger storage room was a feature of the first phyle (*imi-wrt*), which often had the largest storeroom (*e.g.*, in the mastaba of Mereruka). There is no doubt that these five storerooms were made to serve the needs of a priesthood organised into a phyle system. Indeed, the tomb design is particularly impressive and the mastaba warrants further study.

6.5. Tombs with Less than Five Storerooms

In Roth's (1991) review of private individuals with phyle systems eight owners are identified by the tomb design: *i.e.*, the presence of five store-rooms arranged in a unit. The other tomb owners in Roth's inventory of thirty individuals are identified as having a phyle system by other means – textual references. Not all of

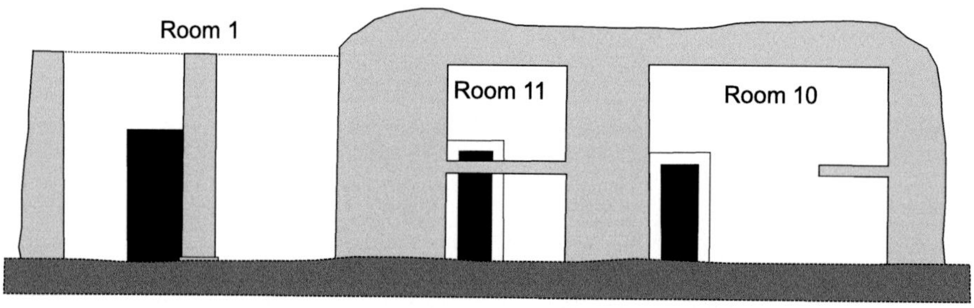

Figure 6.10. Cross-section of the tomb of Ptahhotep (LS 31) showing shelving in Rooms 10-11.

the tombs of these individuals have been identified but many are known. Of these that are known there is nothing distinctive in the plan of the tombs that reveals a phyle system was used. Indeed, the tomb of Nyankhkhnum and Khnumhotep, located underneath the Unas causeway in the east part of the Unas Cemetery, is identified as having used a phyle system by a textual source: a monumental copy of a legal text relating to the mortuary cult being organised into phyles (Roth, 1991: 99). There is only really one room within the tomb that can be easily identified as a storeroom, which is an undecorated rectangular room located on the south side of Room II (Porter & Moss, 1981: plan LXVI). This, and other tombs included in Roth's dataset, asserts that a phyle system could be used within a private mortuary cult without needing multiple storerooms. Other tombs that have more than one storeroom for cult personnel and which may also have had a phyle system, not recorded in documentation, will be discussed below.

6.5.1. The Tomb of Khentika

Khentika's tomb (figure 6.11) lies to the north of the enclosure wall of the pyramid complex of Teti and is a good example of the complexity of multi-roomed mastaba architecture (James, 1953). At the centre of the tomb is a long columned hall (Room 9) that provides access to three undecorated rooms of similar shape and size (Rooms 10-12), all of which are entered from doorways positioned on the southern wall. There is good reason to believe that all three rooms served as storerooms. Room 12 no longer retains its original shape as a later burial shaft was cut through this part of the tomb; the original dimensions of this room almost match those of the other two rooms (2.64 x 1.45 m.) (James, 1953: 29, fig. 11). Rooms 10-12 are approximately the same size (2.62 x 1.38 m. and 2.65 x 1.49 m. respectively) and both contain shelving that James's (1953: 29) describes as, "a shelf of stone built out of the wall at the south end". One might expect these stone shelves to be supported between two courses of the masonry, like in the tomb of Nebet. The depth of the shelf in Room 10 is 0.89 m., with the one in Room 11 having a much shorter depth of 0.31 m. These shelves are narrower than the preserved examples discussed previously. At whatever height they were positioned they are not the type of shelving to create a mezzanine level. The shelving here provides the purpose of supporting objects at a height above ground against the wall rather than splitting the rooms up into two areas. The doorways within Rooms 10-12

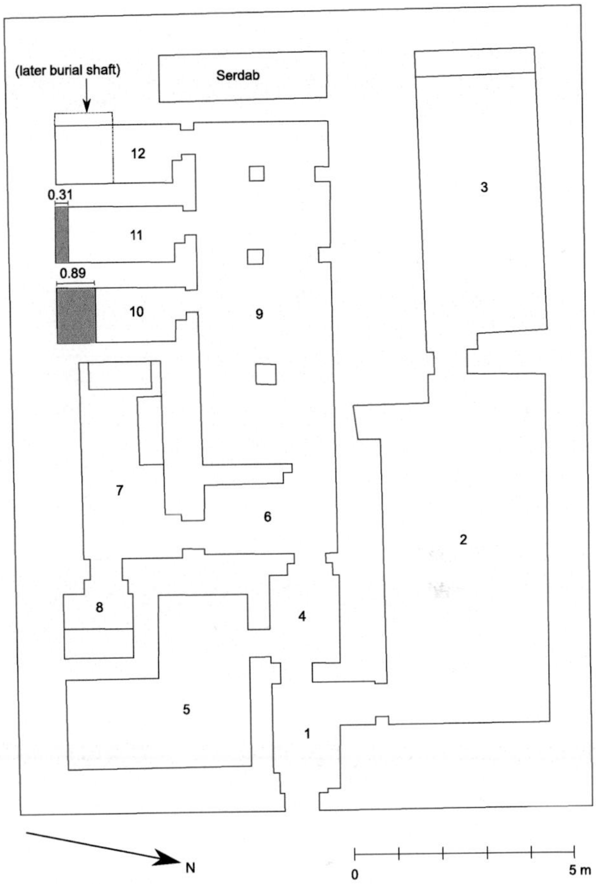

Figure 6.11. Rooms 10-12 in the tomb of Khentika.

are all approximately 0.60 m. in width and 0.20 m. deep, and set within a recess c. 0.90 m. wide and 0.20 m. deep. Wooden doors would have been pivoted at the west side of the doorway, within the north-west corner of the room and would have opened outwards against the west wall. The door fastening methods for these rooms is one popularly used in storerooms whereby a rope attached to the door is passed through a hole cut diagonally through the corner of the outer doorframe (discussed in Chapter 5).

6.5.2. The Tomb of Seshseshet Idut

The arrangement of storerooms in the mastaba of Seshseshet Idut (figure 6.12) in the Unas Cemetery is very similar to those in the mastaba of Ptahhotep (LS 31; figure 6.9). Seshseshet Idut's mastaba consists of nine rooms, some of which are described as magazines by the excavator, Cecil Firth (Firth, 1927: 107). The tomb was built for a vizier called Ihy, probably in the reign of Unas, but inscriptions and decoration were later changed for a king's daughter called Seshseshet Idut during the reign of Teti (Kanawati, 1977: 13, 152 no. 36; Munro, 1993a: 4; Strudwick, 1985: 63 no.15, 83 [under Ihy, no. 1]). Ihy's name is now only visible on one wall of the tomb, and on the sarcophagus in the burial chamber (Macramallah,

Figure 6.12. Rooms C-D in the tomb of Sesheseshet Idut. From: Macramallah (1935: pl. III B).

1935: 36-38). The usurpation of the tomb is important for understanding the layout and construction of some rooms. Reason for the usurpation is not fully known but as Harpur (1987: 38-39) observes the tomb was built in a prime location: "extremely well situated, close to the pyramid of a king no more than a few steps from the mastabas of queens and viziers." Kanawati (1977: 13) and Harpur (1987:65) date the construction of Ihy's tomb to late in the reign of Unas. This may account for the absence of a storeroom adjacent to the offering-room, a design feature that only grew in popularity in the 6th Dynasty. Furthermore, the orientation of the offering-room does not follow the typical 6th Dynasty east-west alignment and removes the false-door from a direct approach route, just as is done in the adjoining mastaba of Unasankh (figure 1.8). Close inspection of the plates within the publication by Macramallah (1935) reveals that there was shelving in Rooms C and D. Plate III B (Macramallah, 1935) shows a view of the east side of the tomb, and in the distance Rooms C and D can be seen with rectangular niches cut within the masonry of the east walls (figure 6.12). The niche in Room D is also visible in plate III A (Macramallah, 1935) which shows a view of the tomb from the south. Unfortunately there is no record of the shelving in the architectural report published by Kanawati and Abder-Raziq (2003).

Both niches are roughly of the same size and position within the wall. Based on published reports (Kanawati & Raziq, 2003; Macramallah, 1935) the length of each niche appears to occupy about two fifths of the wall, which would be approximately 0.70 m. The length covers the whole of the dividing wall between the two rooms, which is 1.40 m. The niches appear to be roughly 0.25 m. in height, which would correspond to the thickness of shelves that would have been slotted in place, about 1.80 m. below ceiling height. It cannot be seen if there are any similar recesses for shelving in Room A. The design of the storerooms with storage shelves, and their arrangement along a narrow corridor, suggests they were used by staff performing ritual services. Though the tomb only has three storerooms the planning is similar to storeroom complexes employed by a priesthood organised in a phyle system. There is no mention of a phyle system within the tomb inscriptions but various members of the mortuary cult personnel who worked in this tomb are named (Macramallah, 1935: 47). The artists responsible for adapting the decoration scheme within the tomb had to work with relief carvings that were made on a thick layer of plaster (*e.g.* Macramallah, 1935: pl. IV B). Macramallah (1935: 2) criticises the workmanship of these artists, but Harpur (1987: 38) acknowledges the difficulty of the task and does not believe poorer workmanship to be indicative of a late date for the re-appropriation work, but the result of working with a difficult medium. It is practical to consider what other alterations might be made to a tomb when it is usurped, in particular changes to the architectural design of the structure. There is some plausible evidence that the storerooms were a later adaptation to the tomb plan by Ihy or by Seshseshet Idut, as part of her appropriation of the tomb. The wall between Rooms C and D is composed of one thickness of blocks, unlike other walls in the mastaba where there is a core of rubble masonry held within two dressed facings of limestone blocks, like Type 3 in Arnold's classification masonry in freestanding walls (Arnold, 1991: fig. 4.72). The walls of the storeroom that meet with the wall that runs east-west are built against it and not bonded into it. Indeed, this is something noted on the architectural plan (Kanawati & Raziq, 2003pl. 53a-b), but there is no discussion of this peculiarity within the commentary. This building technique suggests that these walls are latter additions (*cf.* James, 1953: 16-17), and might reflect the desire for a more contemporary layout when the tomb was usurped, or were changes to the original plan whilst the tomb was being built for Ihy. The close parallels between the layout with the tomb of Unasankh, and to some extent the tomb of Iyneferet, prompt the thought that originally the tomb contained an open courtyard that was later converted for the purpose of accommodating a more elaborate arrangement for the service of the mortuary cult, something that was fashionable with the elite of the time.

6.5.3. The Tomb of Kairer

The lack of decoration and neat masonry within Room C in the tomb of Kairer (figure 6.13) strongly suggests this is a storeroom. At points along the north and south walls there are parallel holes carved within the blocks. The holes pass through the thickness of the blocks and are roughly the same size, varying between 0.09-0.12 m. in width. The holes on the north wall are all c. 1.50 m. above the (unpaved) floor level; and the two holes in the south wall are c. 1.40 m. above the (unpaved) floor level, with another 0.10 m. lower. On account of the shape and arrangement of these holes they are unlike the slots cut into walls for use as footholds in burial shafts sunk into mastaba superstructures for later burials, as

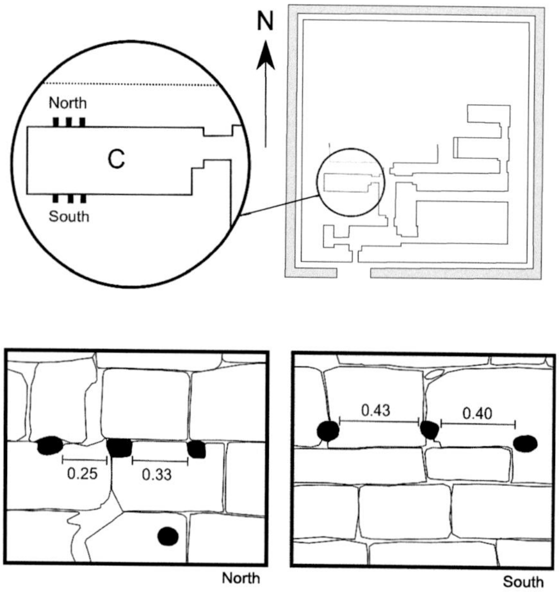

Figure 6.13. Room C in the tomb of Kairer.

seen in other Old Kingdom tombs (James, 1953: 3, 29, fig. 11; von Bissing, 1905: pl. III 4). The holes on each wall are roughly parallel with one another, which must be the result of some architectural reason that is now missing. Given the most likely function of the room being a storeroom for the personnel of Kairer's mortuary cult the purpose of these holes might be related to this function. The location of the holes at the end of the room would provide a suitable position for a shelf spanning the rear half of the room. The width of the holes and the spacing between them suggests that wooden poles may have been inserted into the carved sockets and used to support wooden shelving (figure 6.14). Shelving in similar multi-roomed mastabas is constructed from stone, but it is not improbable that wood could be used for the same purpose. Considering the low quantity of wooden architectural elements preserved within Memphite tombs (through agencies such as reuse, decomposition and removal during restoration) it is most unlikely that this form of shelving would ever survive in the archaeological record and socket holes are the only feature that reveals this technique.

6.5.4. The Tomb of Akhethotep and Ptahhotep (D 64)

In the late 5th Dynasty tomb of the viziers Ptahhotep [II], Akhethotep and his son Ptahhotep, to the west of the Step Pyramid Complex, the excavator, de Garis Davies (1901: 4, pl. I-II), describes an undecorated room with a shelf fitted across the width. Room 7 has a shelf 1.60 m. wide and 1.10 m. deep and is located at just over half the height of the room (figure 6.15). Inscriptions in the tomb mention holders of titles associated with phyles who performed the mortuary cults for Akhethotep and Ptahhotep (Roth,1991: 99-100). This is an example of a tomb without a complex of storerooms that used a phyle system. The shelving in Room 5 suggests its purpose as a storeroom. Perhaps this is the only storeroom for cult personnel, or at least the only storeroom that could be locked.

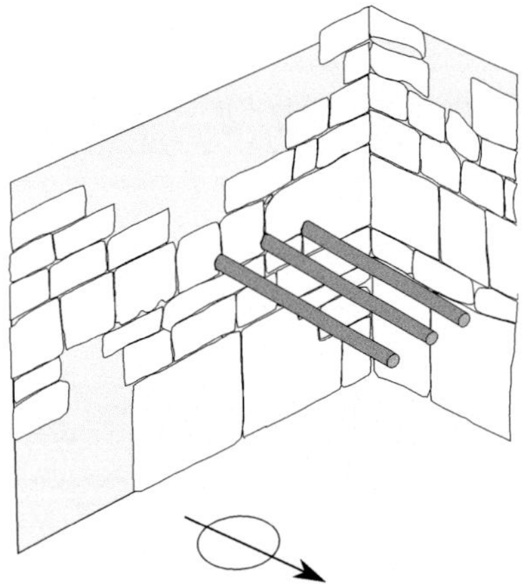

Figure 6.14. Reconstruction showing wooden shelving poles in Room C in the tomb of Kairer.

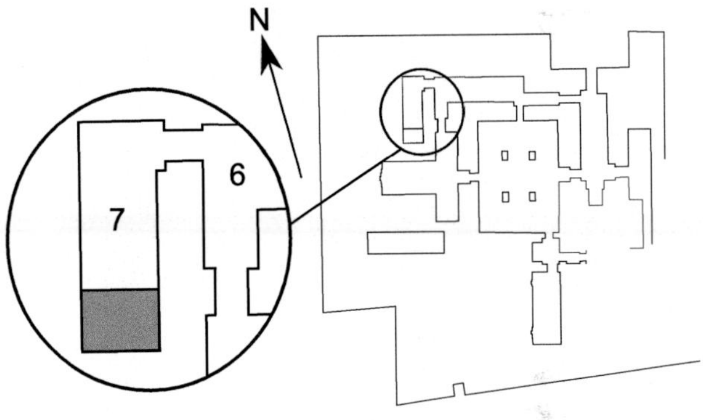

Figure 6.15. Room 7 in the tomb of Akhethotep and Ptahhotep (D 64).

Shelving is not unique to storerooms built in a complex of five rooms used by phyles of priests performing the mortuary cult. Evidence of shelving is seen in individual storerooms. The shelving in these storerooms indicates the different needs of these rooms compared to the storeroom adjacent to the offering-room. The identification of these rooms as storerooms seems certain so it should also be considered what purpose the shelves provided within the private tomb context. Was this just taking the architectural concept from the mortuary temples in its completeness? Possibly so for tombs with a complex of storerooms but the simplest explanation is the practical creation of space within a small room. Shelving at head height frees up floor space and utilises the height of the room. Some goods might also be best stored off the ground. But what other evidence do we have for these rooms? There are very few details about the contents of the phyle storerooms when they were uncovered during archaeological exploration. A rare example being the storerooms within the tomb of Seshseshet Idut that did contain finds which support the idea of temple-like ritual services carried out in the tomb. Room C contained over fifteen pottery vessels and in Room A was a flint knife (figure 6.15), 0.18 m. in length, characteristic of the type used in butchery (Macramallah, 1935: 5).

6.6. Storerooms Adjacent to Offering-Rooms

A long east-west offering room with false-door is a distinctive feature in the internal plans of multi-roomed mastaba tombs (Brinks, 1979: 46; Harpur, 1987: 106-110; Strudwick, 1985: 30-35). The design can be traced to the 5th Dynasty pyramid temple of Sahura at Abusir (Jánosi, 1999: 34; Stadelmann, 2010: 169-182, fig. 134). This arrangement of the false-door within the pyramid temple was further developed in the 5th Dynasty and became part of a standardised layout within the temple. From after the reign of Djedkara the approach to the false-door within an elongated east-west offering-room is through a single columned hall. Very little time elapsed before this form of offering-room was incorporated into non-royal architecture. The tomb of Persen at Saqqara appears to be the earliest known tomb to make the transition from north-south to east-west (Mariette, 1889: 299-301; Petrie & Murray, 1952: 8-10, pl. XIX; Strudwick, 1985: 30, fig. 2.e). Persen's tomb has previously been dated to the reign of Sahura but Bárta (2005: 122-125) believes a later date, in the reign or Nyuserra or slightly after, is more probable. Nyuserra's reign is a time marked by the reorganisation of central administration and innovation in non-royal

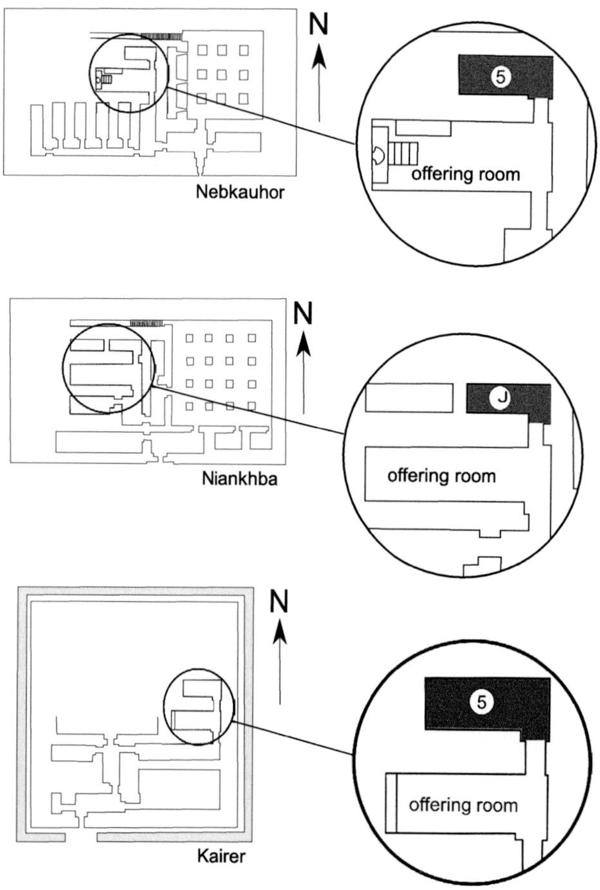

Figure 6.16. Offering-room storerooms in the tombs of Nebkauhor, Niankhba and Kairer.

architecture. As this architectural style spread in use further additions were added, such as a decorated storeroom adjacent to the offering-room. Harpur (1987: 108) included this 'fixed' feature within her study of the orientation and scene content of decoration in Old Kingdom tombs: "In a number of tombs dating between Unis and Pepy I, there is a square or rectangular storeroom, connected to the east-west offering room, which contains reliefs of slaughtered animals, oils, wine jars, and chests on sledges, sometimes being hauled by men."

The common understanding of the side-room is that it functioned as a storeroom, holding supplies required for use within the offering-room. An early example of a single storeroom, with a direct connection to an east-west offering-room, can be seen in the pyramid temple of Neferirkara (Brinks, 1979: 137-139, pls. 13-14). The adjoining tombs of queens Nebet and Khenut marks the transition of this type of storeroom in mastaba architecture, then picked up by high-ranking officials including Nebkauhor, Nyankhba, Neferseshemre, Kairer, Ptahhotep (LS 31), Kagemni, Khentika and Mereruka (including the complex within the tomb for his son, Meryteti) (figures 6.16-6.19). In the tombs of Nebet, Khenut and Ptahhotep (LS 31) the storeroom is located south of the

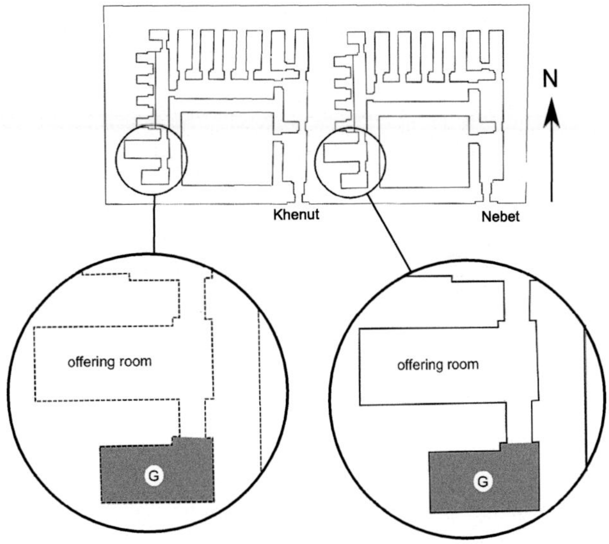

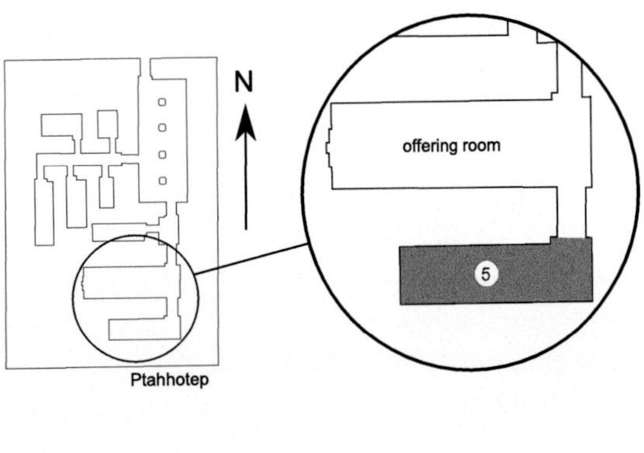

Figure 6.17. Offering-room storerooms in the tombs of Khenut, Nebet and Ptahhotep (LS 31).

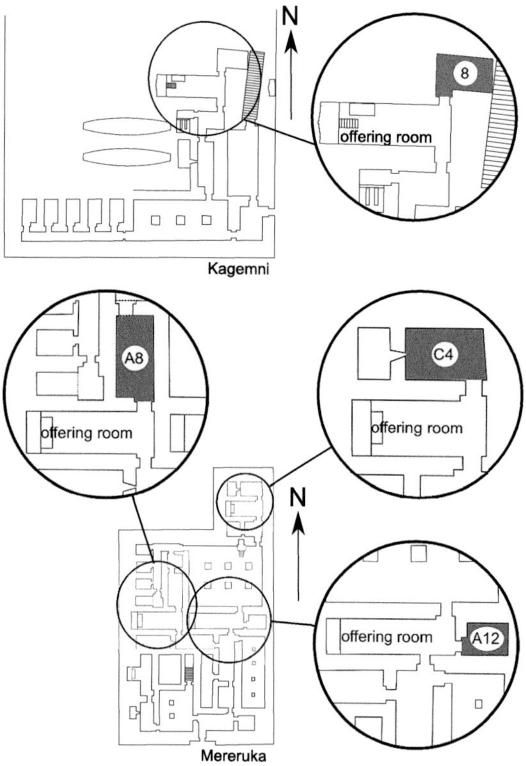

Figure 6.18. Offering-room storerooms in the tombs of Kagemni and Mereruka.

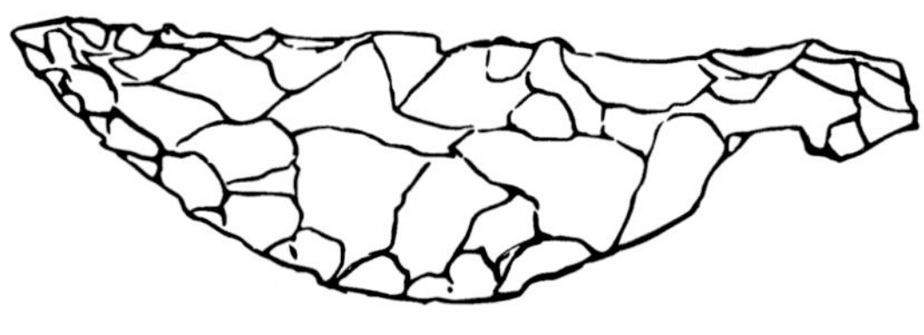

Figure 6.19. Knife from a storeroom in the tomb of Sesheseshet Idut. (From Macramallah (1935: pl. III B).

offering-room (figure 6.17). In all other tomb layouts the storeroom is north of the offering-room (figure 6.16, 6.18). There is one exception in the tomb of Mereruka where the storeroom (Room A12) for the second offering-room for Mereruka (Room A11) is located on the east.

The decorative scheme within these storerooms is quite similar to the scene content within the offering-room (Bolshakov, 1997: 90-91). Indeed, scenes of offering bearers in some offering-rooms move in a direction towards the storeroom and actually turn a corner, making their way on to the thickness of the storeroom, as can be seen in the tomb of Nebkauhor (Hassan, 1975a: 53, pl. XLI B-C). In this vizier's tomb the storeroom decoration scene content includes representations of servants bringing offerings, dragging sledges stacked with sealed vessels containing wine and oils (*e.g.*, *ḥknw* and *sfṯ*) and carrying sealed wooden chests (Hassan, 1975a: 53-56, pls. XLII-XLV). This is the typical repertoire for decoration in this type of storeroom and caused Hassan (1975a: pls. XLII-XLV) to call it the 'chamber of oils'. These storerooms would have been used by family members and priests who carried out ceremonies in the adjacent offering-room. The consistent decorative themes suggest that the storerooms may have held, oils, wine (and whatever was carried in sealed chests) which were required for cult practices. Such goods, and other cult paraphilia, might only have been kept here at times of offering ceremonies – brought out beforehand from (undecorated) storeroom(s) that were the main supply of products and utensils. The storeroom may also have been a place where offerings were prepared before ceremonies took place. Possibly, in addition, the function was symbolic: Harpur and Scremin (2006: 476) describes Room 8 in the tomb of Kagemni as a "symbolic storage-magazine". Bolshakov (1997: 91) believes that storerooms within tombs may not necessarily have been real functioning stores and that as long as they existed the tomb owner would be guaranteed supplies.

Synopsis

Multi-roomed mastabas at Saqqara were constructed from limestone quarried locally along with more distinctive white limestone imported from nearby quarries such as Tura. This is also the case at other parts of the Memphite necropolis but in comparison with archaeological exploration at Giza our knowledge of quarries at Saqqara is more limited. This should be a priority of large-scale archaeological exploration of the necropolis in the future, in order to gain a more holistic understanding of the site. The identification of building materials used in mastabas and their possible sources is not consistent and requires more attention.

Tombs were built using a standard technique. This can be seen in different parts of the Memphite Necropolis and even outside the Nile valley at contemporary cemeteries. The topic warrants closer study but collating evidence is complicated by inadequate architectural details in published records, inhibitive reconstruction work, the inaccessibility of many monuments and the sheer quantity of the data-set. When mastabas were being reconstructed following largescale clearance of the Unas Cemetery in the 20th century little attention was paid to the architecture and the construction techniques employed by the Old Kingdom tomb builders. Wood rather than stone is used as a roofing material with skylights that flood each room with daylight. Visitors to tombs today do not share the same experience as those entering these monuments in the Old Kingdom. Some may notice the empty pivot sockets and bolt sockets in doorways and question who could wander around tombs in the past, what was locked away behind closed doors and who called this tomb their workplace.

Very little has been written on the on the subject of architecture of private monuments. Arnold's architectural study is more inclined to his analysis of royal monuments and is structured by working with masonry as a flat surface or as a cross-section. In restored mastabas modern restoration walls often obscures the cross-section of walls. In places this can be overcome by examining the wall thickness between rooms and corridors (*e.g.*, ideal places being doorways between rooms). This present study has also included mastabas that have not been restored and where the cross-section of walls is exposed. These mastabas, that despite usually only having a few or more surviving courses, lend themselves well to the study of masonry. In addition, archive photographs of mastabas can be utilised to see masonry during excavation and before restoration. For closed tombs and those with inaccessible rooms they form the only record of the interior. However, resources like these are slim, since most fieldwork projects have for a long period failed to make good complete photographic records of mastaba architecture.

Phyles of priests working in multi-roomed mastabas was an imitation of the model used in royal mortuary cults and is a product of the social, political, economic and administrative changes taking place following the reign of Nyuserra. Officials with increasing independence sought to display their wealth and social status not only through the size, materials, craftsmanship and decoration of their tomb but also by the adoption of more elaborate funerary practices and architectural features from royal monuments.

Not all mortuary cults required an arrangement of five storerooms – some are now less visible in the archaeological record. In all mortuary cults there is the need to store cultic equipment of the cult personnel, and possibly the goods to be offered. These rooms can be found in mastabas and there are distinctions between undecorated storerooms and storerooms adjacent to the offering-room characteristically decorated with scenes of oils, wine jars and chests being pulled on sledges. Each type of storeroom fulfilled shared and different purposes based upon who used them, how frequently they were used, what took place inside them and what was stored within them.

Historically, expeditions involved in the recording of Old Kingdom private tombs have prioritised epigraphy, and in the final published record architecture is simply peripheral to texts and art. Until recently there has been little serious analysis of private tomb architecture and the significance of this most prominent aspect of the monument. New technologies available to the archaeologist such as 3D design software and photogrammetry allow better recording of architectural details in tombs. More diverse ways of sharing media through online publishing and web databases facilitate architectural commentaries to be fully illustrated at an economical cost, expanding the data for those who cannot visit the monument.

Bibliography

Aigner, T. 1983a. A Pliocene Cliff-Line around the Giza Pyramids Plateau, Egypt. - Palaeography, Palaeoclimatology, Palaeoecology 42: 313-322.

Aigner, T. 1983b. Facies and Origin of Nummulitic Build-Ups: An Example from the Giza Pyramids Plateau (middle Eocene, Egypt). - Neues Jahrbuch Paläontologisches Abhandlungen 166: 347-368.

Allen, J.P. 1994. Reading a Pyramid. In: Berger, C., G. Clerc & N. Grimal. Eds. Hommages à Jean Leclant. Vol. 4. - Cairo, Institut français d'archéologie orientale (BdE 106): 5-28.

Altenmüller, H. 1974. Zur vergöttlichung des Unas im Alten Reich. - Studien zur Altägyptischen Kultur 1: 1-18.

Altenmüller, H. 1998. Die Wanddarstellungen im Grab des Mehu in Saqqara. - Mainz, Phillip von Zabern.

Altenmüller, H. 2012. Bemerkungen zum Architrav und zur Scheintür des Felsgrabes des Anchi unter Südumfassung der Djoseranlage in Saqqara. - Studien zur Altägyptischen Kultur 41: 1-20.

de Araújo Duarte, C. 2018. Une fausse-porte de l'Ancien Empire au Musée d'Archéologie et d'Ethnologie de l'Université de São Paulo. - l'Équipe Égypte Nilotique et Méditerranéenne 11: 231-242.

Arnold, D. 1988. The South Cemeteries of Lisht I: The Pyramid of Senwosret I. With contributions by Doretha Arnold and an appendix by Peter F. Dorman. - New York, The Metropolitan Museum of Art.

Arnold, D. 1991. Building in Egypt: Pharaonic Stone Masonry. - New York, Oxford University Press.

Arnold, D. 1992. The South Cemeteries of Lisht III: The Pyramid of Senwosret I. With contributions by Doretha Arnold and Felix Arnold and an appendix by Cheryl Haldane. - New York, The Metropolitan Museum of Art.

Arnold, D. 2002. The Pyramid Complex of Senwosret III at Dahschur. Architectural Studies. With contributions and Appendix by Adela Oppenheim and Contributions by James P. Allen. - New York, Metropolitan Museum of Art.

Arnold, D. 2003. Encyclopaedia of Ancient Egyptian Architecture. Translated by Sabine Gardiner & Helen Strudwick. - London, I.B. Tauris.

Aston, B.G., J.A., Harrell & I. Shaw. 2000. Stone. In: Nicholson, P.T. & I. Shaw. Ed. Ancient Egyptian Materials and Technology. - Cambridge, Cambridge University Press: 6-77.

Badawi, A.M. 1940. Denkmäler aus Sakkarah. - Annales du Service des Antiquités de l'Égypte 40: 495-501.

Badawy, A. 1954. A History of Egyptian Architecture. From the Earliest Times to the End of the Old Kingdom. - Berkley and Los Angeles, University of California Press.

Badawy, A. 1965. Ancient Egyptian Architectural Design. A Study of the Harmonic System. - Berkeley and Los Angeles, University of California Press.

Badawy, A. 1966. A History of Egyptian Architecture. The First Intermediate Period, the Middle Kingdom, and the Second Intermediate Period. - Berkley and Los Angeles, University of California Press.

Badawy, A. 1978. The tomb of Nyhetep-Ptah at Giza and the tomb of 'Ankhm'ahor at Saqqara. - Berkley, University of California Press.

Baer, K. 1960. Rank and Title in the Old Kingdom: The Structure of the Egyptian Administration in the 5th and 6th Dynasties. - Chicago, University of Chicago Press.

Barsanti, A. 1900. Fouilles autour de la pyramide d'Ounas (1899-1900): I. Le Mastaba de Samnofir. - Annales du Service des Antiquités de l'Égypte 1: 150-160.

Barsanti, A. 1901. Rapports de M. Alexandre Barsanti sur les déblaiements opérés autour de la pyramide d'Ounas pendant les années 1899-1901. - Annales du Service des Antiquités de l'Égypte 2: 244-257.

Bárta, M. 2005. Architectural Innovations in the Development of the Non-Royal Tomb During the reign of Nyuserra. In: Jánosi, P. Ed. Structure and Significance. Thoughts on Ancient Egyptian Architecture. - Wien, Oesterreichishe Akademie der Wissenschaften: 105-128.

Bárta, M. & J. Krejčí. Eds. 2000. Abusir and Saqqara in the Year 2000. - Prague, Academy of Sciences of the Czech Republic.

Bárta, M. & B. Vachla. 2001. The Tomb of Hetepi at Abu Sir South. - Egyptian Archaeology 19: 33-35.

Bárta, M., V. Brůna & R. Křivánek. 2003. Research at South Abusir in 2001-2002 – Methods and Results. - Památky Archeologické XCIV: 49-82.

Berger, C. & B. Mathieu. Eds. 1997. Études sur l'Ancien Empire et la nécropole de Saqqâra dédiées à Jean-Philippe Lauer. - Montpellier, Université Paul Valéry (OrMonsp IX).

Blackman, A.M. 1936. The Value of Egyptology in the Modern World. An Inaugural Lecture delivered before the University of Liverpool on March 7, 1935. - London, University of Liverpool Press.

Bolshakov, A.O. 1991. The Old Kingdom Representations of Funeral Processions. - Göttinger Miszellen 121: 31-54.

Bolshakov, A.O. 1997. Man and His Double in Egyptian Ideology of the Old Kingdom. - Wiesbaden, Harrassowitz (Ägypten und Altes Testament 37).

Borchardt, L. 1907. Das Grabdenkmal des Königs Ne-User-Re. - Leipzig, Hinrichs.

Borchardt, L. 1910. Das Grabdenkmal des Königs Sáḥu-re. Band 1. - Leipzig, Hinrichs.

Bowyer, J. 1973. History of Building. - London, Crosby Lockwood Staples.

Brinks, J. 1979. Die Entwicklung der königlichen Grabanlagen des Alten Reichs. Eine strukturelle und historische Analyse altaegyptische architektur. - Hildesheim, Gerstenberg (HÄB 10).

Brovarski, E. 2001. The Senedjemib Complex. Part I. Giza Mastabas. Vol. 7. - Boston, Museum of Fine Arts.

Brunton, G. 1947. Burial of Prince Ptah-Shepses at Saqqara. - Annales du Service des Antiquités de l'Égypte 47: 125-133.

Brunner, H. 1986. Tür und Tor. - In: Helck, W., E. Otto & W. Westendorf. Eds. Lexikon der Ägyptologie VI. - Wiesbaden, Harrassowitz: 778-787.

Capart, J. 1907. Une rue de tombeaux à Saqqarah. - Bruxelles, Vromant.

Capart, J. 1927. Documents pour servir a l'Etude de l'art Egyptien. - Paris, les éditions du Pégase.

Cherpion, N. 1989. Mastaba et hypogées d'Ancien Empire: le problème de la datation. - Brussels, Connaissance de l'Égypte ancienne.

Clarke, S. & R. Engelbach. 1930. Ancient Egyptian Construction and Architecture. - New York, Dover.

Daoud, K.A. 1995. The Tomb of Kairer: Preliminary Report on the Fieldwork, Season, 1993. - Göttinger Miszellen 147: 35-48.

Daoud, K.A. 1997. Unusual Scenes in the Saqqara Tomb of Kairer. - Egyptian Archaeology 10: 6-7.

Daoud, K.A. 1998. The Inscribed Stelae of the Herakleopolitan Period from the Memphite Necropolis. - University of Liverpool, Ph.D. Thesis.

Davies, N. de G. 1900. The Mastaba of Ptahhetep and Akhethetep at Saqqareh. Part. I: The Chapel of Ptahhotep and the Hieroglyphs. - London, EES (ASE 8).

Davies, N. de G. 1901. The Mastaba of Ptahhetep and Akhethetep at Saqqareh. Part II: The Mastaba. The Sculptures of Akhethotep. - London, EES (ASE 9).

Davies, W.V., A. el-Khouli, A.B. Lloyd & A.J. Spencer. 1984. Saqqâra Tombs I. The Mastabas of Mereri and Wernu. - London, EES (ASE 36).

Dreyer, G. 2005. Saqqara. In: Spencer, P. Ed. Digging Diary 2004-2005. - Egyptian Archaeology 27: 25-29.

Duell, P. 1938. The Mastaba of Mereruka. Part I & II. - Chicago, University of Chicago Press.

Edwards, I.E.S. 1993. The Pyramids of Egypt. Revised Edition. - Harmondsworth, Penguin.

Eyre, C.J. 1987. Work and the Organisation of Work in the Old Kingdom. In: Powell, M.A. Ed. Labor in the Ancient Near East. - New Haven, CT, American Oriental Society: 5-47.

Eyre, C.J. 2002. The Cannibal Hymn: A Cultural and Literary Study. - Liverpool, Liverpool University Press.

Faulkner, R. 1962. A Concise Dictionary of Middle Egyptian. - Oxford, Oxford University Press.

El-Fikey, S.A. 1980. The Tomb of the Vizier Rē'-Wer at Saqqara. - Warminster, Aris and Phillips (Egyptology Today Series 4).

Firth, C.M. 1926. Preliminary Report on the Excavations at Saqqara (1925-1926). - Annales du Service des Antiquités de l'Égypte 26: 97-101.

Firth, C.M. 1927. Excavations of the Service des Antiquités at Saqqara (November 1926-April 1927). - Annales du Service des Antiquités de l'Égypte 27: 105-111.

Firth, C.M. 1930. Report on the Excavations of the Department of Antiquities at Saqqara (November 1929-April 1930). - Annales du Service des Antiquités de l'Égypte 30: 185-189.

Firth, C.M. & B. Gunn. 1926. Excavations at Saqqara. Teti Pyramid Cemeteries I. - Cairo, Institut français d'archéologie orientale.

Fischer, H.G. 1961. A Supplement to Janssen's List of Dog's Names. - Journal of Egyptian Archaeology 47: 152-153.

Fischer, H.G. 1965. *Bỉ3* and the Deified Vizier *Mḥw*. - Journal of the American Research Center in Egypt 4: 49-53.

Fischer, H.G. 1966. An Old Kingdom Monogram. - Zeitschrift für ägyptische Sprache und Altertumskunde 93: 56-59.

Fischer, H.G. 1996. Egyptian Doors, Inside and Out. In: Fischer, H.G. Ed. Egyptian Studies III. Varia Nova. - New York, Metropolitan Museum of Art: 91-102.

Fitchen. J. 1961. The Construction of Gothic Cathedrals: A Study of Medieval Vault Erection. - Oxford, Clarendon Press.

Fitchen. J. 1986. Building Construction before Mechanization. - Cambridge, MA, Massachusetts Institute of Technology Press.

Gardiner, A. 1957. Egyptian Grammar. Being an Introduction to the Study of Hieroglyphs. Third Edition, Revised. - Oxford, Griffith Institute.

Goedicke, H. 1965. An Old Kingdom Word for Door-Socket. - Journal of Egyptian Archaeology 51: 200.

Goedicke, H. 1971. Re-Used Blocks from the Pyramid of Amenemhet I at Lischt. - New York, Metropolitan Museum of Art (The Metropolitan Museum of Art Egyptian Expedition 20).

Goyan, J., J. Golvin, C. Simon-Boidot & G. Martinet. 2004. La construction pharaonique du Moyen Empire á l'époque gréco-romaine. - Paris, Picard Editions.

Grajetzki, W. 2003. Burial Customs in Ancient Egypt. Life in Death for Rich and Poor. - London, Duckworth.

Grimal, N. 1996. A History of Ancient Egypt. Translated by Ian Shaw. - Oxford, Blackwell.

Gunn, B. 1934. Inscriptions from the Step Pyramid Site. - Annales du Service des Antiquités de l'Égypte 35: 62-65.

Harpur, Y. 1987. Decoration in Egyptian Tombs of the Old Kingdom: Studies in Orientation and Scene Content. - London, Kegan Paul International.

Harpur, Y. 2005. Recording in the Saqqara Tomb-Chapel of Kagemni: A Summary of Work, Opinions and Ideas. - Annales du Service des Antiquités de l'Égypte 79: 115-123.

Harpur, Y & P. Scremin. 2006. The Chapel of Kagemni: Scene Details. - Reading, Oxford Expedition to Egypt.

Harrell, J.A. 1989. An Inventory of Ancient Egyptian Quarries. - ARCE Newsletter 146: 1-7.

Harrell, J.A. 1992. Ancient Egyptian Limestone Quarries: A Petrological Survey. - Archaeometry 34, 2: 195-211.

Harrell, J.A. 2004. In: Spencer, P. Ed. Digging Diary 2003. - Egyptian Archaeology: 24: 26.

Harrell, J.A. 2016. Ancient Egyptian Softstone Quarries. Online: http://www.eeescience.utoledo.edu/Faculty/Harrell/Egypt/Quarries/Softst_Quar.html. Accessed on 5 July 2019.

Harris, J.R. 1961. Lexicographical Studies in Ancient Egyptian Minerals. - Berlin, Akademie Verlag.

Hassan, S. 1938. Excavations at Saqqara 1937-1938. - Annales du Service des Antiquités de l'Égypte 38: 503-521.

Hassan, S. 1943. Excavations at Giza 1932-1933. Vol. IV. - Cairo, Government Press.

Hassan, S. 1955. The Causeway of Wnis at Sakkara. - Zeitschrift für ägyptische Sprache und Altertumskunde 80: 136-139.

Hassan, S. 1975a. Excavations at Saqqara, 1937-1938. Vol. I. The Mastaba of Neb-Kaw-Her. Re-edited by Zaki Iskander. - Cairo, General Organisation for Government Offices.

Hassan, S. 1975b. Excavations at Saqqara, 1937-1938. Vol. II. Mastabas of Ny-ankh-Pepy and Others. Re-edited by Zaki Iskander. - Cairo, General Organisation for Government Offices.

Hassan, S. 1975c. Excavations at Saqqara, 1937-1938. Vol. III. Mastabas of Princess Hemet-R' and Others. Re-edited by Zaki Iskander. - Cairo, General Organisation for Government Offices.

Hussein, A.S.M. 1942. The Reparation of the Mastaba of Mehu at Saqqara (1940). - Annales du Service des Antiquités de l'Égypte 42: 417-432.

Hölscher, U. 1912. Das Grabdenkmal des Königs Chephren. - Leipzig, Hinrichs.

Hölscher, U. 1951. The Mortuary Temple of Ramses III. Part II. - Chicago, University of Chicago Press.

Hölscher, U. & P. Munro. 1975. Der Unas-Friedhof in Saqqara. 2. Vorbericht über die Arbeiten der Gruppe Hannover im Frühjahr 1974. - Studien zur Altägyptischen Kultur 3: 113-126.

Hussein, A. 1942. The Reparation of the Mastaba of Mehu at Saqqara (1940). - Annales du Service des Antiquités de l'Égypte 42: 421.

Ikram, S. 1995. Choice Cuts: Meat Production in Ancient Egypt. - Leuven, Peeters.

Ikram, S. 2003. Death and Burial in Ancient Egypt. - Harlow, Pearson Education.

Isler, M. 1985. On Pyramid Building. - Journal of the American Research Center in Egypt 22: 129-142.

Isler, M. 1987. On Pyramid Building II. - Journal of the American Research Center in Egypt 24: 95-112.

Università di Pisa. 2003. The North Saqqara Archaeological Site Handbook for the Environmental Risk Analysis. - Pisa, Edizioni Plus/Università di Pisa.

Jacquet-Gordon, H.K. 1962. Les noms des domaines funéraires sous l'Ancien Empire égyptien - Cairo, Institut français d'archéologie orientale.

James, T.G.H. 1953. The Mastaba of Khentika called Ikhekhi. - London, EES (Archaeological Survey of Egypt 30).

Jánosi, P. 1999. The Tombs of Officials. Houses of Eternity. In: Arnold, D. Ed. Egyptian Art in the Age of the Pyramids. - New York, Metropolitan Museum of Art: 27-39.

Janot, F., C. Bridonneau, M. de Rosière, L. Cotelle-Michel & C. Decamps. 2001. La mission archéologique du musée du Louvre à Saqqara : une nécropole d'époque tardive dans le secteur du mastaba d'Akhethetep. - Bulletin de l'Institut Français d'Archéologie Orientale 101: 249-291.

Jeffreys, D. & A. Tavares. 1994. The Historic Landscape of Early Dynastic Memphis. - Mitteilungen des Deutschen Archäologischen Instituts, Abteilung Kairo 50: 143-173.

Jeffreys, D. & A. Tavares. 2000. An Integrated Mapping Project for the Saqqara Plateau and Escarpment. In: Bárta, M. & J. Krejčí. Eds. Abusir and Saqqara in the Year 2000. - Prague, Academy of Sciences of the Czech Republic, Oriental Institute: 27-32.

Jequier, G. 1936-1940. Fouilles à Saqqarah. Le monument funéraire de Pépi II. Vol. I-III. - Cairo, Institut français d'archéologie orientale.

Junge, F. 1976. Holzrelief der 6 Dynastie. In: Kaiser, W., G. Dreyer, R. Gempeler, P. Grossmann, G. Haeny, H. Jaritz & F. Junge. Eds. Stadt und Tempel von Elephantine. Sechster Grabungsbericht. - Mitteilungen des Deutschen Archäologischen Instituts, Abteilung Kairo 32: 98-107.

Junker, H. 1938. Gîza III. Grabungen auf dem Friedhof des Alten Reiches bei den Pyramiden von Giza. Band III. Die Mastabas der Vorgeschrittenen V. Dynastie auf dem Westfriedhof. - Vienna & Leipzig, Hölder-Pichler-Tempsky.

Kanawati, N. 1977. The Egyptian Administration in the Old Kingdom: Evidence on Its Economic Decline. - Warminster, Aris and Phillips.

Kanawati, N. 1980. Government Reforms. - Warminster, Aris and Phillips.

Kanawati, N. 2000. The Tomb and Beyond: Burial Customs of the Egyptian Officials. - Warminster, Aris and Phillips.

Kanawati, N. & M. Abder-Raziq. 1999. The Teti Cemetery at Saqqara. Vol. V. The Tomb of Hesi. - Warminster, Aris and Phillips (ACE Reports 13).

Kanawati, N. & M. Abder-Raziq. 2001. Teti Cemetery at Saqqara. Vol. VII. The Tombs of Shepsipuptah, Mereri (Merinebti), Hefi and Others. - Warminster, Aris and Phillips (ACE Reports 17).

Kanawati, N. & M. Abder-Raziq. 2003. The Unis Cemetery at Saqqara. Vol. II. The Tombs of Iynefert and Ihy (reused by Idut). - Oxford, Aris and Phillips (ACE Reports 19).

Kanawati, N. & M. Abder-Raziq. 2004. Mereruka and His Family. Part I. The Tomb of Meryteti. - Oxford, Aris and Phillips (ACE Reports 21).

Kanawati, N. & M. Abder-Raziq. 2008. Mereruka and His Family. Part II. The Tomb of Waatetkhethor. - Oxford, Aris and Phillips (ACE Reports 27).

Kanawati, N. & A. Hassan. 1996. The Teti Cemetery at Saqqara. Vol. I. The Tombs of Nedjet-em-pet, Ka-aper and Others. - Warminster, Aris and Phillips (ACE Report 8).

Kanawati, N. & A. Hassan. 1997. Teti Cemetery at Saqqara. Vol. II. The Tomb of Ankhmahor. - Warminster, Aris and Phillips (ACE Report 9).

Kanawati, N. & A. Hassan. 1999. The Teti Cemetery at Saqqara. Vol. III. The Tombs of Neferseshemre and Seankhuiptah. - Warminster, Aris and Phillips (ACE Report 1).

Kanawati, N., A. el-Khouli, A. McFarlane & N. Maksoud. 1984. Excavations at Saqqara. North-West of Teti's Pyramid. Vol. I. - Sydney, The Ancient History Documentary Research Centre, Macquarie University.

Kanawati, N., A. Woods, S. Shafik & E. Alexakis. 2010. Mereruka and His Family. Part III:1. The Tomb of Mereruka. - Oxford, Aris and Phillips (ACE Reports 29).

Kanawati, N., A. Woods, S. Shafik & E. Alexakis. 2011. Mereruka and His Family. Part III:2. The Tomb of Mereruka. - Oxford, Aris and Phillips (ACE Reports 30).

El-Khouli, A. & N. Kanawati. 1988. Excavations at Saqqara. North-West of Teti's Pyramid. Vol. II. - Sydney, The Ancient History Documentary Research Centre, Macquarie University.

Klemm, D. & R. Klemm. 1981. Steine der Pharaonen. - Munich, Staatliche Sammlung Ägyptische Kunst.

Klemm, D. & R. Klemm. 1993. Steine und Steinbrüche im Älten Ägypten. - Berlin, Springer Verlag.

Klemm, R. 1984. Steinbruch. In: Helck, W., E. Otto & W. Westendorf. Eds. Lexikon der Ägyptologie V. - Wiesbaden, Harrassowitz: 1277-1278.

Koenigsberger, O. 1936. Die Konstruktion der Ägyptischen Tür. - Glückstadt, J.J. Augustin.

Labrousse, A., J.-P. Lauer & J. Leclant. 1977. Mission archéologique de Saqqarah II. Le temple haut du complexe funéraire du roi Ounas. - Cairo, Institut français d'archéologie orientale (BdE 73).

Labrousse, A. & M. Moussa. 1996. Le temple d'Accueil du Complexe Funéraire du roi Ounas. - Cairo, Institut français d'archéologie orientale (BdE 111).

Lacher-Raschdorff, C.M. 2014. Das Grab des Königs Ninetjer in Saqqara. Architektonische Entwicklung frühzeitlicher Grabanlagen in Ägypten. - Wiesbaden, Harrassowitz Verlag.

Lally, M.T. 1989. Engineering a Pyramid. - Journal of the American Research Center in Egypt 26: 207-218.

Lauer, J-P. 1936a. Fouilles à Saqqarah: La pyramide à degrés: l'architecture I. - Cairo, Institut français d'archéologie orientale.

Lauer, J-P. 1936b. Fouilles à Saqqarah: La pyramide à degrés: l'architecture II. - Cairo, Institut français d'archéologie orientale.

Lauer, J-P. 1937. Note sur divers travaux ettetués à Saqqarah en 1936 et 1937. - Annales du Service des Antiquités de l'Égypte 37: 103-115.

Lauer, J-P. 1962. Histoire monumentale des pyramides d'Egypte I, Les Pyramides à degrés (IIIe Dynastie). - Cairo, Institut français d'archéologie orientale (BdE 30).

Lauer, J-P. 1976. Saqqâra: The Royal Cemetery of Memphis. - London, Thames and Hudson.

Lehner, M. 1997. The Complete Pyramids. - London, Thames and Hudson.

Lepsius, C.R. 1849. Denkmäler aus Aegypten und Aethiopien. Band I. - Berlin, Nicolaische Buchhandlung.

Lichtheim, M. 1975. Ancient Egyptian Literature. Vol. I. The Old and Middle Kingdoms. - Berkeley and Los Angeles, University of California Press.

Linacre College, Oxford. 2006. Oxford Expedition to Egypt: Scene-details Database [dataset]. https://doi.org/10.5284/1000009 (York: Archaeology Data Service [distributor]).

Lloyd, A.B., A.J. Spencer & A. el-Khouli. 1990. Saqqâra Tombs II. The Mastabas of Meru, Semdenti, Khui and Others. - London, EES (ASE 40).

Lucas, A. & J.R.Harris. 1962. Ancient Egyptian Materials and Industries. - London, E. Arnold.

Macramallah, R. 1935. Le Mastaba d'Idout. Fouilles à Saqqarah 15. - Cairo, Institut français d'archéologie orientale.

Mackay, E. 1921. The Cutting and Preparation of Tomb-Chapels in the Theban Necropolis. - Journal of Egyptian Archaeology 7: 154-168.

Málek, J. 1986. In the Shadow of the Pyramids. Egypt During the Old Kingdom. - London, Orbis.

Málek, J. 1988. The "Altar" in the Pillared Court of Teti's Pyramid-Temple at Saqqara. In: Baines, J., T.G.H. James, A. Leahy & A.F. Shore. Eds. Pyramid Studies and Other Essays Presented to I.E.S. Edwards. - London, EES (Occasional Papers 8): 23-34.

Mariette, A. 1889. Les mastabas de l'Ancien Empire. - Paris, F. Vieweg.

Martin, G.T. 1988. The Royal Tomb at El-Amarna: The Rock-cut Tombs of El-Amarna Part VII, II. - London, EES (Archaeological Survey of Egypt 39).

Martin, K. 1977. Ein Grarantsymbol des Lebens. - Hildesheim, Gerstenberg (HÄB 10).

Martin, K. 1981. Obelisk. In: Helck, W., E. Otto & W. Westendorf. Eds. Lexikon der Ägyptologie IV. - Wiesbaden, Harrassowitz: 544.

Mathieson, I.M. 2000. The National Museums of Scotland Saqqara Survey Project 1999-2000. In: Bárta, M. & J. Krejčí. Eds. Abusir and Saqqara in the Year 2000. - Prague: Academy of Sciences of the Czech Republic, Oriental Institute: 31-42.

Mathieson, I.M. & A. Tavares. 1993. Preliminary Report of the National Museums of Scotland and Saqqara Survey Project, 1990-91. - Journal of Egyptian Archaeology 79: 17-31.

Mathieson, I.M., E. Bettles, J. Dittmer & C. Reader. 1999. The National Museums of Scotland Saqqara Survey Project, Earth Sciences 1990-1998. - Journal of Egyptian Archaeology 85: 21-43.

McFarlane, A. 2000. Unis Cemetery at Saqqara. Vol. I. The Tomb of Irukaptah. - Warminster, Aris and Phillips (ACE Reports 15).

McFarlane, A. 2003. Mastabas at Saqqara. Kaiemheset, Kaipunesut, Kaiemsenu, Sehetepu and Others. - Oxford, Aris and Phillips (ACE Reports 20).

Meyer, C. 1986. Tura. In: Helck, W., E. Otto & W. Westendorf. Eds. Lexikon der Ägyptologie VI. - Wiesbaden, Harrassowitz: 807-809.

Montet, P. 1925. Les scenes de la privée dans les tombeaux égyptien de l'Ancien Empire. n°24. - Strasbourg, publication de la faculté des lettres de Strasbourg.

Moussa, A.M. 1972. Lintels and Lower Parts of a Wooden Relief-sculptured Door of the Old Kingdom from Saqqara. - Mitteilungen des Deutschen Archäologischen Instituts, Abteilung Kairo 28: 289-291.

Moussa, A.M. 1981. The Offering Table of Khnetika from the Causeway of King Unas at Saqqara. - Studien zur Altägyptischen Kultur 9: 289-295.

Moussa, A.M. 1983. Five Monuments of the Old Kingdom from the Causeway of King Unas at Saqqara. - Studien zur Altägyptischen Kultur 10: 273-276.

Moussa, A.M. 1985 Excavations in the Valley Temple of King Unas at Saqqara (II). - Annales du Service des Antiquités de l'Égypte 70: 33-34.

Moussa, A.H. & H. Altenmüller. 1971. The Tomb of Nefer and Ka-hay. - Mainz, Philipp von Zabern (AV 5).

Moussa, A.H. & H. Altenmüller. 1977. Das Grab des Nianchchnum und Chnumhotep. - Mainz, Philipp von Zabern (AV 21).

Moussa, A.H. & F. Junge. 1975. Two Tombs of Craftsmen. - Mainz, Philipp von Zabern (AV 9).

Moussa, A.H. & N. Nasser. 1979. Two Old Kingdom Falsedoors from the Causeway of King Unas at Saqqara. - Studien zur Altägyptischen Kultur 7: 155-161.

Munro, P. 1982. Der Unas-Friedhof. - Göttinger Miszellen 59: 77-101.

Munro, P. 1983a. Der Unas-Friedhof. - Göttinger Miszellen 63: 81-105.

Munro, P. 1983b. Einige bemerkungen zum Unas-Friedhof in Saqqara. 3. Vorbericht über die Arbeiten der Gruppe Hannover in Herbst 1978 und im Frühjahr 1980. - Studien zur Altägyptischen Kultur 10: 277-295.

Munro, P. 1984a. Der Unas-Friedhoft Nord-West. 6 Vorbericht über die Arbeiten der Gruppe Berlin/Hannover in Saqqara (Teil 1). - Göttinger Miszellen 74: 59-90.

Munro, P. 1984b. Der Unas-Friedhoft Nord-West. 6 Vorbericht über die Arbeiten der Gruppe Berlin/Hannover in Saqqara (Teil 2). - Göttinger Miszellen 75: 73-95.

Munro, P. 1993a. Der Unas-Friedhof Nord-West I. Topographische, historische Einleitung, das Doppelgrab der Königinnen Nebet und Khenut. - Mainz, Philipp von Zabern.

Munro, P. 1993b. Report on the Work of the Joint Archaeological Mission Free University of Berlin/University of Hanover during their 12th Campaign (15th March until 14th May, 1992) at Saqqâra. - Discussions in Egyptology 26: 47-58.

Munro, P. & C. Bieger. 1974. Das Doppelgrab der Königinnen *Nbt* und *ḫnwt* in Saqqara. - Studien zur Altägyptischen Kultur 1: 35-54.

Murray, M.A. 1905. Saqqara Mastabas I. - London, Quartich (ERA 10/British School of Archaeology in Egypt).

El-Naggar, S. 1997. Les voûtes à godrons dans l'Égypte ancienne. In: Berger, C. & B. Mathieu. Eds. Études sur l'Ancien Empire et la nécropole de Saqqâra dédiées à Jean-Philippe Lauer. - Montpellier, Université Paul Valéry (OrMonsp IX): 327-339.

Newberry, P.E. 1900. The Life of Rekhmara,Vezîr of Upper Egypt under Thothmes III and Amenhetep II (circa B.C. 1471-1448). - London, Constable.

Onderka, P. 2009. Tomb of Unisankh at Saqqara and Chicago: Unis Cemetery North West II. - Prague, National Museum.

Petrie, W.M.F. 1938. Egyptian Architecture. - London, Quaritch (British School of Archaeology in Egypt).

Petrie, H. & M. Murray. 1952. Seven Memphite Tomb Chapels. - London, Quaritch (British School of Archaeology in Egypt).

Porter, B. & R. Moss. 1981 [1974]. Topographical Bibliography of Ancient Egyptian Hieroglyphic Texts, Reliefs and Paintings, Vol. III², Memphis, 2nd ed., revised and augmented by Jaromír Málek. - Oxford, Griffith Institute.

Posener-Kriéger, P. 1971. Noms des parties de portes dans les documents d'Abousir', Beiträge zur Ägyptischen Bauforschung und Alterumskunde 12. Zum 70 geburtstag von Herbert Ricke. - Wiesbaden, Franz Steiner: 75-85.

Posener-Kriéger, P. 1986.Wag-Fest. In: Helck, W., E. Otto & W. Westendorf. Eds. Lexikon der Ägyptologie VI: 1135-1139. - Wiesbaden, Harrassowitz.

Quibell, J.E. 1913. The Tomb of Hesy. Excavations at Saqqara, 1911-12. - Cairo, Institut français d'archéologie orientale.

Quibell J.E. & A.G.K. Hayter. 1927. Teti Pyramid, North Side. Excavations at Saqqara 18. Cairo, Institut français d'archéologie orientale.

de Rachewiltz, B. 1960. The Rock Tomb of *Irw-K3-Pth*. - Leiden, Brill.

Radwan, A. 1983. Die Kupfer und Bronzegefässe Ägyptens: von den Anfängen bis zum Beginn der Spätzeit. - München, C.H. Beck.

Ranke, H. 1935. Die Ägyptischen Personennamen I. - Glückstadt, J.J. Augustin.

Raslan, M.A.M. 1973. Academic and Applied Paper on the History of Architecture. The Causeway of Ounas Pyramid. - Annales du Service des Antiquités de l'Égypte 61: 148-169.

Ray, J.D. 1979. The World of North Saqqâra. - World Archaeology 10, 2: 149-157.

Reisner, G.A. 1936. The Development of the Egyptian Tomb Down to the Accession of Cheops. - Cambridge, MA, Harvard University Press.

Reisner, G.A. 1942. A History of the Giza Necropolis I. - Cambridge, MA, Harvard University Press.

Roth A.M. 1987. The Organization of Royal Cemeteries at Saqqara in the Old Kingdom. - Journal of the American Research Center in Egypt 25: 201-214.

Roth A.M. 1991. Egyptian Phyles in the Old Kingdom: The Evolution of a System of Social Organization. - Chicago, Oriental Institute of the University of Chicago.

Roth A.M. 1993. Social Change in the 4th Dynasty: The Spatial Organization of Pyramids, Tombs and Cemeteries. - Journal of the American Research Center in Egypt 30: 33-55.

Roth A.M. 1994. The Practical Economics of Tomb-Building in the Old Kingdom: A Visit to the Necropolis in a Carrying Chair. In: Silverman, D.P. Ed. For his Ka: Essays Offered in Memory of Klaus Baer. - Chicago: Oriental Institute of the University of Chicago (Studies in Ancient Oriental Civilization 55): 227-240.

Roth A.M. 1995. A Cemetery of Palace Attendants: Including G 2084-2099, G2230+2231, and G2240. Giza Mastabas. Vol 6. - Boston, Museum of Fine Arts.

Roth A.M. 2002. The Meaning of Menial Labor: "Servant Statues" in Old Kingdom Serdabs. - Journal of the American Research Center in Egypt 39: 103-121.

Rowe, A. 1942. The Sceptre Sub-Gang of Workmen at Meydûm. - Annales du Service des Antiquités de l'Égypte 42: 339-347.

Saad Z.Y. 1940. A Preliminary Report on the Excavations at Saqqara 1939-1940. - Annales du Service des Antiquités de l'Égypte 40: 675-703.

Saad Z.Y. 1943. 'A Preliminary Report on the Excavations of the Department of Antiquities at Saqqara 1942-43. - Annales du Service des Antiquités de l'Égypte 43: 449-468.

Saad Z.Y. 1947. Royal Excavations at Saqqara and Helwan (1941-1945). - Cairo, Institut français d'archéologie orientale (ASAE supplement Cahier 3).

Sethe, K. 1933. Urkunden des Alten Reichs. Urkunden des ägyptischen Altertums I. - Leipzig, Hinrichs.

Shaw, I. 1998. Exploiting the Desert Frontier: The Logistics and Politics of Ancient Egyptian Mining Expeditions. In: Knapp, A.B., V.C. Pigott & E.W. Herbert. Eds. Social Approaches to an Industrial Past. The Archaeology and Anthropology of Mining. - London, Routledge.

Shaw, I. 2000. Quarries and Mines. In: Redford, D. Ed. Oxford Encyclopedia of Ancient Egypt. Vol. 3. - Oxford, Oxford University Press: 99-104.

Siliotti, A. 1997. Guide to the Pyramids of Egypt. - Vercilli, White Star.

Simpson, W.K. Ed. 2003. The Literature of Ancient Egypt. - New Haven, CT, Yale University Press.

Smith, H.S. 1997. Uncharted Saqqâra: An Essay. In: Berger, C. & B. Mathieu. Eds. Études sur l'Ancien Empire et la nécropole de Saqqâra dédiées à Jean-Philippe Lauer. - Montpellier, Université Paul Valéry (OrMonsp IX): 379-393.

Smith, W.S. 1936. Topography of the Old Kingdom Cemetery at Saqqarah. In: Reisner, G.A. Ed. The Development of the Egyptian Tomb Down to the Accession of Cheops. - Cambridge, MA: Harvard University Press: 390-411.

Smith, W.S. 1949. A History of Egyptian Sculpture and Painting in the Old Kingdom. Second Edition. - Oxford, Oxford University Press.

Smith, W.S. 1981. The Art and Architecture of Ancient Egypt. Revised with Additions by William Kelly Simpson. - New Haven, Yale University Press.

Snape, S.R. 2011. Ancient Egyptian Tombs. The Culture of Life and Death. - Malden, MA/Oxford/Chichester, Wiley-Blackwell.

Spencer, A.J. 1974. Researches on the Topography of North Saqqâra. - Orientalia 43: 1-11.

Spencer, A.J. 1975. Saqqara. Private Tombs of the 4.–6. Dyn. In: Helck, W., E. Otto & W. Westendorf. Eds. Lexikon der Ägyptologie V. - Wiesbaden, Harrassowitz: 400-409.

Spencer, A.J. 1979. Brick Architecture in Ancient Egypt. - Warminster, Aris and Phillips.

Spencer, A.J. 1982. Death in Ancient Egypt. - London, Penguin.

Spencer, A.J. 1993. Early Egypt: The Rise of Civilisation in the Nile Valley. - London, British Museum Press.

Spencer, P. Ed. 2005. Digging Diary. - Egyptian Archaeology 27: 26.

Stadelmann, R. 2010. Die pyramidenanlage des Sahure. In: Brinkmann, V. Ed. Sahure. Tod und Leben eines grossen Pharao. - Frankfurt am Main, Liebieghaus Skulpturensammlung. - Münich, Hirmer Verlag: 169-182.

Steindorff, G. 1913. Das Grab des Ti. - Leipzig, Hinrichs.

Strudwick, N. 1983. Aspects of the Administration of the Memphite Region of Egypt in the Old Kingdom. - The University of Liverpool, Ph.D. Thesis.

Strudwick, N. 1984. Some Remarks on the Disposition of Texts in Old Kingdom Tombs with Particular Reference to the False-Door. - Göttinger Miszellen 77: 35-49.

Strudwick, N. 1985. The Administation of Egypt in the Old Kingdom. The Highest Titles and their Holders. - London, Kegan Paul International.

Strudwick, N. 2005 Texts from the Pyramid Age. - Atlanta, GA, Society of Biblical Literature.

Swelim, N. 1988. The Dry Moat of the Netjerykhet Complex. In: Baines, J., T.G.H. James, A. Leahy & A.F. Shore. Eds. Pyramid Studies and Other Essays Presented to I.E.S. Edwards. - London, EES: 12-24.

Swelim, N. 1991. Some Remarks on the Great Rectangular Monuments of Middle Saqqara. - Mitteilungen des Deutschen Archäologischen Instituts, Abteilung Kairo 47 (Festschrift für Werner Kaiser): 389-402.

Swelim, N. 1994. Pyramid Research from the Archaic to the Second Intermediate Period: Lists, Catalogues and Objectives. In: Berger, C., G. Clerc & N. Grimal. Eds. Hommages à Jean Leclant. Vol. 1. - Cairo, Institut francais d'archeologie orientale (BdE 106): 337-349.

Traunecker, C. 1980. Kalkstein. In: Helck, W., E. Otto & W. Westendorf. Eds. Lexikon der Ägyptologie III: 301-303.

Verner, M. 1994. Forgotten Pharaohs, Lost Pyramids. Abusir. - Prague, Academia Škodaexport.

Vischak, D. 2003. Common Ground between Pyramid Texts and Old Kingdom Tomb Design: The Case of Ankhmahor. - Journal of the American Research Center in Egypt 40: 133-157.

von Bissing, F.W.F. 1905-1911. Die Mastaba das Gem-ni-Kai. 2 Vols. - Berlin, Alexander Duncker.

Watson, P.J. 1987. Egyptian Pyramids and Mastaba Tombs. - Princes Risborough, Shire Publications.

Wilkinson, T.A.H. 1999. Early Dynastic Egypt. - London/New York, Routledge.

Williams, C.R. 1932. The Decoration of the Tomb of Perneb: The Technique and The Color Conventions. - New York, The Metropolitan Museum of Art.

Wilson, J.A. 1944. Funeral Services of the Egyptian Old Kingdom. - Journal of Near Eastern Studies 3: 201-218.

Wilson, J.A. 1947. The Artist of the Egyptian Old Kingdom. - Journal of Near Eastern Studies 6: 231-249.

Wilson, J.A. 1954. A Group of Sixth Dynasty Inscriptions. - Journal of Near Eastern Studies 13: 243-264.

Youssef, M., O. Cherif, M. Boukhary & A. Mohammed. 1984. Geological Studies on the Sakkara Area, Egypt. - Neues Jahrbuch für Geologie und Paläontologie 168.1: 123-144.

Zayed, A. el-H. 1958. Le tombeau d'Akhti-Hotep à Saqqara. - Annales du Service des Antiquités de l'Égypte 55, 1: 127-137.

Ziegler, C. 1993. Le mastaba d'Akhethétep. Une chapelle funéraire de l'Ancien Empire. - Paris, RMN.

Ziegler, C. 2006. The Louvre Museum Excavations at Saqqara. - Egyptian Archaeology 28: 20-24.

Ziegler, C. J-P Adam, G. Andreu, C. Bridonneau, M. Étienne, G. Lecuyot & M-F de Rozières. 1997. La mission archéologique du musée du Louvre à Saqqara. Résultats de quatre campagnes de fouilles de 1993 à 1996. - Bulletin de l'Institut Français d'Archéologie Orientale 97: 269-292.

Ziegler, C. Ed. 2007. Le Mastaba d'Akhethetep. Fouilles du Louvre à Saqqara. Vol. 1. - Leuven, Peeters/Paris, Musée du Louvre Éditions.

About the Author

Ashley Cooke is Senior Curator of Antiquities at National Museums Liverpool, one of the largest Egyptology collections in the UK. Tomb architecture is one of his research interests, which also include ancient Egyptian material culture and the history of collecting. He has worked on fieldwork projects in Egypt since 1997 and has excavated at Saqqara, Tell Abqa'in, the Valley of the Kings and Zawiyet Umm el-Rackham.